CW00672849

DESPATCH RIDER ON THE WESTERN FRONT 1915–18

To the memory of my mother,
Marguerite Elizabeth Venner
(1919-2014)
for her unconditional
love and support

DESPATCH RIDER ON THE WESTERN FRONT 1915–18

The Diary of
Sergeant Albert Simpkin MM

Introduced and abridged by
David Venner

Pen & Sword
MILITARY

First published in 2015 by
Pen and Sword Military

An imprint of
Pen & Sword Books Ltd
47 Church Street
Barnsley
South Yorkshire
S70 2AS

Copyright © David Venner, 2015

ISBN 978 1 47382 740 0

The right of David Venner to be identified as Editor of this work has been asserted
by him in accordance with the Copyright, Designs and Patents Act 1988.

A CIP catalogue record for this book is
available from the British Library

All rights reserved. No part of this book may be reproduced or transmitted in
any form or by any means, electronic or mechanical including photocopying,
recording or by any information storage and retrieval system, without
permission from the Publisher in writing.

Printed and bound in England
By CPI Group (UK) Ltd, Croydon, CR0 4YY

Pen & Sword Books Ltd incorporates the Imprints of Pen & Sword Aviation,
Pen & Sword Family History, Pen & Sword Maritime, Pen & Sword Military,
Pen & Sword Discovery, Pen & Sword Politics, Pen & Sword Atlas, Pen & Sword
Archaeology, Wharncliffe Local History, Wharncliffe True Crime, Wharncliffe
Transport, Pen & Sword Select, Pen & Sword Military Classics, Leo Cooper, The
Praetorian Press, Claymore Press, Remember When, Seaforth Publishing and
Frontline Publishing

For a complete list of Pen & Sword titles please contact
PEN & SWORD BOOKS LIMITED
47 Church Street, Barnsley, South Yorkshire, S70 2AS, England
E-mail: enquiries@pen-and-sword.co.uk
Website: www.pen-and-sword.co.uk

Contents

Map: The Western Front in Outline 1914-18   vi
Acknowledgements   viii
Introduction by David Venner   x
Itinerary   xv
Abbreviations   xviii
Preface by Albert Simpkin, MM   xix

The Diary

1   August 1914: Joining up   1
2   December 1914: Training   5
3   July 1915 – June 1916   13

Narrative One: The Battle of the Somme   45

4   July – November 1916   51

Narrative Two: The Battle of the Ancre   71

5   November 1916 – April 1917   77

Map: Arras sector, April 1917   94

Narrative Three: The Battle of Arras and the   95
taking of Monchy le Preux

6   April – July 1917   107

Narrative Four: The Third Battle of Ypres   121

7   August 1917 – April 1918   125

Narrative Five: The German Spring Offensive   161

8   April – August 1918   167

Narrative Six: The Final Allied Offensive   173

9   September – November 1918   177

Narrative Seven: The Armistice   191

10   November 1918 – February 1919   195

Index   201

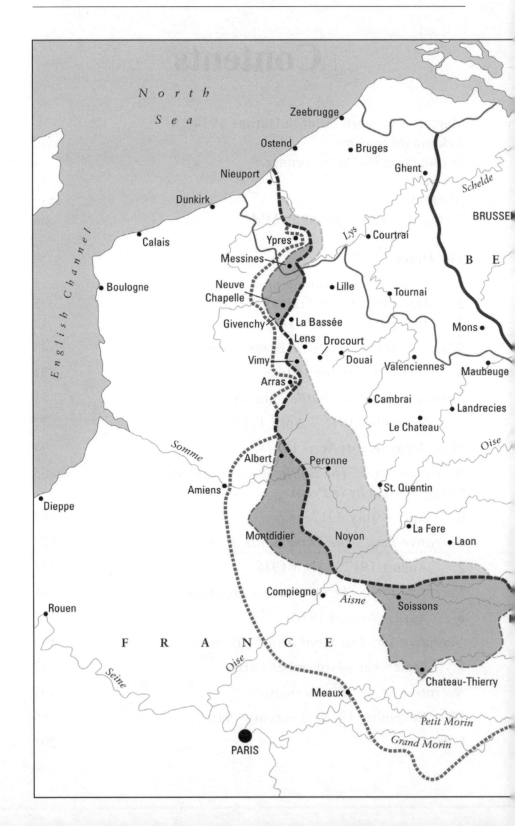

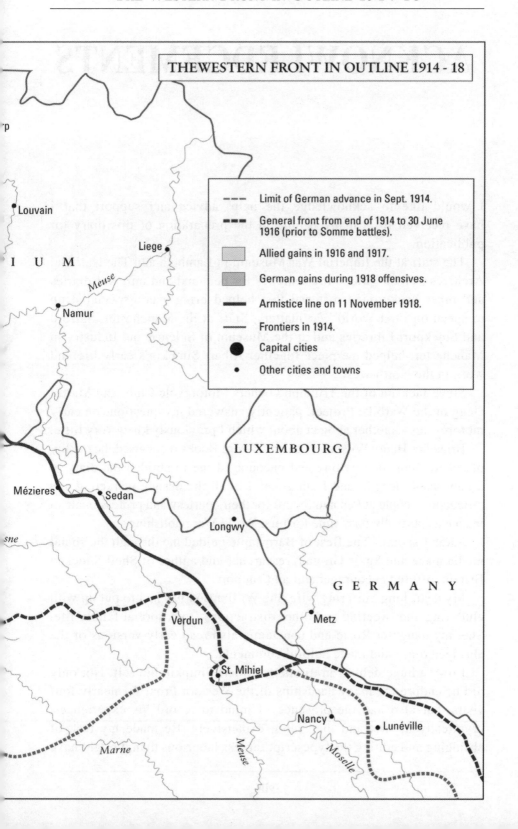

THE WESTERN FRONT IN OUTLINE 1914 - 18

Louvain

I U M

Liege

Meuse

Namur

Mézieres   Sedan

LUXEMBOURG

Longwy

sne

GERMANY

Verdun   Metz

St. Mihiel

Nancy   Lunéville

Marne   Meuse   Moselle

Legend:

- - - - Limit of German advance in Sept. 1914.

━ ━ ━ General front from end of 1914 to 30 June 1916 (prior to Somme battles).

▧ Allied gains in 1916 and 1917.

▨ German gains during 1918 offensives.

━━━ Armistice line on 11 November 1918.

─── Frontiers in 1914.

● Capital cities

• Other cities and towns

ACKNOWLEDGEMENTS

I would like to acknowledge the help, advice and support that I have received from many people in the preparation of this diary for publication.

The staff at the Imperial War Museum in Lambeth and The National Archives at Kew guided my searches for personal and unit war diaries and other background material that helped bring a non-specialist up to speed on First World War matters. Staff at the Manchester, Salford and Stockport Libraries and at the Museum of Science and Industry in Manchester, helped me piece together Albert Simpkin's early life and work in the North-west.

Steve Jackson of the Triumph Owners Motorcycle Club, and Martin Gegg of the Warbike Project, patiently answered my questions on early motorcycles - another subject about which I previously knew very little.

Brigadier Henry Wilson at Pen and Sword Books recognised the quality of Albert Simpkin's writing and encouraged me to abridge the diary to a publishable length; and I am grateful to all the design, marketing and production people at Pen and Sword for their courtesy and professionalism in an exceptionally busy time for First World War publishing.

Sarah Escott of The Best of Barnstaple guided me through the social media maze and Suzie Grogan, researcher and author of Shell Shocked Britain, offered encouragement and support.

My dear, long-suffering wife Sue Williamson has had to put up with cluttering and tweeting and other distractions from normal family life. She, my daughter Rosie and son Jamie also read early versions of the abridged diary and made helpful comments.

I owe a huge debt of gratitude to Albert Simpkin himself. Not only did he endure the many hardships of the Western Front for nearly four years, but also had the presence of mind to record his experiences, cryptically at first and then more expansively. He made my task of abridging and editing the typescript far less laborious than it might have been. I can only hope that he would not have been too upset to see 45,000 of his carefully crafted words end up on my study floor! (For those who wish to read the unabridged version it can be viewed, by appointment, at the Imperial War Museum in London.)

The photographs reproduced in this book are from Albert Simpkin's contemporary collection or were taken by his wife Lily on their visit to the battlefields in 1938.

Finally, thanks are due to my late mother, Marguerite Elizabeth Venner, who brought the original diary back to England after Albert's death in Buenos Aires and encouraged me to get it published. Sadly she did not live quite long enough to see the finished product but I hope that she – and her uncle Albert - would have approved.

David Venner
High Bickington
April 2015

INTRODUCTION

The First World War diary of Sergeant Simpkin came to my notice in 1982 following the death of his widow in Buenos Aires. Another war, between Britain and Argentina over the Falklands, inconveniently started while my mother (their niece) was in Buenos Aires to wind up her estate. The Argentine authorities blocked the transfer of bank balances and other parts of the estate to the UK. All my mother could bring out of the country were some small valuables that could be secreted in her suitcases, together with this diary which was in the form of a bundle of typewritten sheets tied together with string.

A hand-written note stapled to the sheets read:
'This book describes the many actions and the wanderings of the 37th Division in France from July 1915 to the Armistice in November 1918. The author, a sergeant in the infantry, by a miracle survived without serious injury. The writer of these notes served as a despatch rider attached to the 37th Division HQ and took part in all the actions mentioned.'

This strongly suggests that publication was in his mind, although it is not clear why he did not pursue the plan. His typescript runs to nearly 500 pages and contains around 130,000 words. Perhaps then – as now – it was considered to be too long for publication in full. The present volume is an abridged version of the diary, prepared by the author's great nephew.

The entries selected for inclusion provide a fascinating record of the life of a despatch rider on the Western Front: one day dodging shell holes and ammunition limbers to take his despatches to the front, the next observing the quaint but often courageous lives of the local populace. Throughout the diary are colourful and amusing anecdotes about his fellow soldiers, and critical comments on the strategies and tactics employed by the officers.

As an engineer in his pre-war civilian job, Albert took a particular interest in the products of army mechanisation. So when the first tanks and newly-developed aircraft appear in the battle zone, he has some insightful comments to make on their design and effectiveness – or otherwise.

Some of the original entries, covering the main actions of the 37th Division, are much longer passages that go beyond the usual diary form. These cover the battles of the Somme (July 1916), the Ancre (November 1916), Arras (April 1917), and Ypres (the third battle in August 1917). Also described in detail are the German offensive of April 1918, the final Allied offensive in August 1918 and the Armistice. These passages are included as 'narratives' alongside the selected diary entries.

THE DIARIST

Albert Edward Simpkin was born at Salford near Manchester, on 28 June 1885, the eldest child of Walter and Hannah Simpkin. Walter, a printer by trade, was originally from Loughborough but had moved to Salford soon after his marriage. After Albert came a daughter Gertrude and a son Frank. In 1897, when Albert was 12-years-old, Hannah died during the birth of another daughter, Elsie. She was just 39-years-old. Walter, with four young children to look after, soon re-married and two further children were born.

Albert apparently did not get on with his stepmother and much younger siblings and moved into lodgings in his late teens. He received a grammar school education and was apprenticed as an engineer to Crossley Brothers, manufacturers of marine engines, at Openshaw, Manchester. He progressed well in the drawing office, having undertaken further studies at night school and, as war approached, he was well established in a secure and promising career. In the 1911 census, he was described as a 'draughtsman engineer', living with two other boarders in Longsight, Manchester. His landlady, Emma Dawson, appears in the diary as 'Ma' Dawson – Albert often spent his leave here, after making a brief visit to his father and stepmother at their new home in Sheffield.

One of his main interests was motorcycling – a new phenomenon at this time. He owned a Douglas Twin and rode it all over Britain, both on business and for pleasure. This love of motorcycling, combined with an expressed hatred of walking, must have influenced his eventual decision to join up as a despatch rider. But this was not his first choice. At the outbreak of war, Albert's younger brother Frank was called up from the Territorials to join the artillery and in September 1914 he sailed for Egypt. Albert at first tried to join his brother's battery but, being a raw recruit, was turned down. The idea of becoming a 'foot-slogging infantryman' did not appeal to him, although from early diary entries it is clear that he was keen to volunteer at the earliest opportunity; later entries reveal a scathing attitude towards able-bodied men who avoided the draft.

It was as a member of the Auto Cyclists' Union that Albert first heard of the need for experienced motorcyclists to carry despatches. He volunteered at once and this time was accepted. Curiously, he seems never to have considered, or at least does not mention, the possibility of becoming a pilot. Many of the early aviators and Royal Flying Corps pilots were keen motorcyclists; several of his fellow despatch riders left to join the RFC but Albert, it appears, preferred to keep his feet more or less on the ground.

Albert Simpkin's army career began at the Royal Engineers' depot at Chatham in October 1914. In December of that year he was one of ten despatch riders allotted to the 31st Signal Company. All were straightaway given the rank of corporal, apparently so that they could speak to commissioned officers without previous introduction. After 2 months' training at Buxton in Derbyshire, he was promoted to sergeant of his section, a rank he retained for the remainder of the war. Another 3 months at Buxton were followed by one at Tidworth Camp, Wiltshire. So by the time that his training had been completed, the war was almost a year old.

During 1914 and 1915, the war on the Western Front had progressed (perhaps regressed would be more appropriate) from being a war of movement to one of almost static positions. Several inconclusive battles had been fought, with considerable losses to both sides. The names Mons, Marne and Ypres had already claimed their places in the history books. It was against this background that Sergeant Simpkin sailed with the 37th Division from Southampton. The date was 28 July 1915, just a month after his thirtieth birthday.

After the war, Albert Simpkin returned to his job at Crossley Brothers. If he had needed to find alternative employment, he had been given a glowing reference on demobilisation:

'Sgt Simpkin has discharged the duties of NCO in charge motorcycles and despatch riders in the company with marked success. Energetic, keen and reliable in all his work. Exceptionally good disciplinarian and leader of men. Marked organising ability. Throughout his 4 years of active service he has set a splendid example of personal gallantry which has greatly influenced the personnel under his command.'

During the 1920s, he gained a series of promotions and eventually became chief engineer at the Openshaw works. In September 1926, he married Lily Frances Saywell, then private secretary to Sir Kenneth Crossley at the head office in Openshaw. Coincidentally, Lily's mother's family came from Caudry, the village near Cambrai in north-east France where Albert had spent several days before and after the Armistice.

Soon after his marriage, Albert was sent by Crossley to Buenos Aires to assess the possibilities of opening an office in the city. Prospects were favourable, the office was established, and in around 1930 he was appointed manager. Albert and his wife settled amongst the British ex-pat community in Buenos Aires and, apart from visits to relatives in England (and for Albert to the head office), remained there for the rest of their lives. Albert Simpkin died in 1966 when 80-years-old.

The diarist's character comes across strikingly in the following pages. In later life, when I knew him (he and his wife spent holidays at my parents' farm in Somerset), he retained the strength of character and the wit that are so evident throughout the diary. Having survived so many 'near misses' during the war, he seemed intent on making the most of his good fortune. He never spoke of the war (at least, not to me or other young members of the family – I was 15-years-old when he died) but he must have been only too conscious of the extent of his luck compared with that of many of his contemporaries.

One of the final entries of his diary reads:
'Before the war most of my leisure time was spent in search of mildly dangerous sports, motorcycling, speed trials, hill climbing … All that is over, I have had enough excitement for a lifetime, all I want is the peace of the English countryside and the solitude of the hills, lying in the heather listening to the gentle hissing of the wind.'

THE DIARY
Diaries kept by soldiers during the First World War were all kept against army regulations. In his original preface, which is reproduced in this book, Albert Simpkin wrote:

'My notes were always made in a very abbreviated or even cryptic form which were not intelligible to anyone but myself and I now intend to transcribe my notes before the experiences I have recorded pass out of my memory.'

Clearly, the notes could only have provided a rough framework for the eventual diary entries. But in a later entry, he appears to have written his notes as though he was actually in the field of battle at the time: 'As I write this there is a tremendous bombardment going on …' Perhaps this reflects an attempt to retain a feeling of spontaneity and freshness in the style. It seems doubtful that he would have had the time – or the nerve – to write up during the war. I believe that this was done in the first year or two of his return to civilian life – simply because of the detail and vividness of his description of events.

The typescript contains many hand-written corrections and additions. Whole sections appear to have been retyped at a later date: some of the pages were typed on the reverse of business notepaper, with the heading 'Crossley Bros BA'. As noted earlier, Albert Simpkin first went to Buenos Aires in around 1927. My guess is that he undertook this later work on the diary during the late 1930s, at the time of his first return visit to the battlefields.

To me, the diary entries that stand out most strikingly – and disturbingly, for this is not a book for those with a weak stomach – are those describing the colossal waste of life. On a visit to the battlefields in the 1980s, like many others before me, I was overwhelmed by the rows and rows of gravestones in the military cemeteries and the thousands of names on the monuments to those who had no proper burial. In Albert Simpkin's diary one, often solitary, despatch rider makes his countless, hazardous journeys through all the turmoil and, incredibly, survives to record his experiences for posterity.

There is no doubt that Albert Simpkin intended that his diary should be published. I can only hope that, had he been alive today, he would have approved of this final product of his labours.

David Venner

Itinerary of the 37th Division in France and Belgium

[Chapters 1 and 2: The division was being formed and trained in England]
[Chapter 3]

1915	28 July	Le Havre
	5 August	Caëstre	[E of St Omer]
	24 August	Doullens	[SW of Arras]
	5 September	Pas-en-Artois
1916	[23 to 31 January on leave in England]
	21 February	Bavincourt
	21 March	Lucheux
	3 May	Bavincourt

Battle of the Somme
[Chapter 4]

4 July	Pas-en-Artois
14 July	Lignereuil	[W of Arras]
15 July	Bryas
20 July	La Comté	[NW of Arras]
28 July	Comblain L'Abbé
14 August	Bruay
16 September	Barlin
18 October	Rollecourt
20 October	Le Cauroy
21 October	Beauval
22 October	Marieux	[SW of Arras]

Battle of the Ancre
[Chapter 5]

13 November	Varennes
16 November	Engelbelmer	[N of Albert]
24 November	Marieux
14 December	Frohen-le-Grand)
15 December	Flers)
16 December	Monchy Cayeux)	on trek to the North
18 December	St Venant)
23 December	Lestrum)	[N of Arras]

1917   14 February   Noeux-le-Mines

        4 March   Norren Fontes   [W of Arras]

        9 March   Rollecourt

        5April   Agnez Duisans

Battle of Arras
[Chapter 6]

        10 April   Arras (Ritz Place)

        13 April   Agnes Duisans

        14 April   Lignereuil

        21 April   Arras (candle factory)

        1 May   Lignereuil

        19 May   Warlies

        21 May   Arras

        3 June   Lignereuil

        7 June   Bomy   [S of St Omer]

        23 June   Steenbecque

        24 June   Locre

        29 June   Dranoutre

        1 July   Dranoutre

Third Battle of Ypres
[Chapter 7]

        8 August   Scherpenberg

        12 September   St Jan Cappel

        30 September   Zidcote

        3 October   De Zion Camp

        16 October   St Jan Cappel

        10 November   Scherpenberg

        1 December   Scherpenberg

1918   12–25 January [on leave in England]

        1 February   Blaringhem

        17 February   Westoutre

        25 February   Café Belge

        1 March   Café Belge

        28 March   Left for the South

        29 March   Doullens   [SW of Arras]

        30 March   Toutencourt

| | 1 April | Pas-en-Artois | |
| | 8 April | Couin | |

German Spring Offensive
[Chapter 8]

	16 April	Authie	
	24 April	Hénu	
	18 May	Authie	
	6 June	Cavillion	[S of Amiens]
	10 June	Ailly	
	21 June	Pas-en-Artois	
	23 June	Hénu	
	10 July	Ailly	
	21 July	Pas-en-Artois	
	23 July	Hénu	
	21 August	Achiet-le-Grand	[S of Arras]
	24 August	Fonquevillers	

Final Allied Offensive
[Chapter 9]

	5 September	Favreuil	
	12 September	Vélu Wood	
	21 September	Achiet-le-Grand	
	2 October	Havrincourt Wood	[SW of Cambrai]
	5 October	Gouzeaucourt	
	7 October	Bois Lateau	
	9 October	Haucourt	[SE of Cambrai]
	23 October	Caudry	
	24 October	Briastre	
	5 November	Neuville	

The Armistice
[Chapter 10]

	14 November	Caudry	
	1 December	Gommegnies	[E of Cambrai]
	14–28 December	on leave in England	
	29 December	Boulogne	
1919	4 January	Gosselies	[S of Brussels]

List of Abbreviations

AA	Anti-Aircraft
ACU	Auto Cyclists' Union
ADC	Aide de Camp
ADMS	Assistant Director Medical Services
Anzacs	Australian and New Zealand Army Corps
APM	Assistant Provost Marshal (Military Police)
CO	Company Officer
CRE	Commander Royal Engineers
DCM	Distinguished Conduct Medal
DR	Despatch Rider
GOC	General Officer Commanding
GS	General Service
GSO1	General Staff Officer No 1
HQ	Headquarters
MC	Military Cross
MM	Military Medal
MO	Medical Officer
MP	Military Police
NCO	Non-Commissioned Officer
OC	Officer Commanding
QMS	Quarter Master Sergeant
RAMC	Royal Army Medical Corps
RE	Royal Engineers
RFA	Royal Field Artillery
RFC	Royal Flying Corps
Sgt	Sergeant
SM	Sergeant Major
VC	Victoria Cross
YMCA	Young Men's Christian Association

Preface

During my 4 years' service as a despatch rider (DR) I kept a diary. According to army regulations, diaries were not allowed while on active service. Therefore my notes were always made in a very abbreviated or even cryptic form which was not intelligible to anyone but myself. I now intend to transcribe my notes before the experiences I have recorded pass out of my memory.

Looking back, I am sure a despatch rider with a division had one of the most interesting jobs in the army. All day long he was roaming the shell-broken roads and tracks behind the trenches, acting as postman, keeping the staff in touch with the infantry and artillery brigades and auxiliary units located in the divisional area. The DR, as he was always called, saw the war from the 'stalls', sometimes running the gauntlet of the shelling of the roads within range of the German artillery. His greatest danger came from road transport at night, when the ammunition and supplies were sent up the line under the cover of darkness. Worming his way through the horse and motor waggons and the long lines of pack animals, he risked falling under the wheels of vehicles or becoming a target for the hooves of the horses and mules, who had a rabid hatred of motorcycles and showed it by lashing out with their hind legs.

In summer the DR lived in a cloud of dust; in the winter he was plastered with mud. In times of trouble and strife he had no set working hours. He worked on a roster, eating and sleeping when he could. He was the despair of the sergeant major because he could not be subjected to strict army discipline and routine. When the DR left HQ with despatches he might have to find his quarry without the help of a map reference in an area of 10 square miles, often at night, no headlights allowed.

A classic example of finding a needle in a haystack was made by one of our fellows when the division was leaving the Somme. An urgent message had to be delivered to an officer travelling north, who was thought to be on a 10 mile stretch of road crowded with troops and transport moving in opposite directions. It was pitch dark, raining in torrents and blowing a howling gale. The officer would, most likely, be inside a lorry with the infantry. Our DR found his man after a 3 hour search. Even the staff expressed their astonishment and appreciation. They had not expected the officer to be found before daylight.

In times like these the DR relies on his experience and instinct. A failure on his part would be looked upon as a reflection of the whole section.

'Neither snow nor rain nor heat nor the gloom of night stays these couriers from the swift accomplishment of their appointed routes.' There is little doubt that Herodotus had the despatch rider in mind when he wrote these words.

CHAPTER ONE

Joining up

1 AUGUST 1914, MANCHESTER

The newspapers are full of the declaration of war between France and Germany. Six months ago one would have said that war was impossible in these enlightened times, but looking back, it is now plain that Germany has been preparing for war for the past 10 years and her periodic threats were not idle ones, and now she has taken the opportunity of using the Serbian affair as an excuse to declare war.

My brother came home from the Territorials' camp today. From what he has heard it is almost certain that Britain will be drawn into the quarrel. He expects to be called up at any moment.

3 AUGUST 1914, REDCAR

I had to go to Redcar [Yorkshire] today on business. At night in the hotel, I had to listen to a lot of cheap 'Jingos' who were very wrath with Asquith that the government had not declared war. In the hotel was a young fellow about my age who confided to me that he was on his honeymoon and that he was a reservist and would be called up if war was declared. I felt sorry for him having to listen to these fools who would rush into war without considering the consequences.

4 AUGUST 1914

At about noon, I saw a group of people gathered outside the post office reading a telegram posted on the notice board: 'England has declared War on Germany.' There was no excitement. It was evident that the people did not realise its significance. Later in the afternoon, there was a rumour that a naval battle was being fought off Flamborough Head. Crowds gathered on the seafront but nothing could be heard or seen.

5 AUGUST 1914, MANCHESTER

My brother has been called up and spends his time with the officers, commandeering horses for the artillery, which is causing no little stir among the townspeople. One old fellow I know is hiding his horse in the back yard, but from what I have seen of the animal there is little likelihood of its being taken.

1 SEPTEMBER 1914

The country has got the war fever badly. The recruiting stations are besieged but only names are being taken at present. I have put my name down for the RFA – I tried to get into my brother's battery but they will not take inexperienced men.

14 SEPTEMBER 1914

I have been travelling up and down the country almost continuously: Carlisle, North Wales, Cardiff, Devon. I now use my motorcycle for all journeys as I find it quicker and more convenient than the trains. Whilst in Bideford [Devon] I saw one of the German bands who visit England each summer, wandering through the country towns and villages playing for coppers. Nobody was taking any notice of them, except some small boys who were making rude noises. Being enemy subjects, I suppose they are stranded and will be interned. I felt sorry for them. People are saying that the war will be over by Christmas. I cannot believe it – the war has not started and the news does not look good.

I have called at the RFA recruiting office several times, but they have no news when we shall be called up. The infantry are now taking men but I do not care for the infantry. I always hated walking! I do not think I ever walked 5 miles at a stretch; I have almost lived on wheels since I was 12-years-old. I would cycle to the end of the road to post a letter and later I took to motorcycling as the natural sequel to push cycling. The infantry with its 'foot-slogging' has no attraction to me. In the RFA, I should ride a horse or have a seat on a limber or waggon, or at least that is what I thought.

I put my name down for future units which might be formed and waited hopefully for several weeks.

Some of my friends have gone to join the Manchester Pals Battalion and I am greatly tempted to follow them in sheer despair at not being able to get into the RFA.

26 SEPTEMBER 1914

A few days ago I received a notice from the Auto Cyclists' Union (ACU) of which I am a member, calling for experienced motorcyclists to join the army as despatch riders. I filled in the form and today I received word to report to the ACU office in London.

15 OCTOBER 1914

According to the ACU, the army will buy any motorcycle in good condition belonging to the recruits. I have therefore bought a new Douglas Twin as my machine is 3-years-old and getting the worse for wear. I have also bought some heavy wool underclothes in anticipation of the winter as we hear there is a big shortage of uniforms and clothing for new recruits. I have also paid some visits to the dentist to have my teeth overhauled.

I shall not tell my firm that I am joining up until the last moment as I see there is a plan to put all engineers on a civilian basis which will not allow them to join the army.

26 OCTOBER 1914

Travelled to London today. My father saw me off at the station, I felt no more emotion than if I had been making one of my normal business trips, although I expected to be sent to France right away.

27 OCTOBER 1914

A full day. First I went to the ACU office where I found a couple of dozen fellows there for the same purpose as myself. Each one was questioned as to his education, occupation and motor-cycling experience. We were supposed to know something of map reading and French. I have been swotting up my school French which was pretty rusty, but found I had remembered sufficient to ask and answer simple questions.

After this we were sent to Whitehall for medical examination. I passed all right, but several were turned down for ruptures or poor eyesight. We were then passed to another department where, standing in a circle with Bible in hand, we were sworn in a dozen at a time. Just as the officer began to read the oath one fellow blurted out, 'Oh, I can't, I'm a Jew,' which raised a general laugh.

He was told to stand aside and the business proceeded. Then we filled in some forms and lastly received our first day's pay, two brand new shillings – just enough to keep one in cigarettes and a couple of drinks per day. We are now soldiers of the King, the rawest of raw recruits. We were told to report to the Royal Engineers' depot at Chatham tomorrow.

28 OCTOBER 1914, CHATHAM

Presenting ourselves at the depot this morning we were at once promoted to the rank of corporal. It seems all despatch riders have to be corporals which gives them the privilege of speaking with a commissioned officer without previous introduction, or something similar. It is all very mysterious and amusing. What a regular army corporal would say it would be interesting to hear.

CHAPTER TWO

Training

2 DECEMBER 1914, CHATHAM

Today we were issued with a uniform of sorts. It is made of very thin serge with black bone buttons. Some of the fellows recognise it as being similar to those worn by native troops in the tropics. For headgear we have been given a shiny peaked hat like a tram driver's. We have also been issued with a civilian overcoat, two shirts, 'one on and one in the wash' as the Quartermaster said, two pairs of socks, two pairs of boots which look suspiciously like brown paper, a knife, fork and spoon and lastly a piece of cutlery which we eventually identified as an army razor.

Those who have not brought their own motorcycles have been issued with new machines, BSA, Zenith, Rudge, Douglas etc. I have brought my own Douglas for which I shall be paid.

3 DECEMBER 1914

Today we made our first appearance in uniform feeling very self-conscious – even the officers could not suppress a smile. We look like a set of convicts. We have been divided into three sections, about ten to a section. Each section has been allotted to a Signal Company, the 30th, 31st and 32nd. I am in the 31st Signal Company.

We have been told we are being sent to Buxton for training and we are leaving tomorrow. This is rather a disappointment as I expected to be sent to France right away, but from what I have seen of some of these fellows riding I am not surprised. Very few could be called experienced riders.

4 DECEMBER 1914

This morning we loaded our machines in railway vans at the local station, but first we had to empty the tanks and the local taxi drivers got a windfall of free petrol. Crossing London, our section tried to make a procession of pairs but we lost two riders on the way. Arriving at St Pancras we found an RE sergeant waiting to take charge. When the train stopped at Leicester Square I was astonished to hear someone calling my name. I put my head out of the window and a boy thrust a telegram into my hand. For an awful moment I thought it was from my employers telling me to return. It was from Morris saying he had missed the train and was coming on the next. My name was the only one he could remember.

It was past nine o'clock when we reached Buxton, a black night with drizzling rain. What awaited us we had not the slightest idea – a camp with tents we imagined. We were marched off in groups according to our Company. We had a very pleasant surprise to find ourselves billeted in a small Hydro with a hot meal awaiting us. This is soldiering under ideal conditions.

1 JANUARY 1915, BUXTON

We have now been in the army just a month. Our daily routine is usually as follows. We parade at 07:30 washed and shaved. After roll call we go for a route march, then breakfast, followed by drill, with a long break before dinner. In the afternoon we have buzzer practice, flag waving and Morse. Then we have lectures on electricity and the construction of telegraph instruments. If we are to become expert in all these we shall not see France for a long time.

Occasionally we get out on our motorcycles when we indulge in scorching to our hearts' content, much to the alarm of the townspeople who have not seen really fast riding before.

22 JANUARY 1915

One of the section, Morris, has left us to take a commission in the naval machine guns. We gave him a dinner at one of the local hotels and an uproarious send-off. There is a craze for collecting souvenirs: ashtrays from local pubs, name plates and sign boards. The chief souvenir, however, is a huge dinner gong which stands in the hall of one of the billets. It has changed hands several times but it is a point of honour that it must be captured by stealth and not by combat, and it must be kept in the entrance hall.

Hockey on roller skates is the latest craze. Each signal company has a team and some fierce matches have been played, usually with casualties. One of our team, Norman, had his ankle broken last week.

12 FEBRUARY 1915

Today I was promoted to sergeant of the despatch riders' section – why I do not know. I am not senior in service or years, but possibly I am the most experienced rider, and have a good drilling voice. That voice, which used to be such a trouble to me in my teens, loud and gruff, has come into its own. As my mother used to say, 'Keep anything seven years and it is sure to come in.'

3 MARCH 1915

We are now engaged in schemes in which the whole company takes part. Telegraph lines are laid across country to outlying villages where signal offices are set up, usually in a room of the village pub. The DRs keep communication between these offices and HQ which is in Buxton. One of the offices is in Castleton, 10 miles away. There is great competition between the riders to set up the fastest time between the two places.

8 MARCH 1915

One of our riders, Blakeway, had a bad smash yesterday. He is in the cottage hospital with a broken leg, a broken collar bone and smashed fingers. He came in head-on collision with an officer who was learning to ride a motorcycle. The officer had concussion – it is a wonder neither was killed. I am afraid the major will stop fast riding after this accident. According to Blakeway the officer lost his head and came round a corner on the wrong side.

9 MARCH 1915

There is an epidemic of measles in the army, the German variety. Today I felt very seedy and feverish so I went to the doctor and had to go to bed right away. There is a house set apart for measles and scabies which is also very rife.

15 MARCH 1915

Out for the first time today, after 4 days in bed and isolation for the remainder of the time. At one end of the room were men with measles and at the other men with scabies. It is a wonder we did not get the scabies and they the measles.

17 MARCH 1915

I returned to the section today. Blakeway is still in hospital and from all accounts he will be there another month. He has his souvenirs arranged on the mantle-piece of his room. The apple of his eye is the nameplate of a local doctor, and who should walk in one day but the doctor himself. He was a good sport and pretended not to see it, but I have no doubt its cost will be on the bill. Blakeway is having private treatment.

4 APRIL 1915

To keep us fit and amused we have cross country races and sham fights. In one 'fight' we were supposed to storm a fort at the top of a hill. To make things more realistic one of the officers had brought a number of rockets and crackers which the defenders let off at the attackers. One of the fellows managed to stop a rocket in full flight with his face, fortunately with no worse result than a splendid black eye. Everyone agrees they have never seen a finer one. Shaftoe, the owner, is quite a good sport and has allowed it to be photographed from all angles.

10 APRIL 1915

Our training continues, lamp signalling at night, map making and reading, horse riding, telegraph pole climbing with leg irons, wiring; there seems to be no end to it. There are no signs of our going to France just yet. Occasionally, we have 'scheme days' on our motorcycles. We are given a route over the roughest roads and tracks, usually among the hills to test our map-reading and riding ability.

Since arriving at Buxton we have paid for all the petrol used in our motorcycles. It appears there is no provision in the company's expenses for buying petrol. I hope this will not continue much longer or we shall all be broke. I have already spent a lot more than the army has paid which has to be made up from my private account. Although many firms pay volunteers full or half pay, the firm I was with pay nothing.

2 MAY 1915

We hear that we are moving very shortly to Hitchin, which is the HQ of the signal companies and from there we shall be sent to France. This sounds promising.

4 MAY 1915

The DRs travelled down by road, the mechanic and me bringing up the rear to give aid in case of breakdowns. I do not think we rode more than five miles continuously without having to stop to help one rider or another. I am beginning to think that some of these fellows will never make riders. A man should understand his machine as well as be able to ride it.

8 JUNE 1915

The townspeople have been making complaints about the fast riding and the noise of the motorcycles. This morning when the company was dismissed the DRs were told to stand fast.

The OC came over and started to read the riot act. 'This mad riding must stop, all the townspeople are complaining and the next man who …' – the OC paused and looked up the road. A motorcycle could be heard tearing down the Letchworth Hill and the next moment it flashed past the parade like a streak of lightning. The OC exploded: 'Who was that man, Sergeant Major? Bring him up tonight and I will make an example of him.' It was 'Jersey' [Corporal R. Norman] putting his foot in it as usual.

A smile of satisfaction passed over the sergeant major's face, the DRs are the bane of his life. Their happy-go-lucky manner of running roughshod over all army rules is turning his hair grey. 'And when they gets on them motorbikes they goes stark mad – talk about training the young buggers, they want taming first!'

10 JUNE 1915

We are leaving Hitchin tomorrow and we shall not be sorry to go. It is a small town and the country around is very uninteresting.

12 JUNE 1915, TIDWORTH

Six DRs were told to travel by road to Tidworth but only three arrived, myself and two others. Two disappeared and one had a collision with a motor car and we had to leave him behind to get his machine repaired. What use these fellows will be as DRs I cannot think, they cannot ride a few miles without having an accident or losing their way.

The missing riders turned up this morning, one slept in a ditch all night after wandering all over Salisbury Plain without finding us. The plain is covered with camps in all directions.

13 JUNE 1915

We have taken over the complete equipment of the company we are relieving, which includes twenty or thirty mules. The night I arrived in camp there was a continual sound of 'outbursts' from the direction of the horse lines. I couldn't sleep for the noise. At last I asked, 'What's that noise?' 'Oh, that's the mules farting.' I thought the fellow was trying to pull my leg so I said no more, but it was true enough. The poor brutes had not been exercised for days and from the effects of a corn diet their bellies were blown up like balloons.

16 JUNE 1915

The weather has been frightfully hot since we arrived. Our camp is in a hollow, the ground pure chalk which reflects the heat. In the early afternoon it is unbearable.

18 JUNE 1915

One of our DRs – Nunn – has had a bad smash at one of the crossroads nearby, colliding with a motor car. It is a miracle he was not killed. His leg is badly broken so he will be a non-starter when we go overseas. This makes three we have in hospital. Just before we left Hitchin we lost a rider who was taken to hospital for repairs to his face after running into the back of a lorry while on a night scheme. We were not upset when we heard the news as he was very unpopular and the butt of the section.

25 JUNE 1915

Our division, the 37th, was reviewed [at Cholderton] by HM The King today. It was a fine sight, especially the march past which stretched for almost a mile. As the King passed on horseback with our General Gleichen who I believe is a cousin of the King, I heard the King say, 'There are some despatch riders short,' which was quite correct: some were on duty and others in hospital. The 37th Division will be one of the first of the 'Kitchener's Divisions' to go to France.

4 JULY 1915

Another rider went to hospital today. A smash at the same crossroads where Nunn had his accident last week. It is the same prize idiot who tried to move a waggon with his face. He had not been back two or three days. To go to hospital twice in one month must be a record. Anyway, he will not be missed, but this series of accidents is making the DRs look very foolish.

10 JULY 1915

We are to be given five days' leave before we go to France.

14 JULY 1915

I caught the 18:00 train from Salisbury, arriving home for breakfast.

19 JULY 1915

Returned to Tidworth today. I spent my time quietly, visiting friends and putting my few affairs in order. There were no parting scenes thank goodness, in fact I might have been going on holiday.

20 JULY 1915

Our new motorcycles have arrived, all Triumphs. I find they handle rather heavily compared with my light Douglas machine. While I have been away 'Jersey' has been in the limelight again. One morning, having some spare time on his hands, he volunteered to take the general's horse to water. Riding bareback, everything went well until they reached the horse troughs when something startled the horse and it took a jump clean over the troughs. It then tore across the plain at full gallop with 'Jersey' holding on for dear life. The troops waved and cheered which urged the horse to greater efforts, taking ditches and hedges like a hunter, in fact, it was a hunter. After dashing through a farmyard, to the astonishment of some men building a haystack, it headed for home arriving in time to deposit its rider almost at the feet of the general who, pretending not to see the hurried dismount, dryly remarked, 'That horse has been galloping.'

27 JULY 1915

We are under orders to move at eight hours' notice. As the company is considerably over-strength the surplus men have to be sent back to the Reserve Depot. Although it is known more or less who would be left behind it has caused much heartburning now the names are posted. It must have been very difficult to pick out the men who should be left behind because with very few exceptions the company is uniformly good. In our section we have no surplus. All our reserves are in hospital. Two days ago we were one man over-strength but the man himself solved the question by colliding with a waggon which landed him in hospital. He was something of a mystery man, considerably older than the rest. He came from South Africa to join, having worked for some years in the diamond mines, a tough character, a hard drinker, but a poor rider. His age is not less than 40 although the average age is around 24-years-old. I am pleased to lose him.

28 JULY 1915

We were up at 04:00 and by 07:00 we were on our way to Tidworth station. The train left about 09:30 but we did not reach Southampton till 15:00 after a most extraordinary journey. Hour after hour the train kept up a steady forty miles per hour. Where we were taken and how far we travelled in that six-hour journey I cannot imagine. Tidworth is no more than 30 miles from Southampton as the crow flies. The train ran on to the quay and alongside was a small transport steamer called Nirvana, a name which sounded rather ominous.

We sailed about midnight – the night was overcast, not a star showing. The ship was escorted by two destroyers which scurried around like a couple of sheep dogs, disappearing into the blackness and then reappearing where least expected, their white bow wave alone showing their presence.

Daylight was just beginning to show as we entered the outer harbour of Le Havre. In the afternoon we were sent to a rest camp outside the town. We are entraining for the Front tomorrow.

CHAPTER THREE

July 1915 – June 1916

30 JULY 1915, LE HAVRE

At 10.00 we were ordered to go to the railway station for entraining. We had to travel around the outskirts of the town to reach the station. The roads were paved with uneven cobblestones deep in mud and garbage. I never saw such a filthy place. We reached the station with one of our number missing, 'Jersey' as usual. He turned up 30 minutes later having been in collision with a steam tram, fortunately with no worse hurt than a bent mudguard and a few personal bruises. A large covered van was assigned to the DRs. We stacked our machines at either end leaving a space between for ourselves. As we heard that we should not arrive at our destination until tomorrow afternoon we pressed some French boys into our service to buy us some bottles of wine, bread, tins of sardines, pâté, and cheese etc.

About noon the train moved off without the slightest warning. Half the company were on the track waiting for something to happen so there was a mad scramble to climb into the waggons. Slowly at first but gradually the speed increased until we were dashing along at a good ten miles an hour.

Keeping up this giddy speed for a couple of hours, the train suddenly stopped with a bang which brought several motorcycles crashing down and everyone on their feet was thrown to the floor, one fellow collecting a black eye. Picking ourselves up, we all got down on to the track, thinking there had been a collision but we were mistaken, it was our first experience of the normal manner of stopping a French troop train.

We ate, drank, played cards and slept all day, the train slowly meandering along with many halts at wayside stations and sidings, sometimes for hours at a time. Next morning we awoke to find a fine sunny day and the train running along sand hills near the sea. By the aid of a map we found we were near Calais but shortly afterwards the train turned inland and we were left guessing as to our destination: such are the ways of the army.

About mid-day we ran into a fairly large station, St Omer. We noticed that all the people on the platform were gazing upwards in an excited manner. When the train stopped we could hear guns firing and the sky was dotted with puffs of white smoke. A German aeroplane had just passed over the town and had met a hot reception from our artillery. This is the first sign of the war we have seen although we can hear the rumble of guns in the distance.

1 AUGUST 1915, ARQUES, NEAR ST OMER

The Divisional Staff have made their HQ in a large farm. Last night we slept in a barn on deep clean straw. The place was alive with rats which ran over our bodies and sniffed inquisitively in our faces. One of the fellows awoke with a yell, a rat had bitten his ear.

A young artillery man is doing No.1 field punishment tied up to a waggon wheel in the farmyard. The French people are expressing their views in no uncertain manner. It is time this form of punishment was abolished, it is a relic of the flogging days. It does far more harm than good having a bad effect on the troops, making them sulky.

5 AUGUST 1915, CAËSTRE

The DRs had their first real job of work last night. Moving instructions had to be delivered to all units of the division. Several units had lost themselves: some we found miles away from their appointed stopping place having wandered on until the troops could walk no farther so turned into the nearest field. Most of the DRs were out all night and it was daylight before they found the last of the units. It is quite evident that some officers cannot read maps. I hear the staff were in a tearing rage about the matter as they could not go to bed until all the units had been accounted for.

We are now at Caëstre, a village on the main road from Cassel to Bailleul. This road is one of the main arteries leading to the Front. All day long streams of traffic pass through the village, marching infantry, batteries of field artillery, staff cars, motor lorries and horse transport. The guns sound very near and at night the sky is lit with their flashes.

Our infantry are going into the trenches at Ploegsteert and Armentières for a course of training.

We shall remain here until they come back. We have been unlucky with our billet, this time we have a stinking barn with filthy damp straw which has not been changed for months.

I had a narrow escape today. Rounding a corner I found myself going head first into the radiator of a staff car. Instinctively I swerved to the left, which of course was wrong. I realised I had made a mistake so dived for the ditch to avoid a head-on collision. I escaped with a shaking and a severe cursing from the officers.

Riding a motorcycle after dark has a danger we did not foresee. Every camp and HQ has its sentries, who are frightfully keen, challenging everything that passes. It is said that one shot a stray donkey the other night because it did not say 'Friend'. As it is impossible for a motorcyclist to hear the challenge above the noise of the wind and the engine he stands a good chance of meeting the donkey's fate or getting skewered with a bayonet.

10 AUGUST 1915

Today I saw a German aeroplane which I believe was one of the class called the Taube. It sailed along at about 4,000ft, following the main Cassel road, apparently unobserved by our gunners. Half an hour later a group of three came over and immediately the guns of Mont de Cats started shelling them. Mont de Cats is one of the several small hills which stand up like pimples in a zone of perfectly flat country called the Flanders Plain. Others are Mont Rouge, Mont Kemmel and Scherpenberg. The German trenches lie along the crest of a range of low hills which run for several miles forming a semi-circle around Ypres. Our trenches lie at the foot or on the slopes of the hills and thus we are overlooked by the Germans.

Our artillery HQ is in a château which is surrounded by a moat. An old man and his wife live in the château. They are a queer pair – he spends his time fishing in the moat and she is occupied to the full guarding the orchard. One day she found 'Jersey' admiring the fruit and she chased him out with a broom stick, much to everyone's amusement.

The boys play a trick on the old man by dropping a small piece of calcium carbide in the water alongside his float when he is not looking. It makes a stream of bubbles and the old man grips his rod and makes all preparations to land a big fish. For the old dame we have devised another little game calling out, '*Madame, Madame, vite vite, voleurs dans le jardin,*' and out she dashes with her trusty stave ready for battle. '*Trop tarde, Madame!*' everyone cries.

24 AUGUST 1915, DOULLENS

Yesterday evening I was ordered to have three DRs and myself ready to leave this morning with our CO for Doullens. Riding in pairs behind the CO's car, we kept off the main roads as much as possible as they were packed with troops and transport. Beyond St Pol we entered the French area, the traffic thinned out and we saw nothing but French troops. Arriving in Doullens in the early afternoon we became the centre of a large crowd.

We were in some doubt whether it was the novelty of being British or the fact that we were smothered in white dust from riding behind the car.

26 AUGUST 1915

Doullens is a clean little country town. The surrounding country looks fertile and prosperous. The people in these parts are distinctly French, far more so than those in the north. The shops are doing a roaring trade with the British troops but shopping for those who have no French has its difficulties. Today I was in a small grocer's shop waiting my turn to be served. The shop was full of women doing their morning shopping. Bill, our cook, was just in front of me. When it came his turn he thrust out his hand in which he had a round piece of soap and started clucking like a hen, at the same time holding up two fingers. For a moment there was complete silence; Madame must have thought Bill had taken leave of his senses, and then it dawned upon her and she went off into shrieks of laughter as did all the other women. Bill got what he wanted.

1 SEPTEMBER 1915

It has been extremely hot these last few days. There is a river outside the town so we went for a swim but we had the surprise of our lives. The water was so cold it was positively painful. It was amusing to hear the lurid remarks as each one scrambled out as quickly as he had plunged in. The water came from a nearby spring.

3 SEPTEMBER 1915

We are still in Doullens. Our infantry have already taken over part of the Line from the French in front of Pommier. Last night I took a message to the Brigade HQ whose signal office was in the cellars of the *mairie*. The trenches start in the outskirts of the village and the machine guns sounded as though they were less than 100yd away. The Star lights [flares] lit the walls of the houses like bright moonlight. A battery hidden behind the village made the signal office shake and the candles blink. Civilians are still living in the village: I noticed a faint light behind some of the boarded windows.

6 SEPTEMBER 1915, PAS-EN-ARTOIS

We moved to Pas today. Pas-en-Artois, to give the village its full name, is a fair-sized village lying in a deep valley whose slopes are covered with thick woods. The divisional staff have made their HQ in a château which belongs to the Comte de Pas. It is a picturesque old place standing in large grounds.

The signal company have been given the stables as their billet. The NCOs have three small rooms which must have been the servants' quarters. As we are likely to stay here some time we are all busy making ourselves 'comfortable'. Comfort to a soldier means, firstly, a bed, secondly, a shelf and some nails on which to hang his kit and, thirdly, a picture gallery of postcards and illustrations cut from magazines. The bed is generally made up of all manner of bits and pieces, a veritable rack of torture but the pride of its owner. The walls of our room are covered with pictures from *La Vie Parisienne*, left by the former occupants, some French officers. We have a constant stream of visitors, all worshipping at the shrine of Venus. In the next room, occupied by Jock Gunning, a sergeant telegraphist, is a full-sized crucifix minus a leg and an arm, a most depressing room-mate. The French people are superstitious about destroying it so it is left to moulder away.

12 SEPTEMBER 1915

When they took over from the French our infantry found the trenches in a very bad state: mostly very shallow with the sides falling in. There were no dugouts worthy of the name and the French had lived in shelters on the top, having an understanding with the Germans who also walked about in broad daylight. Some of the Frenchmen said that they and the

Germans often visited each other's trenches for a chat. The Germans even went to a French *estaminet* in Berle-au-Bois – this is confirmed by the woman who keeps it. The war around here seems to have been conducted in a spirit of brotherly love. Berle-au-Bois is less than 1,000yd from the frontline. The village is practically intact and most of the houses are occupied. The fields behind the village are cultivated right up to the communication trenches. Our division is the only British division in the area, we have French troops on either side of us.

13 SEPTEMBER 1915

Almost every day we have German aeroplanes over our side of the Line. The French 75s give them a hot reception, their shooting is wonderful. This afternoon a German aeroplane was sailing along followed by a string of shell bursts which were gradually overtaking him, and it looked as though the next would get him, when he made a complete circle which upset the gunners' aim. Very few British aeroplanes are seen in these parts and very few French aeroplanes for that matter.

20 SEPTEMBER 1915

Having nothing to do, I went to Bienvillers to relieve the monotony. Arriving at HQ, I found one of our linesmen just setting out for an inspection of the telephone wires in the trenches. I asked him to take me along. The trenches he was to visit lay in front of Hannescamps. Following a communication trench from the village we took another which zig-zagged up a slight hill towards the frontline. There was not a breath of air stirring and by the time we reached the frontline we were dripping with sweat. The heat of the sun reflected by the chalk walls of the trenches was like a furnace.

Here the linesmen left me to my own devices whilst he searched for a fault. Seeing a steel plate set in the parapet of the trench I was in the act of sliding back a shutter when someone grabbed me by the arm and pulled me away. 'Don't look through there, chum, that plate is marked, one of our fellows was killed there last week. Just you watch.' So saying he pulled back the slide. After 2 or 3 minutes there was a distant crack and the 'phitt' of a bullet passing over. Several more came, some hitting the parapet. The slide was then shut and the firing ceased.

The sniper could see daylight through the loop hole. After this warning I was taken to a proper observation post and had a look at the

German line through the glasses. There were a few Germans working on top well behind their frontline.

The Saxons are opposite us, and when the Saxons are in there is an unofficial armistice. When the Prussians are in there is constant machine gun and artillery fire, especially at night. Last week, early one morning, our sentries in the frontline heard someone calling, 'Hello Tommy,' but our sentry did not reply. The voice called again, 'Hello Tommy', and one of men replied 'Hello', The voice then said, 'We are Saxons, you are Anglo Saxons: we shall not fire if you don't.'

10 OCTOBER 1915

Our part of the line is very quiet. The DRs have very little to do. The days slip by and it becomes a matter of careful calculation to decide the day of the week.

The château is owned by the Comte de Pas. I do not know if it is his real title or merely a courtesy one like our Squire at home. Counts are as common as blackberries in France. The old count makes a picturesque figure going around in a long black cape and wide brimmed hat. His face is long, deathly white with a black beard and a most sorrowful expression. 'Old Misery' the troops call him. He has a great reputation for meanness among the villagers and if a Frenchman says a man is mean there is no doubt about it.

Behind the château is a large wood. Rumour has it that the count was hunting wild boar in this wood and accidentally shot his wife dead. There is a statue in the wood to her which seems to bear out the rumour. He now has another wife, a good deal younger than himself. She only appears in Pas when she wants money and spends the rest of her time in Paris; the villagers say she leads him a pretty dance.

10 NOVEMBER 1915

I had a very interesting journey last night. I had to take a 'special' to Brigadier General Bainbridge of 100 Brigade, who was arriving by train at Amiens at about midnight. It was a beautiful night, bright moonlight, with a clear frosty air, intensely cold. For the first few miles the road wound along a deep valley with dense woods on either slope until it struck the main Amiens road which is broad and straight. There was very little transport on the roads so I pushed along at a smart pace, thoroughly enjoying the ride. Now and again I passed through a sleeping village, not a light showing, the exhaust echoing from the houses like an express in a tunnel. The horizon on the left was lit up with the flash of guns. Arriving at the outskirts of Amiens I stopped at the barricade to show my *laisser faire* to the French sentries.

I entered the town by a wide boulevard lit by glaring arc lights. The place seemed deserted. The station is similar to all large railway stations, a single span glass roof which collects the wind like a funnel. It was colder inside the station than outside. I made enquiries about the time of the arrival of the leave train and was informed it was running two hours late and would not arrive until 02:30 at the earliest. I made friends with the Military Police who took me along to their room where there was a blazing fire. I found one of the MPs came from Bideford where I have spent some happy times in the old 'Steam Packet' public house.

At last the leave train arrived and the problem was how to find the general among a thousand officers and men. I chose the centre of the train as being the most likely place to find him and immediately the train stopped I began in my best drilling voice, 'A despatch for General Bainbridge, despatch for General Bainbridge,' like 'Buttons' in a hotel. A window dropped and an officer called out. I had dropped almost on the exact spot. The general was highly amused at my novel way of finding him. The message delivered, I set off on the return journey. The wind bit to the bone and there was a suggestion of snow in the air. When I got back I took a stiff tot of rum which I had hoarded for these occasions and tumbled into bed.

4 DECEMBER 1915

Jock Gunning has been on leave and brought back a bottle of whisky which he doled out. My share was half of tumbler full. It was just before going on parade and without thinking I knocked it back – on an empty stomach too – with a 'Thanks Jock, Scotland for ever.' Very soon I began to realise I was a wee bit 'foo', when I bent down I nearly fell over, but nobody noticed it. Then as luck would have it the major sent for me. There was a fierce battle going on between body and will power. Fortunately I managed to pass the ordeal.

15 DECEMBER 1915

Christmas will soon be here again and the main topic of conversation is leave. There has been a brisk business in the buying and selling of leave dates. The Christmas leave has been sold for 100 Francs to a fellow we all detest. At the present allotment rate I should be going home about the end of January.

In spite of the Line being so quiet we have two or three casualties each day. Almost every morning going up to the brigade in Bienvillers I meet a burial party. These casualties are mostly from sniping and trench mortar fire. The German mortars are called *Minenwerfers* or 'Minnies' for short. They throw a huge bomb, far greater than an ordinary shell, which explodes on contact. It has a slow flight and can be seen flying through the air turning over and over like a crazy barrel. It explodes with a tremendous roar making a hole large enough to bury a haystack. The mortar which fires it gives a low 'woof' and the next moment there is a general cry 'Minnie up' and everyone searches the sky for the black object to judge its line of flight. Fortunately it is not very accurate and most of them fall harmlessly in no-man's land or behind the trenches.

27 December 1915

The DRs' Christmas dinner was a great success. Soup, fish, goose, plum pudding and all the usual trimmings. The wine list was wonderful for its variety: something to suit everyone's taste.

The dinner was held in one of the village *estaminets*, 'La Poste'. The French people cooked it and we all agreed that they upheld the French reputation in the art of cooking.

After we had drunk every toast we could invent as an excuse for a glass we adjourned to the DRs' billet for entertainment and refreshment. Everyone had to give a song, no excuses accepted, and so it went on until midnight. By this time some of the boys were *hors de combat*. Blakeway's singing mixture, champagne lashed with cognac, accounted for quite a few: it's alright for swans but a bit strong for canaries. Shaftoe acted as wet nurse, putting them to bed as they fell out of the ranks. If Shaftoe decided they had enough, to bed they had to go. We ended up with 'Auld Lang Syne'.

We had invited the old sergeant major. Although he is a seasoned cask he had overlooked that he had to carry it down three flights of a narrow winding staircase. It was suggested we should rope ourselves 'alpine fashion' with the SM in the middle, one steadying him from above and two from below. Blakeway encouraged us with blood-curdling yells which he said was yodelling.

The old SM was as merry as a sand boy. Two of us escorted him through the village singing at the top of our voices. Arriving at his billet we had to call out the QMS from his bed to help our charge up the stairs, by that time he had become very heavy. And so to bed.

1 JANUARY 1916

New Year passed without the usual festivities. Everyone was on duty. An attack from the Germans to mark the New Year was expected, but nothing happened. At midnight our artillery gave them a lively 10 minutes' bombardment to remind them of things to come, which produced very little retaliation. Possibly it was to prevent the troops fraternizing as they did last year in some sectors. I wonder where we shall be this time next year. Let us hope it will all be over.

We are having wretched weather, raining every day, everywhere deep in mud. Some of the boys are making fancy mudguards for their motorcycles. After an hour's riding we are plastered with mud from head to foot and the only way to clean oneself is to wash down with buckets of water.

7 JANUARY 1916

Some wild stories have been going around about the DRs' Christmas revelry. One fool yarn has it that we carried the SM home on a stretcher which is hitting below the belt. The SM carried his liquor like a gentleman and was merry and bright until we left him when he said he would not be long out of bed, 'after he had taken his nightcap'.

8 JANUARY 1916

Our artillery has been very active during these past few days, so it looks as though the shortage of ammunition was a temporary one. A battery of 60 pounders has been added to our artillery strength which has been stirring up trouble and the Germans are retaliating on Bienvillers. These guns seem to be a very old-fashioned type. Apparently they have no recoil chambers.

Each time they fire they jump back a couple of feet and have to be re-laid. I think they must be something left over from the Boer War.

9 JANUARY 1916

Some shells dropped in Souastre today - it was the first time it has been shelled. The inhabitants blame us for it. Bienvillers is shelled almost daily but several civilians are still living in their homes, which in some cases are partly demolished. They sleep in the cellars at night and during the day they live on top, hoping that they will have time to reach safety when the shelling begins.

10 JANUARY 1916

Noticing a stranger at the Bienvillers HQ today who seemed to command much deference, I asked one of the signallers, 'Who is that little blighter?' 'Don't you know', was the reply, 'that's Winnie, he is visiting his friend General Barnes.' Churchill made a tour of our trenches and experienced the pleasures of 'Minnie' dodging.

12 JANUARY 1916

Sir Douglas Haig was at our HQ today but only stayed a few minutes. We are expecting a gas attack at any moment. The wind is favourable, northeast. We have endured intensified drill in gas masks for the last three weeks. The helmet is a simple bag made of three thicknesses of flannelette soaked in some chemical, the greater part of which is glycerine. A celluloid window is sewn into the front of the bag for seeing through when the helmet is worn. The lower part of the helmet has to be tucked inside the tunic collar which is then buttoned. One's hair and neck become sticky. It is far from being popular. An interesting letter from an infantry officer who had lately been in a gas attack was issued as a Divisional Order. He made a number of observations about the effects of the gas. It destroys the lung tissue, producing violent coughing and choking which quickly affects the heart. The helmets withstand the gas but the wearer must not walk about or in any way upset the normal pulse of the heart. The helmet must be absolutely airtight and moist or the gas is not kept out. To me it seems a very primitive affair.

The officer said there were many casualties due to men walking about whilst the gas attack was in progress and, feeling short of breath, took off their helmets. When they did this they started coughing violently and could not put them on again. Strange to say the gas did not seem to affect dogs: all the regimental pets survived. A white pigeon flying over the trenches fell dead. The effect of the gas is felt 3 or 4 miles behind the trenches.

17 JANUARY 1916, PAS

A beautiful morning, the first really fine morning for a long time.

18 JANUARY 1916

Wigg, one of our DRs, went to hospital last night, badly scalded in the face due to a tin of sausages exploding. Everyone is highly amused, except poor Wigg. Coming off duty about midnight he decided to supper on a tin of sausages. Placing the tin on top of the stove to warm it fell into the fire.

Wigg was trying to fish out the tin with a couple of pokers when it exploded and the contents caught him full in the face like a poultice. The explosion knocked over the stove and the fire was scattered all over the room. Most of the boys were asleep at the time so it was a rude awakening.

Now we are wondering what will happen if he is sent home 'wounded'.

23 JANUARY 1916

Started my leave today. I did not get much sleep last night being fearful of oversleeping and missing the bus. I was up at 05:30, collected my kit and made my way to the village square where the bus was waiting. It was dry and dark with a bitter wind blowing. The 'bus' was an open lorry with planks nailed across for seats. There was quite a crowd and it looked impossible that it could hold all of us but we managed to jam ourselves in somehow. A good many were infantry who had come from the trenches just as they were, their boots and puttees thick with chalk mud.

It was daylight when we reached the railhead – Doullens – and after several false alarms, getting into trains and having to get out again, the leave train came along. The contrast between our train and those we had thought were ours was rather violent. Ours consisted of a string of the most ramshackle coaches imaginable. Most of the windows were without glass, there were wooden seats with straight backs - it looked as though the train had been delayed whilst they searched for the oldest coaches they could find. However everyone was in a good temper at the thought of going home. The train trundled along, I am sure it never exceeded twelve miles an hour and never more than ten miles at a stretch without stopping.

At 22:00 we were outside some big terminal station with arc lights and there we waited for over two hours. The station proved to be Le

Havre. After being cooped up like chickens for 16 hours some of the men were getting cramps. We had a long march across the town to the docks where we found a steamer waiting. The three decks were filled like sardines - everyone had to put on a life-belt but what use it would have been if we had been torpedoed I cannot imagine. Making a pillow of my kit I fell asleep immediately and did not awake until the boat was entering Southampton Docks.

A train was waiting for us for the journey to London. We were in third class carriages in good condition – what a contrast to the other side. The interest the people took in the train, waving and cheering, made us feel like heroes. We arrived in London about midday. I caught the next train to Manchester and made my way to my old lodgings. 'Ma' Dawson welcomed me like a long lost son.

25 JANUARY 1916, MANCHESTER
Awaking first thing this morning, my first sleep in a real bed for several months, I could not collect my thoughts but when I saw my khaki clothes it brought me to my senses with a shock.

31 JANUARY 1916
My leave finished today. I have had a quiet but enjoyable time visiting old friends and now I have to return. I took the night train to London and made my way to Victoria as the day was breaking. The scene at the station was a queer mixture of pathos and humour. The platform was packed with relatives and friends seeing us off. Weeping women rubbed shoulders with others dancing to the strains of a concertina. Quite a number were a few sheets in the wind. As the train left, a roar of cheering went up until we were out of sight.

This leave taking is very depressing and we were all silent and moody for the rest of the journey. A few said they would not take another leave, it was not worth it. I hope there will be no occasion for another leave and that all will be over very soon and we shall be coming home for good.

We had a quiet crossing from Southampton to Le Havre and it was still dark when the boat docked. Not a word was spoken, not even a curse, as we marched to the station. We might have been a chain-gang, setting out for Siberia – it was certainly cold enough. We were issued with bully and biscuits and told that tea would be issued along the route. Fortunately, most of us had brought food from home and a bottle of wine from a shop near the station. The train was similar to the one we came in but in worse condition if it were possible. It looked impossible that the train could hold the crowd of troops waiting but we packed ourselves in. The French third class carriage is about one degree better than a cattle truck, just a long box on four wheels divided into compartments by low wooden partitions which form a back rest. The space between the seats was so narrow that I could touch the opposite seat with my knees. No windows, simply a door – without glass – which let in the wintry blast. We had to sit with our legs interlocked and we endured this torture for 12 hours.

This is a volunteer army. We have counter jumpers and bank clerks in the commissioned ranks and stockbrokers and men of substance in the ranks. One thing which rankles with me is the great difference in the treatment of the officers and the other ranks. Even a sergeant major has to muck in with the privates when travelling, whilst the lowest 'pip squeak' [officer] travels first class. This snobbery raises the gorge of the volunteer soldiers, many of whom have left better jobs to join the army than the officers who order them about. It was dark when we detrained at Doullens where we found the old 'bus' waiting to take us to the scene of our labours, as a wag put it.

2 FEBRUARY 1916, PAS

Very little has happened whilst I have been away. A little pantomime has been going on for some time. One thing we miss is a hot bath. We 'borrowed' a barrel from a local brewery and cut it in half to make a tub. For convenience of transport it was knocked down into a bundle of staves. It was a common sight to see a fellow trying his skill with a circle of onlookers all giving advice, mostly ribald. To build the tub became a job for anyone with some spare time on his hands but so far it has defied everyone including myself.

7 FEBRUARY 1916

A beautiful bright day but very cold and windy. Our motorcycles are showing wear and tear in all parts. The mud and bad roads this winter are showing their effect, practically every wearing part requires renewal. Unfortunately there are no spares available and we have to make up one good machine from two old ones. We are told there are spares on the way but they have been saying this for a couple of months. At the same time it is wonderful how the machines stand up to the terrible roads we have out here which are broken up by the heavy transport.

9 FEBRUARY 1916

Early this morning we had snow on the ground. It disappeared by noon with the brilliant sun but it is extremely cold. The air was so extraordinarily clear that both sides put up their observation balloons and there was heavy artillery fire all day.

I have just remembered an amusing incident in the train from Le Havre to Doullens. Right opposite to me in the carriage, our legs and knees interlocked, was an old Jock. His age could not have been less than fifty which made me wonder how he managed to get into the army. His face was the colour of old leather, heavily seamed. His nose had been badly broken and badly set and its colour a deep purple. A pair of pale bleary eyes deeply set under shaggy eyebrows, and a large loose mouth fringed with a ragged moustache, completes the description of his rugged features.

The first few hours of the journey he slept with heavy breathing, rolling about with the motion of the train like a jelly. Sometimes he would pitch forward onto my knees and at other times he would roll sideways, much to his neighbours' annoyance – they were also trying to get a bit of sleep. The jolt would awaken him but in a few minutes he was fast asleep again. I have been constructing a little picture of the raw time he had been having, a real Scotsman's joyday, unlimited thirst and unlimited whisky.

At last he was fully awake and looked around, carefully scrutinising each of us in turn. Then he became thoughtful and we wondered what he was going to do next. After scratching his chin and giving some vigorous sniffs he dived into his greatcoat pocket and brought out what appeared to be a bundle of handbills. He then searched his pockets again and produced a battered spectacle case. Carefully adjusting his spectacles on the only straight part of his nose he began reading, his lips silently forming each word. Whilst he was absorbed in his task the wink went around, everyone was watching with amused interest. Having finished his reading, he gave a nod of appreciation, took off his spectacles, put them in the case and then, wetting his thumb, he distributed his bills around. They were pamphlets on the evils of strong drink.

11 FEBRUARY 1916

It is extraordinary what simple folks there are in the world. I do believe if a call were made for recruits for the Horse Marines it would bring thousands tumbling over each other to join. One of our DRs who has a weakness for leg-pulling inserted an advertisement in *The Times* agony column. 'Wanted, a housekeeper to run a despatch riders' mess in France. Send full particulars, etc.' A hoax is a form of humour which does not appeal to me but Blakeway did the whole thing on his own without telling anyone.

When the replies came he explained what he had done. He had received over one hundred replies. Shuffling the letters like cards he dealt them around to anyone who would promise to reply to at least two. Some of the letters in their simplicity were very funny. One candidate for the honour of stewing our stew asked if she could bring her little dog and her mother, another asked if she could bring her table linen and silver. A few saw through the hoax and sent humourous replies. One letter which I got said she had a friend on the staff of the division and she was going to ask for further details. This rather shook Blakeway and he asked me to write by return and explain that it was a leg-pull. I must say we spent a very merry evening reading the replies and I hope the kind folks will forgive us. They provided an hour's entertainment in this gloomy place.

15 FEBRUARY 1916

Today I received a letter from my brother saying he had left Gallipoli and returned to Egypt to take a commission in the artillery. He expects to be sent to Salonica. I am glad he is out of Gallipoli.

16 FEBRUARY 1916

Violent wind and rain all day. This awful weather seems to have no end. Having no fires, it is impossible to dry our clothes. Riding a motorcycle in this weather forces the rain through every crevice of one's clothing and we live in a damned moist condition day and night. Several of us went up in a body to see the OC about getting a transfer into the RFC. He said he would mention the matter to the general, but he couldn't let all of us go at the same time. I mentioned the matter to the SM who is an old RE. He was highly indignant that we should wish to leave the REs. He says as we are 'specialists' we are not allowed to transfer to any other regiment.

21 FEBRUARY 1916

The Division HQ moved to Bavincourt today. It is much smaller than Pas, lying on the north side of the Arras-Doullens road and consists of a church, a château, half a dozen farms and fifty tumble-down houses all floating in a lake of mud. During the morning I was superintending the loading of our stores, when the APM [Assistant Provost Marshal – i.e. Military Police] came into the château yard in a great state of agitation. 'Sergeant, do you know what your men are doing? They are looting, looting I say, go immediately and find out what they are doing.' The APM is an inveterate stutterer and it took him quite a time to get it out and even then I could not grasp what he meant but I hurried off to the DRs' billet at the other end of the village to find out what they were up to. It seems that 'Jersey' and Blakeway had been sleeping on an old box mattress which was in the billet and they had decided to take it along with them to Bavincourt. It so happened that they had the mattress hanging on a rope lowering it from the attic window, as it would not come down the narrow winding staircase. At that moment the APM was passing. 'Looting, that's what that is', said the APM. The mattress isn't worth half a crown, but it looks serious as 'Jersey' and Blakeway have been put under open arrest.

22 FEBRUARY 1916

This morning broke brilliantly fine with a biting cold wind blowing. Shortly before midday the sky clouded over and snow began to fall, fine and powdery like flour, and gathering in drifts. In the afternoon I had to take a despatch to Doullens when the storm was at its worst. Half way there the back wheel collapsed and I had to wait until the mechanic brought me a new one.

Towards evening it got colder still and it snowed all night. The barns in which the troops are billeted are in a most ruinous condition and the pigstys are full in preference to the barns. The sergeants have struck lucky, we have a small room over the stables of the château which is luxury compared with some of the billets.

There were many aeroplanes out this morning before the storm. We saw a fight between one of ours and a German. After a lot of manoeuvring our aeroplane dived almost vertically over the German, his machine gun going all the time. The German immediately ran for his own lines, slowly descending and appeared to alight inside Adinfer Wood, which is just behind their lines. We have heard that Blakeway is to be charged with looting which is a serious crime on active service. It seems ridiculous – these old 'dug outs' have nothing better to do than make the troops' life a misery. They take a fiendish delight in 'criming' every little thing which is not in accordance with army discipline.

24 FEBRUARY 1916

The day broke fine with bright sun, a welcome change but it is still freezing. The trees are laden with snow, everywhere looks like fairyland. During the morning, a German aeroplane came over reconnoitring. Our AA guns opened fire, pumping shells into the air without the slightest effect and as usual a number came down unexploded. One crashed through the roof of the stable where the staff officers' horses were stabled, passing through the main supporting beam of the loft floor. The whole weight of the loft floor with its load of hay fell on the backs of the animals below, killing one and injuring another.

One night when at Pas we heard what we thought were shells falling in the woods around the château. At the same time we heard an aeroplane over the village. The shells and the aeroplane were not connected at the time but it now looks as though we are going to have night bombing. Last night several shells fell in the woods at the back of the château. It is now reported that they were bombs from a night-flying aeroplane. This is the first time that it has been confirmed that aeroplanes can fly at night and drop bombs, although I have often thought it might be possible.

25 FEBRUARY 1916

Last night we had 15° of frost. Today snow has been falling all day, filling all sunken roads and ditches level with the surface of the fields. During the afternoon I had to make a journey to Doullens. On the outward journey I had the wind behind me. In Doullens the roads were covered with ice. A new artillery brigade which has just detrained at the station had half their horses lying on the ground, holding up the traffic. Having no frost nails in their shoes the poor animals were too frightened to move. As soon as they were got on their feet they fell down again. I took a toss myself trying to avoid a civilian, with no worse hurt than a bent foot rest. On the way back I had to face the blizzard. The fine snow stung the eyeballs like needles.

Late in the evening the brigades sent word that two DRs who had left hours before had not arrived. I went out to try and find them. I found the motorcycle of one abandoned in a snowdrift 2 miles from his destination so concluded he had continued on foot. The other I found struggling with his machine in a deep ditch filled with snow. It was impossible to judge where the road ended and the ditch began. I helped him get his machine on the road again and saw him on his way.

26 FEBRUARY 1916

The weather is a little milder today. All resting infantry have been pressed into service cutting through the big drifts on the main roads to get the transport through.

The water in all the village wells is pretty bad, which is not surprising as there is no system of drainage. Privies and great piles of farmyard manure are often placed near to the wells and there is bound to be seepage. The British army post warnings that well water is unfit for drinking. The French go one better, they put up a sign headed by a skull and crossbones to emphasise the danger. Neither the French nor the British notices frighten the villagers, they use it as no doubt did their fathers before them and seem to thrive on it. This bad weather has brought all hostilities to a standstill.

28 FEBRUARY 1916

The snow is melting rapidly and everywhere is deep in mud. I do not know which is the greater evil, snow or mud. Snow turns to water but mud sticks closer that a brother. According to the *Daily Bulletin* (or 'Sketchy Bits' as we call it), which is issued daily from Army HQ giving a résumé of the war news, two enemy aeroplanes were brought down on this part of the Front during yesterday's air fights. Our AA batteries have recently been equipped with guns of a more powerful type. When we were at Pas several shells fell in the grounds of the château and one at the feet of a sentry on guard, fortunately without hurting him. This annoyed our general who sent a despatch to the officer in charge of the battery. 'Present my compliments to the officer in charge of the AA battery that the aeroplane is not over Pas but his shells are falling around my headquarters.'

3 MARCH 1916

Blakeway's court martial came off today: he was acquitted. We had been preparing 'our' case for some time. We consulted one of our officers who was reading for the Bar before he joined up and he advised us to find the owner and induce him to sell the bed and obtain an ante-dated receipt. When Blakeway produced the receipt the case collapsed and he got off.

5 MARCH 1916

A few nights ago one of our patrolling parties between the lines met a German patrol in no-man's land: a fight ensued. One German was killed and another, badly injured, was carried into our trenches. Next morning at stand-to our men in the frontline heard a voice calling in English from the darkness, 'Good morning, gentlemen.' No-one answered. Again the voice called 'Good morning.' The officer in charge of the platoon replied, 'Good morning.' The voice then asked,'Can you tell us anything about our two comrades you captured yesterday evening?' He was told that one was dead and the other badly wounded. The voice replied, 'Thank you, gentlemen,' and was heard no more. He had crept up to our wire to enquire the fate of his friends.

7 MARCH 1916

Today must be an important date in the calendar of the French Catholic Church. There was a procession headed by the priests and two young boys in white surplices coming out of the church. All the time the bell was tolling. When the procession reached the end of the village the priests began to retrace their steps and as they passed, the people came out of their houses and joined the procession which finally entered the church. I suppose it has something to do with the beginning of Lent.

10 MARCH 1916

The weather is bitterly cold – I cannot remember weather like it. One of our DRs met with a bad accident on the night of the eighth. He collided with a transport waggon in the darkness and was picked up unconscious. Up to the moment he has not come round. He had delivered his despatches to the brigades and was on his way back to HQ. I was out before daylight searching for him. I followed the route he would take but could find no trace of him. I then went to the first aid station at Gaudiempre. There were about twenty stretcher cases awaiting removal, a number unconscious. I could not recognise any of the faces and was on the point of leaving when I noticed one of them had leather leggings. Making a closer inspection I identified 'Jersey' but not by his face. His head and face were swollen to the size of two, a fearful sight. He had a fractured skull and was snoring horribly. I am afraid there is little hope for him.

13 MARCH 1916

The first fine day we have had for weeks – a fact worth recording. What a difference it makes when old Sol shows his face. 'Jersey' has not yet recovered consciousness, one of our fellows visited the hospital today.

15 MARCH 1916

It is marvellous what a change the last few days of sunshine have made to the countryside. Last week we were in the depths of winter and there was no sign of spring. Today the fields are tinged with green and the trees and hedges are showing signs of life. We appreciate the first warm days of spring more than the balmiest days of summer.

20 MARCH 1916

We did not move yesterday as was expected. It looks as though the Germans got wind that we were going to move – their artillery was very active shelling all roads and tracks behind our lines. On the Pommier-Bienvillers road, which at one point can be seen from the German side, several transport waggons were hit and some horses killed. The German aeroplanes were also out in force keeping a close watch on our front. One flew so low that our AA guns could not depress enough to fire at him. He wandered around our back areas at not more than 200ft. His wireless signals to his batteries were picked up on our side.

22 MARCH 1916, LUCHEUX

We are now in a picturesque little village which dates back to feudal times. The surrounding country is hilly with deep woods. The ruins of an old castle stand on the hillside. At one time the village was surrounded by walls: some parts remain and the entrance at one end is through a massive stone gateway. Lucheux is noted for its waters which have medicinal properties. It is bottled and sold like Vichy water. I must say the beer is the worst I have ever tasted – perhaps the water makes bad beer.

25 MARCH 1916

The weather has turned very cold; we have snow and sleet all day. The DRs' cup of misery is filled to the brim: we have to take a refresher course on 'stables'. This is our new sergeant major. I do not mind riding, but grooming, feeding, watering, wiping their tails and not forgetting harness cleaning from early morning to late at night, are the dullest jobs I can imagine.

A horse's life in the army is one of pampered ease, especially if it should belong to a signal company. He is fed, watered, exercised and groomed three times a day. The probability is before he was taken over by the army, he was groomed once a week and that with a curry comb which we are not allowed to use, and he was lucky if he got one square meal a day. The army horse is often better housed than his willing slaves. These pampered pets do about one day's work in seven. At a rough estimate one half of the horses in the army are engaged in transporting forage for the other half.

20 APRIL 1916

We have now been at Lucheux for a month. It has been a painful surprise for all of us. When we heard that we were moving back for a rest we imagined a life of slippered ease but the time has been spent in daily parades, drills and kit inspections, besides stable training. I suppose all this is to keep us from brooding over our troubles. Everyone is longing to get back to the Line again. Most of our section are determined to take commissions as soon as they can.

21 APRIL 1916

I had a long run today to take a 'special' to an officer who was supposed to be in a village 30 miles away. When I got there I was informed he had left and was now in a village 20 miles further on. Arriving there I was told he was now stationed in a place not 6 miles from Lucheux, where I found him in the Belle Vue aerodrome on the Arras-Doullens road. I had covered 100 miles over the most awful roads to find a man 6 miles from our HQ.

22 APRIL 1916

Today I had to deliver a despatch to a battery in the outskirts of Arras. After delivering the message I continued into Arras to look up some DRs of another division who had invited me to see the sights when I came their way. The town is badly damaged by shellfire but the streets are narrow which gives a feeling of safety. Most of the houses are built of soft white stone. The outer walls of many are missing, leaving the interior exposed to view, with furniture still in the rooms and pictures on the walls. Hardly a pane of glass is unbroken and the curtains flap in the breeze. Many streets are blocked by fallen masonry.

The Hotel de Ville which stands in the Grand Place has been pounded to fragments. It was one of the glories of France. The Grand Place is surrounded by ancient houses four or five storeys high, mostly in the Spanish style, dating back to the Spanish occupation. Most are damaged beyond repair. What will future generations say about the wanton destruction of these historical monuments, which have stood for centuries and took centuries to build?

I found the DR who had invited me to see the sights, one being an observation post in a factory on the outskirts of the town. Through a slit in the walls we looked down on a cluster of ruined houses about three hundred yards away, the village of Blangy. We hold one half and the German the other. Not a sign of life could be seen, in fact it looked quite peaceful, being bathed in hot sunlight. It was hard to realise that snipers were keeping watch for the unwary. Behind the town our artillery was hard at work, the shells passing over like a gale of wind. Before leaving I helped my friends finish a bottle of white wine. There is no shortage of wine in Arras for those in the know.

4 MAY 1916

Just before daylight a tremendous bombardment broke out which lasted almost an hour. It seemed to be around Monchy. Later we heard that the Germans had made a big raid on our trenches and caused us many casualties and we lost a number of prisoners.

9 MAY 1916

We have a divisional concert party called the 'Barn Owls' whose duty is to entertain the troops when out of the line. The concert party is made up of amateurs and one or two professionals, run by a brother of Paul Rubens, the composer. One of the party had a fine baritone voice and his songs were very popular. Last week he applied to go back to his battalion as he wished to be among his old pals again. His battalion was in the trenches and the day he re-joined he was killed in the attack made by the Germans on the night of 4 May. His helmet was brought to HQ. It had a bullet through the crown, he must have been killed instantly. As everyone knew him it has cast quite a gloom. During the afternoon I saw a parade of Leicesters [regiment] who are detailed to make a raid in retaliation for the raid the Germans made the other morning. The colonel was addressing the men in true military style. I caught the words: 'And you are going over the top.' By the tone and manner the colonel might have been addressing a gang of delinquents. When will these old army dugouts realise they are dealing with men who have volunteered and not a lot of conscripts or men like himself who could find no other job but the army?

10 MAY 1916

Warm and cloudy. Everyone is talking about the big attack which is to be made on the Front. The attack is to be preceded by a tremendous bombardment. Artillery is already massing behind the lines, new batteries arrive daily.

13 MAY 1916

Last night we lost our mascot, deserted with his collar and chain. When we were in Lucheux we dug out a fox cub in the woods and made him the company mascot. He had grown quite tame and would sit outside his kennel and take an interest in everything that was going on, occasionally giving a short yelp like a playful pup.

Every company has a mascot of some kind. The supply column has a monkey which makes endless interest for the children. The other day 'Jacko' as usual was the centre of a group of children when a large dog pushed his way in. Immediately 'Jacko' took a flying leap and fastened himself on the dog's back by teeth and nails. The dog gave a howl and set off down the road at full stretch with his monkey jockey still fastened to his back. The funniest thing was to see the tails of both animals wag in unison as the dog twisted and turned trying to dislodge his rider. Eventually 'Jacko' sprang off on to the top of a wall while the dog continued its flight in a cloud of dust.

14 MAY 1916

Heavy rain with high winds. Our batteries in and around Pommier seem to annoy the Germans who are blasting the village to pieces. The few remaining inhabitants are leaving. Today I met a procession of farm carts laden with furniture and bundles of bedding followed by the farm stock: a few cows, some with calves, some pigs tethered in a cart making a horrible noise, and finally the inevitable goat. Some of the old folks were riding in the carts perched on the bedding holding children, while others were wheeling barrows filled with oddments. It must be heart-breaking for them to leave their homes, probably for the first time in their lives. A sad sight. Our people at home have not tasted war.

17 May 1916

A perfect day with cool winds. The German reconnoitring aeroplanes were out early this morning. They have got wind of something unusual on this front, there is no doubt. Our new AA batteries gave them a hot reception, unexploded shells and pieces of those which exploded came raining down making everyone fly for shelter. They say the ammunition is from the USA.

18 May 1916

There was a stampede of horses in the village yesterday evening. Several men were hurt, one seriously. It is said that the stampede was caused by the back-firing of a motorcycle. Fifty or sixty horses went full-stretch gallop down the village street jammed like herrings, knocking down everything in their path, running into carts, trees and well heads. Several had to be shot.

19 May 1916

One of the men who was hurt in the stampede has died, a bad business and the DRs are blamed for it. There is to be an enquiry. There is one type of motorcycle which always backfires when starting, the old-type Triumph; fortunately there are very few left and it is now obsolete.

21 May 1916

Very hot. We endured an hour of gas helmet drill this morning. I do not know of anything which ruffles our tempers more than using these gas helmets. About 10:30 the Germans started to shell the RE dump on the Arras road, big stuff too. We fully expected that when he had finished with the dump he would turn his attention to the village. All horses were rushed out of the village into the fields behind and the villagers took to their cellars. After an hour of shelling they stopped, we were not troubled. There is little doubt it will be our turn soon, as several German aeroplanes have been over the village during the past few days having a good look at us.

Very little damage was done to the dump, RE materiel can take a lot of punishment without much effect. The most serious damage was to the *estaminet* at the crossroads which was hit, and a cow in the field behind was killed. Hard luck, now there will be a shortage of *café au lait*.

24 MAY 1916

This morning I had to take a 'special' to Mailly Maillet, which lies 12 miles south of our position. During the last few weeks we have heard so much about the 'Big Attack' which is to begin at any moment, and with nothing happening we began to think it was one of these latrine rumours which are always floating around. From what I saw in Mailly there is no doubt that something big is coming off and shortly too. Every village is packed with troops and dumps, and every convenient spot is occupied by batteries. Early this morning all leave was cancelled until further notice. One of our DRs who has been waiting almost a year for his leave was due to go today.

Blakeway, who had a misunderstanding with the APM over the bed, left us today to take a commission. This leaves us with only six of the originals who joined up at Chatham. When Blakeway applied for a commission he thought he was going into the RFC but he was afterwards told he would have to put in a certain amount of time in the infantry first.

26 MAY 1916

General Haig and General Allenby called at the Division HQ today for a conference with our general, most of which took place on the steps of the château. I had a look at them through field glasses from the cover of the stable loft. From the expression on their faces the subject of their conversation was of grave importance.

1 JUNE 1916

The big attack still hangs fire. By this time, the news must have reached Timbuktu as there are spies everywhere.

2 JUNE 1916

One of the DRs, Wigg, left us a couple of weeks ago for the Flying Corps. We all felt very envious of his good luck as Blakeway's experience has put a damper on our ideas of getting into the RFC. One of Wigg's pals called at the aerodrome today to see how he was getting on. Unfortunately he arrived just after Wigg had been in trouble for firing on one of our machines. Wigg's version was that he was acting as observer when the pilot gave the signal that a 'Boche' aeroplane was about. Seeing an aeroplane ahead, Wigg jumped to the conclusion that it was an enemy and let fly at it with his machine gun. The aeroplane dived to get out of range and as it did so it showed by its markings that it was one of ours. Fortunately the aim was off the mark. When the aeroplane recovered from its dive the pilot ranged alongside and shook his fist vigorously at Wigg. The upshot of the affair was that Wigg had to go before the OC.

3 JUNE 1916

Thunderstorms off and on all day. Early this morning, one of our wireless operators who knows French caught the news that a big naval battle had been fought in the North Sea. The news was confirmed later in the day and from all accounts we do not seem to have done too well. [Battle of Jutland]

7 JUNE 1916

About 09:00 this morning one of our DRs came to me with a very mysterious air. 'Have you heard the latest?' I replied: 'No, what is it?' He then said, 'Go to the signal office and see for yourself, I'm not going to spread the rumour.' I was just on the point of going out on a run and thinking it was a fool catcher, I thought no more about it. Later in the day we heard that Kitchener had been lost at sea. Everyone is asking, 'Why was he going to Russia?' [Lord Kitchener did in fact drown, along with all but a few of the crew on board HMS *Hampshire*, when she struck a German mine on 5 June. Kitchener was intending to talk to the Russian Government to try to boost their flagging enthusiasm for the war, and to improve coordination between actions on the Eastern and Western Fronts.]

8 JUNE 1916

The DRs are building a sidecar to carry their spare kit. There is always difficulty in getting it carried when we move because it has no official status. The DR section is the *bête-noire* of the sergeant major:

he delights in thwarting our little stratagems to smuggle it in the GS waggons. When our sidecar is finished it should relieve the SM of a large amount of worry on our account. We have called in old Jim Bate, the farrier, to help us bend the frame and whilst watching him work at his forge the conversation turned to Kitchener and his untimely end. Jim is a reservist who went through the Egyptian campaign. He related a little incident which brought him in contact with Kitchener.

The engineers were assembling a gunboat which had been sent from England in sections to be put together on arrival in the Sudan. This boat was to carry stores and ammunition for the troops who were following the river towards Khartoum. When the boat was assembled it was found that part of the boiler furnace was missing. It looked as though the boat would be delayed until the missing part arrived from the base some hundreds of miles away. Jim then suggested to his officer that a search should be made in a native village nearby and an armed party was sent to beg, borrow or steal any piece of iron they could find.

The party returned in a few hours with a collection of old iron which made even Jim scratch his head to know what to do with it, but he set to work and by dint of much hammering and forging he managed to weld the mass into a piece large enough to make the missing part. At this stage Kitchener arrived on the scene. He had heard that the boat was held up and he had come to see what was being done about it. To give Jim's description, 'He stood by the forge fire, just as it might be you sergeant and watched us work, and by God it was hot I can tell you, the sweat ran off us in streams. Several officers were with him and one ventured the remark that he didn't think it would do, but Kitchener said nothing. After a time we began to bring the metal into shape and Kitchener, giving me a nod, turned on his heel and walked away without a word.'

Another little story I heard today from 111 Brigade signal office: one of our aeroplanes was forced to land behind the village due to engine trouble. In landing the machine was badly damaged through hitting a tree, fortunately without injuring the pilot or observer. The pilot came into the signal office to telephone to his unit: 'Hello, I've just landed behind Bavincourt after a strafe with a Zeppelin. Left wing gone, engine out of frame. Send along a hammer and a few nails!'

10 JUNE 1916

The railhead at La Herlieu was shelled again today by the German long-range naval gun. When a German aeroplane came over to direct the shelling, our AA batteries set up a fearful racket to frighten the aeroplane away. The shelling continued from 04:30 until 10:30, one every two minutes. Very little material damage was done but we had eight killed and wounded. Whilst the firing was going on there was great excitement at the siding, moving some railway vans loaded with gun sights and other valuable stores, which are said to be worth £1,000,000. It is a remarkable thing that the German bombardment coincided with the arrival of these vans. There is little doubt there are spies about.

11 JUNE 1916

The good news from Russia comes as a gleam of sunshine in this dull gloom of inactivity and uncertainty. [The 'good news' was that of the efforts of the Russian Army in the war. An attack against Germany's ally Austria compelled General von Falkenhayn, Supreme Commander of the German Army, to withdraw troops from the Western Front. This boosted British hopes for a successful offensive on the Somme.]

14 JUNE 1916

A heavy bombardment in the direction of Arras put us on tenterhooks. Has the big attack started? The News Bulletin, however, merely reported 'a lively artillery duel' and so we go on living in a state of tension.

17 JUNE 1916

Today is the first fine day after a long period of wet cold weather. German aeroplanes have been very scarce during the bad weather but today we had them over in droves. I counted nine machines in one flight. They sailed over at a great height and proceeded inland making a reconnaissance of the country behind the lines south of our sector. Our AA guns banged away, covering the sky with shrapnel smoke without turning them a hair. Later in the day, another flight of five came over but this time our aeroplanes were waiting for them and a lively fight with machine guns crackling took place and our aeroplanes chased them in the direction of Amiens.

18 JUNE 1916

Wigg has been sent back from the RFC. His escapade of firing on one of our own aeroplanes proved too bitter a pill for the OC to swallow. Wigg said he might have got away with it but he made a foolish mistake when he was being examined by the OC and some other officers. It happens that he was at the Blue Coats School at the same time as the OC and during the examination Wigg inadvertently used the OC's school nickname. That tore it!

Wigg told us some interesting yarns about spying by the aid of aeroplanes. One of the commonest methods of obtaining information from spies working for the Allies in enemy territory is by carrier pigeons, which are either dropped in baskets by small parachutes or by an aeroplane which lands and delivers them to the spy who is lying in wait.

A more daring way is to convey spies by aeroplanes and land them in some lonely spot well behind the lines and return for them at a pre-arranged time. I have no doubt this is easy if the conditions on the German side are the same as here. There are vast stretches of sparsely populated country where it would be possible for an aeroplane to land and get away without being seen. The French farmer, like his British brother, is usually abed and fast asleep by 21:00.

20 JUNE 1916

The big attack still hangs fire, but today the OC told me to visit all the brigades and arrange cover for the motorcycles in case of bombardment. People in the villages near to the Line have been warned to leave. I passed several pathetic little processions of farm carts loaded with furniture, bedding, crates of fowls and farming implements, followed by their livestock, moving towards the rear.

23 JUNE 1916

A big thunderstorm broke this afternoon and whilst it was at its height the German artillery started a heavy bombardment and our artillery retaliated as though trying to smother the noise of the thunder. As the storm died down the guns ceased firing. These surprise bombardments are becoming quite frequent nowadays. It is supposed the Germans are trying to make us show our artillery strength and the positions of our batteries.

25 JUNE 1916

A flight of twelve German Albatross aeroplanes came over our front at noon dropping bombs. The sky was covered with banks of broken clouds which gave them good cover. Passing in and out of the clouds made them a difficult target for our AA guns. Bombs were dropped on several villages causing a number of casualties among the civilian population.

26 JUNE 1916

I was at the Brigade HQ in Bienvillers this morning. Some batteries of 6-inch howitzers have taken up positions behind the Signal Office. The guns are being fired as rapidly as they can be loaded and this has been going on for the past 12 hours. The telegraphers say they cannot hear anything or do anything, it is like living inside a big drum. The last few panes of glass have been shattered and most of the roof tiles have fallen off with the concussion. The Germans are searching for the batteries and several farm buildings have been hit. To me it seems to be a foolish thing to place a battery almost on top of a Brigade HQ.

28 JUNE 1916

My birthday. The weather has broken down completely. It rained in torrents all morning and intermittently for the remainder of the day. Yesterday was more or less the same. It is bitterly cold for the time of the year. Rumour has it that our infantry attack was timed for yesterday morning but was postponed on account of the weather. The trenches on this part of the Line are cut in solid chalk and when it rains the surface is like butter which makes it impossible to get a foothold.

All villages and roads behind the trenches are being shelled continuously. The lower end of Bienvillers is particularly hot and the few remaining houses are being reduced to rubble. The road between Pommier and Bienvillers is sniped by German field guns. From the wreckage of our horse transport some waggons had been caught.

Being my birthday I entertained the boys to tinned lobster and white wine. I hope I shall be able to do the same next year. At the rate the war is progressing it will last another three years at a minimum.

29 JUNE 1916, BAVINCOURT

This morning we received news that the 55th Division has made a successful raid on the German trenches after discharging gas. They found the German dugouts full of men in a state of collapse. A number of prisoners were taken. It is refreshing to hear of the 'Boche' tasting a dose of his own medicine, though it is a fiendish business.

Just before I arrived at the brigade office in Bienvillers this morning there had been a bit of excitement. A party of infantry were sat around the farmyard fitting detonators to hand grenades.Through a defective pin a striker was released and a bomb was due to go off in four seconds. Fortunately the man who held the bomb had the presence of mind to throw it into a heap of dung where it exploded harmlessly. They were getting ready for a raid which comes off this evening.

NARRATIVE ONE:

The Battle of the Somme

**Although the 37th Division were held in reserve for the
main attack starting on 1 July, Albert Simpkin heard first
hand reports of the action from fellow despatch riders and
witnessed the return of the survivors of the battle.**

I have it from the 'horse's mouth' that unless the weather is impossible our
attack will start tomorrow at daylight. As far as we know our division will
not take part. The 46th Division on our right will attack Gommecourt, a
small village which stands on rising ground overlooking our trench system
between there and Fonquevillers. On the right of the 46th Division is the 55th
who will attack at the same time and from there right to the south of Albert
the British line will attack and advance.

It has been common knowledge for a month or more that we have been
planning for this and the Germans have had weeks to prepare their defences.
There will be no element of surprise. The weather and the condition of the
chalky soil will be a big factor in success and failure.

(1 July) The day has arrived. Those not on duty were awakened at 04:30
and told to stand by. A heavy mist lay on the ground which blanketed the sound
of the bombardment; all that could be heard was a dull throbbing roar. News
came in before 07:00 that the infantry of several divisions between here and
Albert had attacked but nothing was known about how they were faring.

Everyone was intensely excited and I found it very nerve-trying waiting
for something to do. I was relieved when I had to take a 'special' to 111
Brigade in Bienvillers. As I passed through Pommier I could see that it had
been shelled heavily since yesterday. Half of the church tower was down
and there was a big hole through the roof. I had the roads to myself, not a
soul about.

In Bienvillers the road was almost blocked by bricks from the battered houses. The batteries around the Brigade office were still firing on Gommecourt where it was said our infantry are unable to make headway. I was told the German artillery fire was almost as strong as ours. About five hundred shells have fallen in the village since early morning: the lower end has been reduced to rubble.

Our aeroplanes have been masters of the air all day – hardly a German aeroplane has shown itself. During the morning, when the attack was at its height, one of our observing planes saw a column of German infantry marching into Bucquoy which is about two miles behind the German lines. This news was passed to our batteries and in a few minutes every gun was trained on the village.

At midday news began to come through and we heard that the Fourth Army had advanced about 1 mile on a 6 mile front, north and south of Albert and consolidated their position. They have taken about 1,300 prisoners. Nearer, at Gommecourt which is strongly fortified by deep dugouts and a network of deep trenches protected by wide belts of wire, the situation is not clear. The 46th Division attacked with moderate results. The flanks took their objectives but the attack on the centre failed and the flanks had to fall back again. As I write this there is a tremendous bombardment going on, fiercer than anything I have ever heard, directed on Gommecourt, blasting a path for the infantry. It is inconceivable that anything can live after such a tornado.

The 55th Division have captured some lines of trenches and 150 prisoners. From the latest reports our casualties have been enormous. I saw a telegram this evening stating that the average number of sitting and minor cases was 1,100 per hour. It didn't mention stretcher cases.

Being off duty I turned in but sleep was impossible so I got up again. The noise and concussion stunned one. The sky was lit with a blood-red glare while the horizon was ringed with the dancing flashes of the guns. To add to the excitement a night-flying aeroplane passed over the village dropping bombs. One fell so close as to bring down the ceiling of the HQ farm.

On the morning of 3 July, I saw a party of Notts and Derbys, survivors of the 46th Division who had found their way back to our lines during the night after being marooned in the German lines. I never saw such scarecrows. They were caked with mud from head to foot, some with half their clothes torn off their backs; very few had either helmet or equipment. There was an officer with them in no better condition. One of them, a corporal, told me he accounted for the failure by the fact they passed over the first and second lines with little opposition but when they were making for the third line the Germans appeared behind them. Instead of abandoning their trenches and retiring as our men supposed, the Germans who were in deep dugouts, came out and machine-gunned our men from the rear: a terrible disaster which cost us 6 or 7,000 men.

The General of the 46th Division [Major General the Hon E.J. Montagu-Stuart-Wortley] has been sent back to England; I saw him saying goodbye to our general this afternoon. There is an air of gloom everywhere. The news from the south is scrappy. Certainly there is no breakthrough as everyone expected. The fighting is savage butchery. Wave after wave of infantry are sent over to take a single trench. The Germans are defending every foot of ground with the greatest fury. I have no military knowledge but it seems the wrong policy to advise the enemy weeks beforehand that we are going to attack at a certain sector by a great concentration of guns, troops and stores and to give them further warning by prolonged bombardments. Surely an element of surprise and bluff is necessary.

The newspapers from home are full of news about the fighting. According to the majority of reports the whole affair was just a rough and tumble and the 'Tommies' had quite an enjoyable time. One paper describes the Gommecourt attack as a feat. What that means is only known to the writer of the article. It certainly was a feat to lose 6,000 men in less than 6 hours and probably half of them killed.

The weather seems to be in league with the Germans. We have had thunder all day, the rain descending like waterspouts. All the trenches in this region, and also in the south are cut in chalky clay which when wet makes it impossible to get a foothold.

110 Brigade have gone to replace 63 Brigade of the 21st Division which has lost more than half its infantry in the recent fighting. The new brigade arrived today and were played into the village by the Divisional band. They appeared to be in good spirits, a great contrast to the stragglers of the 46th Division.

We were all anxious to hear how the attack in the south was going on, from first-hand information. As soon as the troops were dismissed to their billets I button-holed a corporal who was only too willing to tell me his experiences. He confirmed that the Germans have sent their best and most experienced troops to oppose our attack. In one sector, held by the Prussian Guards, they climbed out of their trenches and fought our men in the open. A terrific struggle took place but our men made such good use of their Mills bombs the Germans were simply blown to pieces. Our infantry call the Mills bomb 'Tommy's friend'.

Several battalions went into action with their rifles slung, relying solely on bombs, one in each hand for the first attack. The Germans are greatly superior to us in machine guns: our casualties have been enormous.

I saw Blakeway, one of the old DRs who took a commission. He is with the 10th Loyal Lancashires as signalling officer and his regiment have been through the thick of the fighting. He gave me a very graphic description of his experiences and what he had seen. Hell must be a pleasant and salubrious place compared with the Somme. The German losses have been great but nothing like as great as ours. An attacking force always loses more than the defenders. From the description of the artillery and machine-gun fire it is wonderful that anyone survives the storm of bursting shells and the hail of bullets. The slaughter has been terrible: bodies lie unburied in their hundreds, festering in the sun and attracting myriads of emerald-green flies which cover the bodies, making them look as though they were clothed with shimmering green armour. Fragments of flesh, dismembered bodies, legs and arms are littered around, putrefying, causing a most terrible stench.

In the hot sun a body turns as black as coal in a few hours and swells to an enormous size, bursting the clothing. Eyes stand out like hat pegs, mouths gape with tongues protruding from the pressure of the imprisoned gases – the pawns of the war game. In many places the Germans had thrown their dead out of the trenches and formed a rampart of bodies. In other places they had simply flung their dead down the dugout stairs.

The amount of artillery we are using is prodigious. Before our infantry attack the whole area is flattened out. Not a thing could remain alive above ground after the storm of fire. The German have anticipated this and built deep dugouts capable of holding hundreds of men. Some of these dugouts are fitted with electric light, kitchens and sleeping accommodation, in fact, all the comforts of barrack life below ground. The living quarters of the German officers in these dugouts are even luxurious. The walls are boarded and painted, in some cases draped with fabrics. They are furnished with beds, tables and chairs taken from the French houses. In one case Blakeway told me there was a small greenhouse and a plot of grass at the entrance.

Most of these dugouts are 30 to 40ft deep, connected by underground passages. They have caused our old 'has-beens' a great surprise; they never imagined in their wildest dreams such elaborate dugouts existed. The German infantryman, when not on duty in the trenches, lives in comparative comfort and complete safety which must reduce their casualty and sick list.

Our infantry had a grand time ransacking these dugouts, wine, beer and tobacco being the most coveted loot, but souvenirs were thick and plenty. In one or two of the most pretentious dugouts, probably occupied by the German Staff, women's clothing was found which seems to show that the officers had feminine company to solace them whilst in the trenches, though rumour has it that the clothing had been used for a baser purpose to which certain cliques of the German Army are addicted.

Our losses in front of Pozières have been terrible. The Germans held the village which was situated on a ridge and gave them a view overlooking the surrounding country. Pozières was looked upon as the key to Bapaume. The position consisted of a network of trenches protected by belts of barbed wire with deep dugouts to shelter their troops from shellfire. In this redoubt they had concentrated 200 machine guns, not to mention trench mortars and riflemen. Over ten attacks were made before it was captured. Our first attacks were mown down to a man, the Germans defending with the greatest desperation. After our 'Brass Hats' had expended about half a brigade they decided to suspend attacks whilst the position was subjected to a four-day intense bombardment. The attacks were then resumed but even then the waves were thinned out until only a few stragglers managed to enter the village to be swallowed and nothing further seen of them. At last a few men managed to get right through the village and establish themselves on the opposite side, but not in sufficient numbers to clear up the dugouts and deal with a number of machine guns which were still active. Nor could they hope to withstand the counter-attack which would surely be made by the Germans. As a complete brigade had practicably been wiped out, the Anzacs were brought up to relieve the survivors. They advanced with little loss and consolidated the position. The papers at home have given all the credit to the Anzacs for capturing Pozières which is quite inaccurate and has caused a lot of bitter comment from the home troops who made such tremendous sacrifices.

Much of the news given in the home newspapers is completely inaccurate. Many times I have seen victories claimed for absolute failures. I suppose the people at home must be fed with a certain amount of successes or they would grow despondent. I doubt if this is a good policy. In my opinion it is better to tell them the truth and then they will know what they have to face and what steps ought to be taken if we are to win.

Thirst and hunger have caused our men great suffering as often it is impossible for the ration parties to reach them or the ration parties are wiped out before they reach their destination. The terrible nervous strain causes great thirst. Fearful agonies are suffered by the wounded. Blakeway told me it almost sent him mad to hear the wounded lying between the lines calling for water. Some of the wounded were lying in the open for 3 days before being rescued. Some were screaming, others praying and singing which could be heard above the roar of the bursting shells. The German machine guns fired incessantly, sweeping the top of the trenches, making it absolutely impossible for anyone to go and help them. When they were brought in their wounds were gangrenous, some with skins as yellow as a guinea from loss of blood. The Glory of War.

The fruit of victory for all this terrible carnage is an advance of 6 miles on a front of 10 miles. Hardly a square yard of this ground is untouched by a shell hole; not a house remains standing and not a tree. Mametz Wood has disappeared: all that remains are a few splintered stumps. If the truth were known every square yard of this area won has cost us a casualty. To me it seems quite wrong even according to the rules of war. Undoubtedly our staff have miscalculated the strength of the enemy or at least they have miscalculated the strength of their defences.

A great many prisoners have been taken but the fighting has been so bitter that very little quarter was given. There are many tales of stark ferocity being handed around which are best left unrecorded.

CHAPTER FOUR

July – November 1916

10 JULY 1916, PAS-EN-ARTOIS

I was awakened at 03:00 by an orderly to report that one of our DRs was missing. He left about 22:00 last night with a special message for a brigade somewhere beyond Albert. He had not returned nor had the signal office received confirmation that he had delivered his despatch. When a DR delivers his despatch his arrival is telegraphed back to his brigade or division.

Reaching the HQ in Albert, I found the DR had arrived and left some hours previously. The reason why they had not confirmed his arrival was that the lines were down. A week ago the trenches were just outside the town but now they are 3 miles away. The town has been badly battered, most of the houses are in ruins, especially around the cathedral which stands in an open space once occupied by streets and houses.

The cathedral tower and wall being of massive construction have withstood the shelling though in a ruinous condition. The dawn was beginning to show and as I passed I looked up at the statue of the Madonna on top of the tower leaning at a crazy angle. The main body of the church and the tower has been gutted by fire and the heat has caused the iron framework of the dome on which the statue stands to wilt over. In daytime the statue glinting in the sun can be seen for miles around. Lower down the town is a large steel building, its girders twisted and bent, showing the power of modern explosives.

The next place I had to call at was a small village due south of Albert. I tried to take a short cut to avoid the traffic but like most short cuts it proved the longest in the end. I found myself in the midst of old trenches and shell holes over which I had to lift the machine – the road had not been opened for traffic. I must say, however, the country does not show the effects of heavy shelling as in the north. The village I had been seeking had been on the edge of the trenches but it showed very little damage. I found our DR had called there some hours before so I decided to chase him no further and make for home. By this time, I was feeling ravenously hungry so begged a breakfast from a cook of a heavy battery who were in action in the next field. Luke warm tea and cold bacon were very welcome, it being 'too late for breakfast and too early for dinner', as the cook remarked.

A good part of the traffic coming from Albert was ambulances filled with wounded. I happened to see one case sitting beside the driver. He was holding his hand to his face, blood streaming through his fingers, the front of his tunic and his sleeves smothered with blood. If this poor fellow had to ride outside what was inside?

Although I got only a momentary glimpse as I went by, it brought to mind some of the puerile stuff I had read in the daily papers from home describing the fighting. Most of them treat the matter in an attempt to be humorous. It would do some of these writers good to see a clearing station as I saw one during the Gommecourt attack. Over 200 stretcher cases waiting their turn for attention. Many already dead, pools of blood everywhere. Even if it is not policy to tell people the plain unvarnished truth there is no reason why these 'penny-a-liners' should try to make cheap humour out of this ghastly business. I arrived back about noon after doing well over 100 miles.

11 JULY 1916

A fine day. Returning from the Brigade HQ this afternoon I met two old women entering the village with their donkey cart loaded with bedding and their bits of furniture. There were returning to their home in the village. Less than a month ago all the people were cleared out of the villages near the line but now they are dribbling back. Quite a few, I am afraid, will find their houses badly damaged if not razed to the ground. The old ladies seemed very pleased with themselves and were all smiles as they gave me a bonjour. It is extraordinary that these old folks are willing to take the risk of living in a village which is shelled every day. I hear that the gendarmes had to be called in before many of the villagers would leave.

12 JULY 1916

Our artillery is still in the Line backing up another division. There is a foolish rumour going around that the Corps General will not use our division as a unit because of our general's ancestry which is mostly German. From what I remember he is no more German than some of the

Royal family. It does seem extraordinary that ours is the only division which has not been in the fighting. [See entry for 25 August 1916.]

We are still holding the Line in front of Monchy, Pommier and Bienvillers with our one remaining brigade and the remnants of the two brigades from the 21st Division.

At 09:00 I took a 'special' to the artillery brigade. It was an operation order for a bombardment to begin at 10:00. At one point the road passes over a low hill which gives a view of the trenches. The bombardment started on time, I paused for a minute to watch, it looked like a firework display. When I got back the staff were all in bed. Picking out a quiet corner in the signal office I lay down, 'all standing', as I was on duty. Lulled by the tinkling of the telegraph instruments I soon dozed off and the next thing I heard was the early morning DR coming on duty.

13 JULY 1916

Dull and threatening weather. At last we are moving: tomorrow, somewhere north. An Anzac Division has arrived in our area, a fine-looking lot, all tall and lean.

14 JULY 1916, MOVED TO LIGNEREUIL

The divisional staff have quartered themselves in the château which is set in the midst of a well-wooded park with long drives lined with big trees set at regular intervals, a sight worth seeing. The stables and courtyard are very picturesque. The DR were out half the night searching for some of these small units who take a delight in losing themselves. It was getting daylight before some of the riders could turn in. The map reading of some of these officers has not improved from the time they arrived in the country.

15 JULY 1916, MOVED TO BRYAS

The staff have again taken over the local château. This one is far more elegant and modern than the one of Lignereuil. The château is built of pure white stone which would have gladdened the heart of Marie-Antoinette. In front of the house is a large terrace with several flights of steps with stone balustrades.

16 JULY 1916

Last night I saw an airship which I am sure was a Zeppelin. It was a dark night with stars showing but there was a slight ground mist. I was passing through a small village where some troops are billeted when a sentry rushed into the centre of the road waving his arms and rifle. 'Put out your light! Put out your light!' he shouted. As we are a long way behind the lines I was using my headlight. 'Look up there', he said. Immediately over us was a long black shadow as big as a row of houses. I judged it to be about 300ft high. It drifted over quite slowly without a sound and disappeared into the blackness.

A few minutes later we heard the engines start. The sentry, who was really scared, said it had been hovering over the village for some time, starting the engines and then stopping them again. I reported the matter to the OC this morning but he seemed sceptical as no-one else had reported seeing it, and there it rests but it looks as though we missed a fine opportunity of bringing down a Zeppelin. Thinking it over there is little doubt he was dropping spies. The DRs' sleeping accommodation has variety enough to please everyone. Some sleep in 'bivvies' [tents], some in pigstys, some in hen cotes, while for myself I have taken possession of a derelict farm cart.

17 JULY 1916

This morning I took a 'special' to a brigade behind the Souchez front. The countryside is a pleasant change from the flatness of the Somme. Small villages perched on the hillsides make the scene quite picturesque. As a contrast, to reach it I had to pass through the colliery district of Houdain, filled with mine-shafts, refuse heaps and chimneys vomiting black smoke. The houses were mean and untidy and the roads deep in coal dust.

20 JULY 1916, MOVED TO LA COMTÉ

At first sight Le Comté is one of the best villages we have struck so far. It is some distance from the main road and seems to have been overlooked as a training centre. The staff have taken over the local château as usual. The DRs have pitched their 'bivvies' on a hillside overlooking the village. The red-tiled roofs and the white church among the trees makes a restful picture.

21 JULY 1916

Today I went to Bruay, a large colliery town where the pits are still working although the town is shelled frequently by long range guns. Like all modern mining towns the houses are built in long monotonous rows. On the road I met parties of miners returning home. In these parts they wear baggy trousers and loose blouses made of calico, while on their heads they have a 'sou'wester' made from stiff leather to protect their heads from contact with the roof.

24 July 1916

My old enemy the hay fever has been troubling me very much just lately. Spending so much time on the dusty roads aggravates the complaint. To sneeze eight or ten times in succession is quite a common occurrence. It amuses the boys a lot but I do not get much amusement out of it. It gives me a temperature and a violent headache. My eyes and the passages behind my nose burn like fury.

27 July 1916

Our stay in La Comté is coming to an end much earlier than we expected. We are moving tomorrow to a small village on the Arras – Bruay road and taking over part of the Line in front of Vimy. Behind our front are the villages of Carency and Villers-au-Bois whilst in front is Souchez; all these names are famous from the early battles of the war. Carency and Souchez changed hands several times in the fighting between the French and the Germans and the losses on both sides were enormous. On the left of our sector is the hill Notre Dame de Lorette, from the top of which can be seen the town of Lens in the enemy's country.

31 July 1916, Comblain L'Abbé

We have pitched our 'bivvies' under the trees in a large orchard behind the château. We have had some scorching hot weather during the last few days and today has been one of the hottest days of this year.

There is a cemetery in the village where over a hundred French soldiers are buried. Several Germans are buried in the cemetery too and their graves are kept just as trim as the others. I was impressed by the simple epitaph on the headstones of the French soldiers: '*Mort pour la France*'.

2 August 1916

The hot weather continues. We had three German aeroplanes over the village this morning and our AA guns gave them a hot reception. Pieces of shrapnel were showering down all around us. I picked up a piece, as large as my hand, which dropped with a 'fizz' a couple of yards away.

This afternoon I had a message for the Advanced Centre in the trenches. The way lies through Carency village which is now a heap of ruins. A quarter of a mile beyond the village the communication trench starts. At one time this spot was in the midst of a wood but only a collection of tree stumps remains, looking as though a tornado had passed over.

I left my machine and took to the trench. It was a stinking hot day and as the ground is chalk, the walls of the trench reflected the heat with double intensity.

After half a mile of tramping to and fro around the traverses, I was sweating like a bull. I found the Report Centre at Cabernet Rouge, which was once an *estaminet* on the Arras road to Béthune. The entrance to the dugout is through what was the cellar of the *estaminet*. Only a few bricks of the original building remain.

As I had some time to wait I asked one of the signallers whom I knew to show me the sights. He took me up to an observation post from where we could look at the town of Lens which is some four miles behind the German front line. It appears to be quite a modern town with rows of bright red brick cottages. On the outskirts are some collieries, their pithead gear leaning at all manner of fantastic angles.

Just in front of us was Vimy Ridge and in the intervening valley were the ruins of the Souchez sugar factory. The Germans hold the crest of the hill while we hold the lower slopes. Not a tree nor a blade of grass is left – nothing but craters and shell holes looking like the surface of the moon. There is no proper trench system, our infantry occupy the various craters and shell holes which they connect by short trenches.

A slow bombardment was going from both sides; some of the shells were falling in the valley below us while others were passing over us directed at the batteries around Carency. On the skyline in the direction of Loos are the remains of some modern colliery plants being slowly dismembered by shellfire. To the right are the ruins of Givenchy village over which the jet black plumes of shrapnel were bursting. Quite an interesting quarter of an hour. Picking up my despatches I returned by the communication trench to the road.

3 AUGUST 1916

This afternoon I had to take a message to Mont St Eloi, a small village which stands on a hill overlooking the trenches. I was seeking our artillery general but found he had left half an hour before so I took up his trail in another direction.

The dust and heat of the past two weeks has been hellish. Why could we not have had this weather for the Somme attack, it would have made a great difference. The wells are already showing signs of running dry. Our horses have to be taken to a place over 2 miles away for watering.

4 AUGUST 1916

Rather cooler today, a welcome change. Last night just after 22:00 a bombardment started. Word came that Arq was being shelled, a village two miles away which is the HQ of a cavalry division. Shortly afterwards droves of stampeding horses came galloping through the village: a pleasant prospect for someone to find and catch them.

Today is the anniversary of our entering the war. Our artillery started early in the evening and kept up a heavy bombardment all night.

5 AUGUST 1916

At 02:15 the Germans blew two mines which shook the ground like an earthquake. We are four miles away at least but the telegrapher on duty in the signal office said that it made the instruments dance on the tables. We have no news of what damage was done.

At 08:00 a German aeroplane flew over the village almost skimming the tree tops and made off towards the Line wobbling and twisting as though he was damaged.

8 AUGUST 1916

Cooler today. At 08:00 we heard a perfect 'hurricane' of rifle and machine-gun fire coming from the direction of 'Cabaret Rouge'. The Germans made a raid and as the majority of our infantry are inexperienced drafts, the Germans had it all their own way until the 153rd Field REs came to the rescue and drove the Germans out of our trenches.

It is rumoured we are coming out of the Line for a few days rest and training. Some of the new drafts we received just before we took over this front had only been in the army three weeks.

10 AUGUST 1916

Early this morning, 03:00 to be exact, I had to take an accumulator and a wireless set to the head of the communication trench. Not a breath of wind was stirring and every sound seemed to be magnified. As the road beyond Carency is strafed on the slightest provocation I felt sure that a noisy motorcycle would draw fire, but nothing happened.

13 AUGUST 1916

The successes of the Russians and Italians makes good reading. I notice that 'Cabaret Rouge' is mentioned in the papers today. Not a vestige of the house remains above ground but the cellar is the entrance to a big dugout which is fitted with electric light and running water. Its position on high ground gives a view of Lens, Loos and Hullock across the Vimy Ridge. The ground around seems to have been used by the Germans as a cemetery as whenever a new trench is made layers of bodies are found. A corporal in charge of a party digging a cable trench said it was like cutting through a graveyard.

15 August 1916, Bruay

Heavy rain in the morning. We moved to Bruay today. It is a filthy place with rows and rows of mean houses. As there are not sufficient barns we are to be billeted in private houses.

16 August 1916

Last night I slept in a bed, the first for 9 months which is worthy of record. A hot night and a stuffy room however made sleep difficult and I longed for my 'bivvy' in the orchard. The Germans are shelling Béthune again after 12 months' silence. The first shell fell in the market place on market day, killing and wounding thirty or forty civilians, mostly old folks. A real bolt from the blue.

22 August 1916

After a period of quietness we had quite a gale of activity today. Special messages were the order of the day and at one time there were as many as eight DRs burning the road at the same time. The reason was that one of our old brigades is re-joining the Division after a month on the Somme.

24 August 1916

Weather fine but cool. I changed my billet today and not without good cause. For some days I have been troubled with a bad rash which I thought were heat spots. They itched terribly. At last I decided to see the doctor who laughed and said it was the bite of vermin. I was somewhat sceptical but that night I examined the bed I have been sleeping in and found every known species of vermin, bed bugs, lice and some I was unable to christen. I straightaway got leave from the OC to go and get a bath after which I changed all my underclothes. I have got a new billet in a miner's cottage which is spotlessly clean.

I was speaking to an MP corporal today who gave me a description of how he had to take part in shooting a deserter. 'Private so-and-so was shot at 05:00 for desertion' occasionally appears in routine orders. The accused is seated on a chair, the back of which rests against a post. His legs and hands are bound to the framework of the chair and a rope is passed around his body and tied to the post. The APM, a doctor and the Military Police are present. A smoke helmet is placed over the prisoner's head and the doctor pins a white disc over his heart. The five MPs then take their stand at ten paces and on a signal from the APM. they fire at the white disc from a kneeling position.

One of the last deserters to be shot ran the gauntlet for over nine months before being caught. He deserted at Armentières and changed into civilian clothes. Speaking fluent French he passed as a civilian for a long time without raising suspicion.

25 AUGUST 1916

Our infantry have been taken away again and lent to another division, so here we are, 'All dressed up and nowhere to go'. All manner of rumours are about; one is that we are all being sent to base as reserves. There is certainly something mysterious about this inactivity. Whilst we were at Pas before we came up here I heard a whisper, which came from pretty high places, that the army generals will not use our staff for anything except defensive operations because our general is supposed to have German sympathies due to his origins. His grandfather came over with the Georges and furthermore he is a cousin to the King. The whole affair is mysterious and there is something more than coincidence in it. [Major-General Albert Edward Wilfred Gleichen was the son of Admiral Prince Victor of Hohenloe-Langenburg and Laura, daughter of Admiral of the Fleet Lord Seymour. He was titled Count Gleichen until August 1917 when he changed his name, with the King's consent, to Lord Edward Gleichen. Clive Hughes, formerly of the Imperial War Museum, concludes that there is no concrete evidence that the 37th Division was held back on account of the General's German ancestry. The division was a mixture of units previously raised as army troops, and as such had less cohesion than most Kitchener Divisions. This may have influenced their deployment in action at first, as two brigades were attached to the 34th Division for the Somme operations during July and August 1916, and the division was only deployed as a whole in the final Ancre battle of November 1916 – after Gleichen had left. While the reasons for his removal are not clear, his subsequent career in the Intelligence Bureau would tend to suggest that his loyalty was not questionable.]

This evening's 'Sketchy Bits' gave a very interesting account of an escape from the Germans by a private of a Scottish Regiment in the 9th Division.

He was one of a party of fourteen who were bombing some German dugouts in Longueval in the attack on that place on about 3 July. They were chasing the Germans down the underground passages connecting the various chambers when they were suddenly overwhelmed by superior numbers. They were taken prisoners and marched to a 'cage' in the rear of the German line, in the vicinity of Flers. A 'cage' is a barbed-wire enclosure in which prisoners are placed until they have been examined by the intelligence officers.

For some reason or other, probably lack of transport, he was kept in the cage for several days with some men from various regiments. Shells from the British guns were falling all around them at times and at last one fell inside the enclosure and in the confusion he managed to escape. He wandered for 4 days hiding by day and moving at night, trying to find a way through the German lines. He lived during this time solely on unripe apples which he found in the orchards of ruined farmhouses. He was at length discovered and captured.

His next experience was to undergo a cross-examination by the German intelligence officer who was sceptical about his story. The officer said he was a spy and not a soldier but our man said he could prove he had been wounded; thereupon he was made to strip and fortunately he was able to show his wounds, sustained at Loos. He was then sent to work with a German labour battalion, unloading trains at a siding, but even this place was shelled almost daily by the British guns and on one occasion eleven Germans were killed by one shell. During the time he was working at the siding his sole food was black bread and maize coffee with a mess of macaroni for dinner. He only tasted meat, tinned, three times during the month he was in captivity.

At dawn one morning the siding was shelled very heavily and the Germans fled in all directions. Whilst the coast was clear our man took the opportunity to escape again. Cautiously moving by night and hiding by day he made towards the trenches. Then, creeping from shell hole to shell hole, he eventually found himself in no-man's land. He was now within 100yd of the barbed wire of the British trenches but to attempt to get through would have meant certain death. As he lay cowering in his shell hole a German patrol passed him and he feigned death. Once, his shell hole was actually occupied by part of a German patrol. Early next morning a British patrol came over, and showed him the passage through the wire.

28 AUGUST 1916

The chief item in the news today is the declaration of war against Austria and Hungary by Romania, and Italy against Germany.

4 SEPTEMBER 1916

We heard by wireless this morning of a Zeppelin raid over England and that one had been brought down.

12 SEPTEMBER 1916

I cut some verses from Punch magazine called '*Madame*' which struck me as very good and must have been written by someone who is intimate with life just behind the Lline:

> '*At dawn she tows the spotty cow*
> *To graze upon the village green*
> *She plods for miles be'ind a plough*
> *An' takes out washing in between.*
> *She 'ears the guns boom day an' night*
> *She sees the shrapnel burstin' black*
> *The sweaty columns march away*
> *The stretchers bringin' of 'em back.*'

These French farm women are real heroines. All men under 55-years-old are away in the army. Only the old men, women and children are left to work the farms and fields. The fields are often shelled yet they plough, reap and sow with the utmost sangfroid. Not only have they to face danger but often they are hampered by troops billeted in their barns and all manner of restrictions preventing their free movement and the use of the roads.

Working from dawn to dark, wet or fine, they face it with a reasonably good temper with no thoughts of publicity or reward. It makes one rather tired seeing these photographs of war workers at home, rigged out in all manner of queer costumes looking as though they were part of a musical comedy.

I read an article in a weekly newspaper supposed to be an authoritative one on the use of pigeons in wartime. After reading the article one might think that pigeons do the greater part of the work of keeping the staff in touch with the trenches. There are pigeons out here that is true, but one might live quite a long time without being aware that they existed, except the poor devil of a despatch rider who has to carry the wretched birds to the trenches. The staff ignore them and the DRs curse them.

When not 'on duty' in the trenches the birds are kept in a black and white bathing-van affair on wheels and the work of looking after these pets provides a cushy job for an ex-pigeon fancier. The pigeon can fly from the trench to the loft but from the loft to the trenches he has to be carried in a special basket. This contains compartments for about twelve pigeons. It is the size of a packing case and is strapped to the back of an unfortunate DR. Riding over rough roads with this pigeon basket on one's back in a stiff side wind is a feat of strength not to mention the painful results to one's back. I know of no other duty which causes so much bad language as taking up the pigeons. As one of our section remarked: 'If those ruddy birds understood English they would know that they are not exactly popular.'

When the birds arrive in the trenches they are kept for a day or so and then released unless they have been used for ration purposes, which has happened more than once. When released, they return with some simple message such as the direction of the wind or anything which occurs to the sender. The message is enclosed in a small aluminium cylinder which is attached to the bird's leg.

I have yet to hear of a message of any importance being sent by pigeon. While so much depends on the vagaries of the birds it is too risky to send important messages by carrier pigeon. It would be quite a tragedy if a bird arrived with a message and refused to enter the loft. I can imagine a pathetic little scene with all the staff gathered around the loft throwing corn and whistling in the approved fashion trying to entice a perverse bird from the housetops. What is really wanted is a bird of that famous Lancashire strain, a cross between a parrot and a pigeon.

14 SEPTEMBER 1916

Very cold. I heard the other day how a corporal of the 9th Division Signals captured fifteen prisoners single handed. The corporal was following the infantry after an attack, laying a telephone line by hand reel in a village which had just been captured. He was busily laying his lines when a German suddenly appeared from a hole in the ground. The corporal grabbed his rifle and took a sight when the German threw up his hands crying: '*Kamerad, Kamerad.*' Whilst he was wondering what to do with his capture, a string of them filed out of a dugout until fifteen stood around with their hands in the air. For a moment the corporal was too flabbergasted to know what to do, but he managed to get them in line and marched them towards the rear, hoping to find someone who would take charge.

After going some distance he met a sergeant coming forward with a party, but he refused to have anything to do with the prisoners. The corporal was now in a dilemma: the infantry were waiting for the line he was laying yet he could not leave the prisoners to their own devices. A little further on he met a lance corporal with several men. This time he did not wait for any arguments: he ordered the lance corporal to take over the prisoners. His exploit came to the ears of the staff and he was awarded the DCM. It is a good story and I hope it is true. I should not like to think the corporal missed his DCM.

18 SEPTEMBER 1916

I went to Bully Greney today, a large mining village immediately behind the Line. The communication trenches start in the outskirts of the village. Most of the houses are in ruins or badly damaged by shellfire. A number of civilians are still living there, leading a perilous life, rushing to their cellars when shelling takes place which is pretty often as the Germans make a point of dropping a few each hour to keep the pot boiling. The village is less than 3,000yd from the front line yet the women hang out their washing within sight of the Germans.

19 SEPTEMBER 1916, MOVED TO BARLIN TODAY.

Cold and rained in torrents. We have a billet over an *estaminet*. Unfortunately the *estaminet* has little to sell but French beer and grenadine, both of which sit heavily on English stomachs.

The division has taken over part of the Line with the villages of Bully Greney and Aix Noulette as headstones at either end. I made a tour of all the roads and villages behind our front to get the lie of the land. Judging by the damage it must have been a hot quarter at one time though it is quiet enough at present. Aix Noulette itself is smashed to pieces. It lies in a shallow valley and the only road into the village is under direct observation from the German side which gives one a conspicuous feeling. The road surface is a succession of badly-filled shell holes.

23 SEPTEMBER 1916

In the village of Aix Noulette there is an *estaminet* in the cellar of one of the houses which is run by a woman and her daughter. About half a dozen civilians still live in the village. We have had very fine weather for the past few days which is a point worth recording after the bad weather which has lasted for weeks. The wind is blowing from the south and we can hear a tremendous bombardment which must be on the Somme.

26 SEPTEMBER 1916

The bombardment in the south still goes on. This evening we heard that we had taken Thiepval and Combles which is good news. Several German aeroplanes were over today, they seem to be taking a keen interest in this front just lately.

29 SEPTEMBER 1916

Fine and warm. The *News Bulletin* tonight gives a very interesting account of a bombing raid, early yesterday morning, on an important railway station and junction by a squadron of our aeroplanes. The raid was a particularly audacious one because the Germans have three aerodromes around the junction. To distract the attention of the Germans from the main object of the raid, an ingenious ruse was used.

Whilst twelve large aeroplanes were bombing the station, three of our light aeroplanes arrived simultaneously over each of the aerodromes and dropped smoke bombs which enveloped the ground with a thick smoke and prevented the Germans seeing what was going on. In addition to smoke bombs an occasional explosive bomb was dropped to keep their aeroplanes on the ground.

Before the Germans had recovered from their confusion the raid was over. The station buildings and the sidings were completely wrecked. As our aeroplanes were making for home they caught sight of three trains approaching the junction, following each other at short intervals. The first train was bombed and derailed, and before the second and third could stop they had crashed into the derailed train.

The trains were filled with troops who naturally got down on to the track to see what had happened. Their curiosity was soon satisfied as our aeroplanes swooped down and swept the packed masses of men with their machine guns. The troops broke and ran across the fields towards a village but our aeroplanes chased them even into the village streets. All our aeroplanes arrived back safely, hardly a shot having been fired at them.

5 OCTOBER 1916

I heard a weird story when at the brigade in Bully-Greney today. A few civilians still live in the village. One of them was an old man who lived alone in the ruins of a house near to the signal dugout. He was well known to the troops who called him 'Souvenir Jack'. Any day when things were quiet he could be seen rooting among the ruins searching for nose caps. Other times he might be seen digging out the shell holes in the fields behind the village for the same purpose. Nose caps were not the only object of his search – dud shells were equally acceptable. It is said he had commission from a company in Paris to supply an unlimited number of nose caps which presumably are sold to souvenir buyers.

Jack had a workshop in which he had stacks of dud shells from which he removed the nose caps at leisure. To stand and watch Jack remove a nose cap sometimes by hammer and chisel was a good test for the nerves and any stranger who chanced to stray into the workshop whilst Jack was at work usually came out faster than he went in. Dud shells, like tame tigers, always turn on their keepers sooner or later. One day a shell came through the wall of a house, the lower rooms of which were used as a mess by the brigade NCOs. It was assumed that the shell had come direct from the German side; no-one thought that Jack might be responsible. Someone happened to look in his workshop next day and found the old man's mangled remains. Poor Jack, no more will he be seen with sack over shoulder. *'Bon souvenir, Jack?'* *'Oui, Bon.'*

6 OCTOBER 1916

We have lost one of our old hands, Shaftoe. His eyes have been failing just lately and he found he could not ride at night. Never a fierce rider, but taking his own time he always got there. A great faddist, teetotaller, non-smoker, anti-everything, his only vice seemed to be an inordinate love of marmalade which was a stock joke for the tame humourist. To enter into argument with Shaftoe was flying in the face of Providence. Talking the hind leg off a donkey was child's play to Shaftoe.

Another old hand who has been with us a long time is Scarlett. He went to hospital today and it looks as though he will be evacuated. Scarlett is another character. A confirmed pessimist of melancholy countenance and a very red nose which belied his drinking capacity: he drank very little. That nose will be sadly missed by all. Quiet by nature, occasionally he would explode and give vent to a string of oaths of the old army sergeant's vintage which would leave the listener spellbound. 'Never knew 'e 'ad it in 'im.'

12 OCTOBER 1916

I saw a peculiar sight today in the village of Coupigny. A batch of about 200 prisoners, Germans, who had been working on the roads in the district were being marched through the village. The sight of the Germans sent the women mad with rage. Shrieking at the top of their voices they hurled themselves on the guards and tried to get at the Germans, screaming choice bits of invective and drawing their fingers significantly across their throats. The prisoners seemed quite terrified. The scene reminded me of tales of the Revolution. After the prisoners had gone many of the women broke into torrents of tears.

18 OCTOBER 1916

Moved from Barlin today to Rollecourt, our first day's trek. The weather was dull, cold and showery.

21 OCTOBER 1916, MOVED TO BEAUVAL

Bitterly cold. Last night I paid a Franc for the privilege of sleeping on a stone floor in a private house. The only consideration was that it was better than sleeping in a stinking barn with 100 men crammed into space enough for thirty.

These divisional moves provide the DR with plenty of work. His day starts at 06:00 when the orders for the day have to be delivered to all units throughout the division before they get on the move. His despatches delivered, he hurries back to HQ to try to catch the cook for some breakfast before the cookhouse moves. After a wash and a shave he leisurely packs his kit and sets off for the next HQ for the night. Arriving about noon before the staff have set up shop he has an hour or so to look around. The cookhouse will not arrive until 18:00. He must, therefore, fend for himself for dinner, civilian fare is what he craves. If the place boasts a restaurant he gets a lunch of sorts: an omelette or *oeufs* and chips with a bottle of *vin ordinaire*. Next he looks for a place to sleep for the night because it will be after midnight when he returns. Fixing on a likely place he reserves it by dumping his kit, though more often than not he finds when he returns that the billeting officer has jumped his claim.

About 16:00 the staff make their presence known by sending a few 'specials' and things begin to warm up until the grand finale when orders for all units have to be delivered giving routes and orders for the morrow's march. These arrive about 21:00. The riders divide the despatches between them according to areas. Locations are checked with the map. Routes are carefully studied and mental notes made of the run of the roads. Some of the directions are a bit sketchy and some have no address at all, these latter are the bugbear of the DR. Finding a unit in a 20 mile area on a dark night is where the experienced DR comes in. All day he is making mental notes of the various units he sees on the roads, bits of information picked up when delivering his despatches and an instinct of where they ought to be will often put him on the right track. Sometimes, however, the missing people have to be tracked down by the process of searching every village and every road until they are found.

Finding one's way at night in a country without signposts needs careful study of the map before starting out. Short cuts across country byways at night are seldom successful; it generally ends in getting hopelessly lost in a labyrinth of roads not marked on the map. The surest and quickest way is to use the main roads, even if it means travelling a few miles farther.

As we have to ride without lights, eyesight is very important for night-riding. Some with good eyesight in the daytime are quite blind at night. We have lost some men due to this weakness. There is always a certain amount of light even on the darkest night but roads lined with trees have to be negotiated with care as the only way to guide oneself is by the opening in the tree tops. Running from an open road into a tunnel of trees at high-speed produces a few hectic moments until one finds a new horizon. In complete darkness all sense of direction and sense of balance is lost. I should imagine it is impossible for a blind man to balance a bicycle.

22 OCTOBER 1916, MOVED TO MARIEUX

Poured in torrents all day with high wind and bitterly cold. The roads are simply wicked, deep in mud and a succession of pot-holes. A continuous stream of motor lorries passes in either direction day and night. The roads are narrow and leave little room for overtaking. Riding a motorcycle at night in this traffic is a nightmare. To overtake means cutting out at the right moment and dashing ahead in the narrow lane between the lines of traffic and diving for shelter behind a lorry when the space closes in. As the traffic is bunched up tight it is sometimes difficult to find an opening. A fall in this traffic – well, I should not like to.

23 OCTOBER 1916

The division have made their HQ in the château. We are in the farm building behind the château which is a very old building standing in its own wooded grounds surrounded by high walls. A beautiful spot, a pity one cannot appreciate the beauty under the present conditions. It rains continuously and we are plastered from head to foot with mud. When will the rain cease?

It is said the division is going into the Line for a 'stunt' but when or where nobody knows. The country around is packed with troops, it is easy to see trouble is brewing.

27 OCTOBER 1916

Last night I went out to find an infantry battalion. The map reference showed them to be in the middle of a stretch of country lying between Engelbelmer and Mesnil. The night was pitch black with rain and mist. I had a pretty hectic time on the road dodging the transport and more than once I had to dive into the ditch to avoid getting run over by ammunition limbers at the gallop.

At last I reached a crossroad which bounded one end of the area in which I hoped to find the battalion. Leaving my machine by the roadside I set off across the fields threading my way through a maze of horse lines, waggons and store dumps. Beyond the horse lines I found myself in the midst of a battery of big howitzers which burst into song just as I arrived. The flash of the guns dazzled me, one moment it was as light as day and the next I was groping my way in pitch blackness. Some distance in front of the battery I entered a wood with more horse lines and dumps. The wind was showering the rain from the trees in sheets. Seeing a light in a tent I pushed my way in to make enquiries and look at my map. No-one had seen the battalion. The map reference given showed them to be about 300yd in front of the wood.

I went forward and found myself in open country which seemed to be part of an old trench system full of big shell holes. Fortunately, I could pick my way by the light of the flares from the trenches, otherwise it would have been impossible to cross this area. Having travelled what I judged to be 300 yards I stopped and looked around but could not see a sign of the battalion. Waiting for the flares I searched each point of the compass. Suddenly, in an extra bright glare from the trenches I caught sight of something on the skyline which looked like a haystack. I decided to go and find out what it was; it was the tents of the missing battalion, everyone asleep, not even a guard on duty as I could see. Bawling out at the top of my voice I was taken to an officer's tent where I delivered my despatch to a sleepy officer who was distinctly peeved to be awakened at that hour. His annoyance was a pleasure to me after the trouble I had taken to find them.

Returning to the road I spent an anxious 10 minutes searching for my machine. I must have passed and re-passed it several times before I spotted it. I began to think someone had scrounged it. What a night it was, raining and blowing harder than ever. Fortunately the 'old bus' started at first kick.

On the way back I fell to wondering what was in that precious message: probably a telling-off for the OC for allowing his men to march with tunic collars unbuttoned or something similar. Then I imagined a little scene in the HQ mess. After a good dinner the General turns to his GSO1, 'We must send a stiff note to so-and-so, I saw his men marching in a most slovenly fashion this morning, I don't know what the army's coming to. Send him a special.'

I got back about 02:30, raining heavens hard. Handing in my docket, I tried to impress a sleepy signal clerk what a hell of a time I had had finding that perishing battalion, but he wasn't interested. After sluicing myself down at the pump to remove the mud, I turned in.

29 OCTOBER 1916

Pouring rain all day. What with the weather, the mud, the food, the lice, this is Hell and no mistake. We are 'lousy as cuckoos' as the old sweats say. I delouse my shirt each day catching them wholesale but the next day there are just as many. No baths or clean underclothes. The roads are seas of thin runny mud. We and our machines are plastered with it. How the machines stand up to it is extraordinary.

3 NOVEMBER 1916

I saw some tanks for the first time today. I was disappointed, I had imagined something entirely different, something more imposing. To me they look very crude affairs, something designed and manufactured in a hurry. Larger than a motor lorry yet smaller than a cottage, but resembling neither. Some say they resemble a toad, I fail to see it. The nearest description I can give is they have the shape of an eye but the most extraordinary thing about them is a pair of wheels sticking about 6ft from the back. I believe the object of these wheels is to guide the affair. Their movement is like a snake but when they strike rough ground they waddle like a duck. If ugliness is useful in warfare they may have some value, but a well-directed shell would put them out of action.

4 NOVEMBER 1916

Tonight I had despatches for Engelbelmer and the Brigade post in Mesnil. I cursed my luck as it would mean a long walk over a disused road which is honeycombed with shell holes, making it impossible to use a motorcycle over it by night. Arriving at Engelbelmer, I was more than pleased to find a couple of runners waiting for me, to take the despatches to Mesnil. The roads were jammed with transport of all kinds travelling at a crawl with frequent stoppages for traffic blocks, every driver cursing his neighbour. I had several narrow escapes of getting knocked down, it was a case of every man for himself.

7 NOVEMBER 1916

Our sleeping quarters is a loft over a stable about 8 by 6yd. In this space twenty-six men sleep in wire frame beds arranged in tier system. When they all get up and dress at the same time the congestion is trying to the temper. This congestion does not often trouble me as I have no fixed hours. I go to bed when I can and get up when it is my turn for duty. One humourist made quite a good joke about the crowding. He complained that he found he had shaved someone else's face instead of his own.

11 NOVEMBER 1916

A fine but dull day. Last night was clear and bright with a full moon as bright as day. The German aeroplanes were over in droves dropping bombs. I passed through Beauval just after two big ones had been dropped, fortunately they fell just outside the village; no-one was hurt but all the windows and roofs in the vicinity suffered. At Doullens, however, there were many casualties among the civilians. Our AA guns blazed away without doing a ha'porth of good. The German aeroplanes were also firing on the roads at the transport. At one spot I was quite near, everyone thought it was our own machine guns firing at the aeroplanes until we saw sparks from the bullets striking the pavé. It was all over in a few seconds. Although the road was packed with transport nobody was hit as far as I could tell.

Everything indicates that a big attack is coming off on this front. All the villages are crowded with troops, and batteries occupy every spot where they can be concealed. Last night at midnight our guns started a tremendous bombardment which has continued all day. There are two 15-inch guns on this front, their deep boom can be heard at intervals above the roar.

NARRATIVE TWO:

The Battle of the Ancre

The River Ancre is a tributary of the Somme, lying to the north of it, with a confluence just to the east of Amiens. The Battle of the Ancre in November 1916 was a follow-up to the Battle of the Somme and the 37th Division was heavily involved in the action.

Last night the air was very still and the noise and concussion of the bombardment shook the place like an earthquake. We got orders at 23:00 to move up to Varennes. The attack comes off tomorrow at daylight. We follow the Naval Division and take over after they have attacked.

We arrived in Varennes at midday; the signal office is in a farmhouse. The farmer evidently resents our intrusion and his awkwardness led to a quarrel with the French interpreter. It commenced with a wordy argument, their noses about three inches apart with much waving of hands like a couple of fighting cocks getting ready to scrap. Then they started pushing one another about, their arms going like windmills. The troops gathered around in a circle, cheering and laughing. This exhibition went on until the combatants were exhausted, then the interpreter went off to see the mayor and I understand he had the farmer fined. The French peasant farmer is the limit of meanness. He does not care a damn whether the French or the Germans win so long as it does not affect his pocket or his personal convenience. Patriotism to him means looking after number one.

The staff kept us on the go until the early hours of the morning. Fortunately our runs were short. The bombardment started at midnight, but the mist and drizzle muffled the sound of the artillery and all we could hear was a dull rumble although we are less than two miles from the front line. About 06:00 the fire slackened and the attack was launched. At 08:00 news began to come through. The right division was doing well and had reached its objective by taking Beaucourt Hamel. Soon the wounded were coming into the dressing stations.

Later they began to arrive in their thousands, brought in every kind of vehicle from motor lorries to GS waggons. Next we had a sight of the spoils of war, batches of prisoners being marched through the village on their way to the 'cages'. Poor miserable devils, plastered with mud, faces white as death, wearing curious scuttle-shaped helmets The right division gained all their objectives in the first attempt. The centre division was held up for sometime but finally overcame the resistance. From a description I got from one of our wounded, the attack was made in the thick mist and our troops got within a few yards of the German first line trench before the enemy were aware they were being attacked, and they had no time to call up their reserves. When our men advanced to take the second line the Germans were quite alive to the situation and put down a fierce barrage of shellfire which caused most of our casualties. The machine-gun fire was nothing like so deadly as usual, no doubt due to the thick mist.

This evening we hear that a German Brigadier General and his staff have been taken prisoner. The gallant general waited in a dugout until the fiery blast had passed over and then emerged and gave himself up. They were all attired like the lilies of the field, all spick and span as out of a band-box. As the little procession marched down the road in the charge of a couple of grinning 'Tommies', it made quite a sensation. It is said that the general protested vigorously at having to 'pad the hoof' and demanded a motor car but all available horse transport was being used to bring in the wounded.

We captured over 3,500 prisoners in yesterday's attack. Hundreds of Germans came out of their dugouts to give themselves up. Some had not eaten for 4 days as it had been impossible for rations to reach them, so intense was our shelling of their back areas. To their credit they formed themselves into stretcher parties without being ordered. The RAMC say their help was invaluable as at that time there were hundreds of wounded still lying in the trenches.

There is a dressing station on the road between Engelbelmer and Martinsart. I called there to pick up their returns. Hundreds of wounded were lying in the open awaiting their turn for attention, some on stretchers, some lying on straw which had been laid on the ground. God, what a sight, plastered with mud and blood, faces yellow from loss of blood, many already dead and still the waggons and lorries rolled up. Waiting for the returns in the midst of this shambles was just as much as I could stand. Several asked me for a drink which I had not got, but I gave away the few cigarettes I had with me. Among them were a fair number of Germans and I noticed that the orderlies made no distinction between friend and foe.

112 Brigade lost over 1,100 men: they were caught in a tremendous barrage before they reached the frontline. Beaucourt was captured with over 400 prisoners.

The Germans made a big counter-attack this afternoon – I was at the Advanced HQ when it commenced. The first we knew about it was a rattle of machine guns and then our artillery went mad. The staff were standing on the roof of the dugout using their field glasses but there was too much smoke to distinguish anything. Soon afterwards we heard that the German attack had been beaten off; our infantry had been expecting a counter-attack and were waiting for them. We are now at the Advanced HQ which is in a roadside dugout, with the general, GSO1, a few telegraphers and six DRs. The day has been gloriously fine but bitterly cold with high winds which freeze one to the marrow. There is no room in the dugout for the DRs so we have brought our own 'bivvies' which give precious little protection against the wind and cold. There are no trees or houses for miles and the wind sweeps down the valley.

The infantry of the 63rd Division are coming out of the trenches. Their battalion were paraded near our HQ today. Some of the platoons could only muster five or six men whilst twenty seemed to be the most any could show. I cannot remember a more miserable night. I turned in at about 01:30 but I could not sleep for the terrible cold; I had a violent headache and felt feverish. One blanket and a greatcoat is not much protection against 10 or 15° of frost and a strong wind. Every half hour I got up and went outside to flap my arms and stamp around to restore circulation but directly I lay down again I started to shiver violently and I began to think I was sickening for an illness. Then I remembered I had a flask of rum in my kit bag so I took a good pull which stopped the shivering and I spent the remainder of the night alternately dozing and taking nips of rum. I was glad when an orderly came to roust me out at 05:30 for a run to Corps HQ.

Some of the 63rd Division infantry belong to the Artists' Rifles. They were the first to enter Beaucourt which they say bristled with machine guns. I noticed that the tunic and trousers of one man had large patches of dried blood and he told me how it happened. His chum was showing him a small wound in his hand and jokingly remarked, 'I wish it was a Blighty', the next instant he was blown to pieces by a shell which fell at his feet but left the other man unscathed.

About midday the OC said he thought the DRs should be able to ride as far as the Advanced Brigade Post in Beaucourt and could I go and check. I took a Canadian boy with me who had been attached to us from the Corps. We managed to ride as far as the old German front line but it was impossible to ride further. The road beyond here was a succession of huge craters, most of them 20ft in diameter, which must have been the work of our 15-inch howitzers. At the bottom of some of these craters I saw the bodies of men of a kilted regiment, their flesh as black as coal; no doubt they fell in the attack of last July. Many bodies of those who fell in yesterday's attack were also lying where they had fallen.

A narrow path weaves its way among the craters following the old road to Beaucourt. At one time the river banks here had been fringed with poplar and willow trees; all that now remains is a few blasted stumps. On the other side of the river are the slopes of Thiepval of terrible memory in last July's push.

The rear Brigade HQ had taken possession of German dugouts – the one used by the signallers had been a QMS stores. Most of the stock had been brought to the surface and spare clothing was strewn about the trench. The German greatcoats were made of a felt-like material which I should imagine is more water-proof than ours, which soak up the rain and weigh a ton when wet. Another thing I noticed was a waterproof lining to their tunics: a tip which might be copied by our authorities.

As there was no particular hurry I continued on a voyage of exploration. The trench was seldom more than 6ft deep but every thirty yards or so were entrances to dugouts, at least 20ft deep, all connected by underground passages. In one dugout I tried to enter, the stairway was blocked at the bottom with a layer of bodies six or eight deep. Many dead Germans were lying in the trench and a number of ours also. The amount of discarded equipment lying around was simply enormous. From the hundreds of German steel helmets it looked as though every German had thrown away his helmet rather than be encumbered with it.

In some places it was possible to re-construct little episodes of the attack. Here was a small drinking cup half full of coffee lodged on the side of the trench, doubtless left by one of those on guard but the attack was made before he could finish it. There was a dead German with a field dressing in his hand, he had died before he could apply it. Lying on the parapet in another part of the trench was the corpse of a German Red Cross man, his equipment of dressings still in his belt. Near to his outstretched hand was a stick bomb as though he had been in the act of throwing it.

Many German machine guns had been left behind, beautiful pieces of work, heavier than our Vickers-Maxim. At one spot set in a small sap was a Minenwerfer gun sitting on a concrete base. On either side of the gun were cubby holes filled with ammunition. The gun was a short stocky affair and the shells were as large as our 12-inch howitzer ammunition.

At last I found a dugout entrance that was not blocked. Just inside I stumbled over a body of a German with his gas mask on. I turned my flashlight on and had the fright of my life. In one of the top bunks was a man, his head and shoulders hanging over the side as though in the act of springing out. For a split second I thought he was alive and I felt the blood rush to my head, but the next instant my reason told me he was dead by the colour of his face and the glaze of his eyes. Poor devil, he had been awakened out of his sleep to meet his death and his last act was to raise himself to look over the side of his bunk when a bomb exploded at the bottom of the stairway.

The parapets of the trench around the dugout entrances were piled with German dead where they had been thrown to keep the trench clear. It was obvious that they had been surprised and tried to fight their way out. We have heard a lot about the size of the German dugouts in the Somme area but here is a string of them inter-connected by underground passages, capable of sheltering a full brigade.

Higher up the trench I came across the body of one of our men badly mutilated, one of his arms had been blown off and half of his face was missing. The front of his tunic was shredded like wool and the ammunition in his pouches had exploded. A pretty ghastly sight but it raised no more feeling in me than one feels in a butcher's shop. War brings one down to the level of animals. Next I caught sight of one of our tanks on the skyline. It was stuck in a big shell hole and its crew were busy digging it out. It had come to a standstill about 10yd short of the trench but near enough to rake it with machine guns. I had now seen as much as I had time for so I returned to pick up my companion whom I had left waiting at the signal office for the runners coming in from the battalions over the river.

We then set off alongside the river towards Beaucourt. Some distance ahead we could see shells falling. It looked unhealthy to say the least but a steady stream of men were passing through it, ration parties, stretcher bearers and odd groups of men bunched together for companionship. The Germans know this is the only path to our frontline and were keeping up an intense barrage. It was surprising how coolly everyone took it. No hesitation or mad rushing, though they were gambling with death itself. The stretcher bearers stepped out at a smart pace, only breaking into a trot when a shell fell uncomfortably close. The noise was far more trying to the nerves than the shelling. The only thing I can liken it to is living inside a drum with a mad drummer pounding the outside.

On the right of the path we passed the ruins of Beaucourt station; a fragment of wall still remained on which the name could just be distinguished. The remains of two or three railway waggons were still standing on the rails, the woodwork splintered and shattered – it was a marvel how the pieces held together. Around the station many bodies were lying, mostly our men who fell in yesterday's attack.

A little further on we came to a crossroads with a barricade of farm carts. The road to the left went to Beaumont Hamel while straight ahead went to Beaucourt. We now became conscious that bullets were buzzing all around us but I put them down to strays. At that moment we caught sight of a signal flag in the distance but when we got there it was only a runners' post. Along the bank were dozens of funk holes in which men were sheltering in a deucedly uncomfortable position, chin on knees.

A runner came out to answer our enquiries and whilst he was giving us directions to the Brigade there was a tremendous scream. Everyone fell flat except myself who stood stock still like a frightened hen too astonished to move. The shell burst less than 5yd behind me; fortunately it fell in soft earth, just missing the hard roadway by inches. No harm was done except I was peppered with earth and stones. It passed so close to my head that I could have sworn that I felt its hot breath.

In front was a flat field about 200yd wide with a steep bank bounding the side nearest to the Line. The face of the bank looked like an ant heap – hundreds of men were busy digging themselves in. It was an ideal situation, facing away from the line, too steep to be reached by shell fire. The Germans seemed to know of its existence and were trying to reach it. The ground at the foot of the bank was being pounded with huge crumps throwing up fountains of earth and black smoke. Small parties of men were dashing across the field, running the gauntlet of the shells. We were startled by several men running past us as hard as their packs and equipment would allow them. We could not understand the reason for this tremendous hurry, but it gave us the feeling that we ought to be running too.

It was now getting dark and our eyes were fully occupied in keeping to the track and avoiding falling into the shell holes. Suddenly we were surrounded by the sound of zipping and whining of bullets. A German machine gun was sweeping the road and this explained the other fellows' hurry. We followed their example and doubled as hard as we could for the next 100yd and then walked and trotted all the way to the signal dugout, where we found a linesman busy repairing the terminal board which had been smashed by a piece of shell. We picked up some messages for HQ and set off again. The track lay through a succession of huge shell holes filled with water – this was the old no-man's land. There was still a red glow in the sky which reflected on the water, making it easy to pick one's way. It was a marvellous sunset, a deep blood red, a fitting end to a day of carnage.

31st Company Despatch Riders at Buxton and their countries of origin.
Left to right:
Cpl Little (S Africa)
Cpl L Shaftoe (England)
Cpl W T Hobson (England)
Cpl A E W Wemys (England)
Cpl Nunn (England)
Cpl B D Garnier (Ceylon)
Sgt A E Simpkin (England)
Lt Griffin (England)
Cpl W E Powell (Argentina)
Cpl A W Wildig (England)
Cpl R Norman (Jersey)
Cpl J Torrey (USA)
Cpl A E Scarlett (England)
Cpl R C Washington (Egypt)
Cpl H E Jones (England)
Cpl C B Wigg (Canada)

Albert Simpkin in May 1915 on being promoted to sergeant.

Albert Simpkin on his army issue Triumph Model H motorcycle, 1915.

Albert Simpkin, third from right, with fellow despatch riders at Buxton.

R.E. Signal Company
Christmas Card, 1916.

Mrs Emma Dawson, Albert's
landlady in Manchester –
she appears in the diary
as 'Ma' Dawson.

F. B. WYLES,
PHOTO ARTIST

37th Division Despatch
Riders' Christmas card,
1917.

Albert Simpkin on his
Triumph Model H
motorcycle, 1917.

Pas-en-Artois, December 1915. The two-storey building is the Hotel de la Poste, where the DRs had their Christmas dinner.

Pas-en-Artois, February 1916: the rear of the DRs' billet – from the attic window Corporal Norman and Corporal Blakeway lowered the box mattress which led to Blakeway's court martial.

Café de la Mairie, Lestrum, December 1916. The sergeant major's billet where the company sergeants had their Christmas dinner.

Dickebush was one of the 'hotspots' of the Salient, being shelled almost continuously. Café Belge was occupied by the DRs in March 1918.

Blangy railway cutting: the dug-out made by the Germans and used by the 37th Division as a signal office in April 1917.

The rebuilt Hotel de Ville in Arras – all but razed to the ground when the 37th Division arrived in March 1917.

The pillbox used by Major
General Bruce-Williams during
the attack on Monchy

Albert Simpkin visiting the
memorial at Monchy le Preux
to the men of 37th Division lost
in the action on 10 April 1917.

CHAPTER FIVE

November 1916
– April 1917

19 NOVEMBER 1916, ENGELBELMER

Last night it rained in torrents with a tremendous gale. I finished at about midnight and was thanking my stars that I might get a few hours of undisturbed rest, when I found our 'bivvy' was blown down flat and apparently had been like that for several hours. Fortunately it had not taken flight altogether. I was struggling to get the 'bivvy' erected again when my partner turned up and between us we managed to get it up, double staking all the guys, but with the soft, rain-sodden ground it looked as though it might fly away at any moment. Everything inside the tent had got soaked but fortunately we had left our greatcoats rolled in our waterproof sheets which had kept them fairly dry.

The wind was forcing the rain through the canvas in the form of a fine mist. It was quite evident we should be soaked in a short time. I then remembered I had seen some large canvas trench sheets in a field about half a mile away. We decided to go and fetch one. We had to cross a stretch of country full of shell holes and old trenches and seemed to fall into most of them. We found the sheets still there and not a soul about to hinder us but they were larger than we imagined and when rolled up in their sodden condition they weighed 'a ton'. We had quite a trip carrying that sheet and arrived back wet through with sweat in spite of the cold wind.

We were busy fixing the sheet over our 'bivvy' when another couple of unfortunates came to say that their shelter, which was a hole dug in the side of a clay bank with a sheet of corrugated iron on top, had caved in on them. I mentioned the canvas sheets and left them to it. We crawled inside, lit our Primus [stove] and surrounded ourselves with a good warm fug. It blew a gale all night. This is a very exposed place, right in the middle of a bleak stretch of country without a tree or shelter of any kind.

Marples, one of the brigade linesmen, was killed yesterday afternoon. He was one of the old originals who trained at Buxton.

20 NOVEMBER 1916

After frost, snow and gales we are now wallowing in mud. There is no mud equal to chalk mud: it is as slippery as butter and as sticky as glue. On the roads it varies in consistency from that of a thin watery 'soup' to that of dough. The latter variety picks up on the tyres of the waggons and lorries like a snowball gathers snow and falls off in huge clods. Motorcycle mudguards get choked very quickly and bring the machine to a standstill. We have taken off our mudguards and the result can be imagined.

21 NOVEMBER 1916

The smell in the trenches and all around is stifling. It is a combination of explosives, burnt wood, decaying vegetable matter, stale cooking, sweat and urine, a 'witch's broth' of foul smells.

22 NOVEMBER 1916

I went to La Boisselle today, passing through Albert which was full of resting troops. They are living in whatever shelter they can find in the ruined houses and cellars. There was a big change in the appearance of the town since I passed through it last July. The streets have been cleared and many civilians have returned and a number of shops have been opened.

We are expecting to be relieved any day now. We have lost a lot of men and we are supposed to go right back for rest and training. The three Canadian DRs, Mount, Munro and Larkin, all good lads and willing, went back to the corps today. They had been lent to us for this push.

23 NOVEMBER 1916

The River Ancre, which has been in the limelight so much just lately, is little more than a good-sized brook which meanders through a wide reedy swamp, once the home of many fine willow trees. Most of these are now lying on the ground in all manner of fantastic angles. The few that remain standing are split and shattered, most of them broken off half way.

24 NOVEMBER 1916

The weather has returned to rain and the roads are in a fearful state. Most of the DRs have given up their machines as not only do the guards get choked with mud but the chains and belts get so clogged as to break. It is quicker to use any lorry or waggon which comes along. It is surprising what ingenuity some riders will use to reach their destination. The prize tale is told by 'Titch' our smallest rider. He started on a GS waggon, then rode for several miles on the luggage grid of a staff car and then changed to a lorry and reached his destination. Coming back he used a succession of lorries until he got within 2 miles of 'home' when he finished on the back of a spare mule.

25 NOVEMBER 1916

The division is coming out of the line tomorrow. No-one will be sorry; everyone is absolutely fed up with the mud and cold. I am looking forward to a good sleep and to feel really warm. It seems ages since I had more than three hours of unbroken sleep.

26 NOVEMBER 1916, MOVED TO MARIEUX

Heavy rain and a gale all night. The dressing station lower down the valley was flooded out during the night. Many stretcher cases were awaiting removal by the ambulances. All these had to be hurriedly loaded into GS waggons and any transport which could be found at a moment's notice. A 10 mile journey in open waggons for most of them – pouring in torrents at 03:00 in the morning.

27 NOVEMBER 1916

Rain and sleet all day. I hear we shall be here for several days until our infantry are fit to march. They have had a terrible time these past few days. The trenches were deep in mud and water.

One bit of news which awaited us when we got back to the château was the death of the old billygoat who was a feature of the landscape in these parts. He was the largest and most stinking specimen of goathood I have ever met. He was old, how old nobody knew but if ripeness of smell was any guide he must have come out of the Ark. He had eyes the size of saucers and hoofs like young dinner plates. He would make a meal of anyone's shirt left out to dry. One of his favourite tricks was to lie down at the foot of the ladder which led to the loft where we slept. He would take up his position when everyone was asleep. The rich smell would ascend. Shouting would not move him, he had to be forcibly ejected. Then an argument would start as to who should go down the ladder to chase off the intruder. 'Now then So-and-So, you smelled him first, it's your job; if you hadn't wakened us we wouldn't have known anything about it.' 'I'll fix the bugger' says the volunteer; grabbing his rifle he clambers down the ladder, barefooted, giving vent to his feelings in a torrent of blasphemy. A 'whoof' from the old goat as he receives a hearty prod from the business end of a rifle and off he shoots into the courtyard, his hoofs rattling like castanets over the cobblestones. More blasphemy from the prodder as he painfully climbs the ladder, clad only in his short shirt, 10° below, a chorus of chuckles from those under the blankets and off we go to sleep again.

18 DECEMBER 1916, MOVED TO ST VENANT

St Venant is a small town about 8 miles north of Béthune. We are to stay here for a few days. From what I have seen of the town it is one of the cleanest we have seen in France: a very welcome change after our experience of the last few months.

The past few days whilst we have been on the move have been most trying. We have been on the go day and night like sheepdogs shepherding a flock.

19 DECEMBER 1916

The prices in the shops and restaurants are reasonable – a great contrast to the south. We have billeted ourselves in a small hotel called the Clef d'Or. Sleeping in beds, Ye Gods! There is a delicious humour in the situation. Two nights ago we were sleeping in pigstys, fairly clean but a bit odorous with plenty of straw borrowed from a nearby stack, but we were 100 per cent better than trying to sleep under a thin canvas 'bivvy' on a bleak hillside on the Ancre in a gale of wind, sleet or rain.

The Clef d'Or is also a restaurant. In the evening we take the restaurant dinner with full complement of wines, finishing off with the usual coffee and cognac. After that we settle down to bridge and some mild gambling games. This high life will last as long as the money holds out; fortunately we had a month's pay in hand when we got here.

22 DECEMBER 1916

We said good-bye to St Venant today. Oh saint of blessed memory who named this town, may his bones rest in peace. We have had a splendid time, one of the best we have had out here, just enough duty to remind one that there are other things besides eating and drinking.

Last night, we had a farewell dinner at the Clef d'Or which was a gorgeous affair. After dinner there was a poker game with eight players, a pure gamble. It lasted 2 hours and by that time only three survived to play for the spoils. Then we had a sing-song with all the old 'smutty' numbers and finally Garnier gave an exhibition of his famous bottle feat. This consists of lying full length on the floor with a bottle balanced on his forehead. Whilst rising he balances the bottle and finally stands on his feet amid the plaudits of an admiring crowd. A good trick which he does to prove he is not drunk, but I doubt if he could do it when sober.

23 DECEMBER 1916, LESTRUM

We moved to Lestrum today, on the road between Béthune and Merville. The village consists of one long straggling street with houses on either side. The surrounding country is absolutely flat and very low lying. All the fields are intersected with dykes and some of the roads run along the top of the embankments. The roads are narrow and full of sharp bends; woe betide the rider who runs off the road in the dark. The practice of lining up for rum issue at any point of call where the issue is in progress, whether by invitation or by sheer impudence, will have to cease or there will be some new faces in heaven.

24 DECEMBER 1916

Lestrum is turning out better than we expected. The people are a very decent lot and appear to be glad to see us. All our thoughts are concentrated on our Christmas dinner. There has been no time to make much preparation but four DRs are scouring the country for any delicacies they can find. One has gone to Lavantie to a certain *estaminet* which used to have a good stock of wines, liqueurs and champagnes. Another has gone to Béthune and Aire to try to find a goose which will be as scarce as hen's teeth by this time. May success attend their noble efforts.

We have been allotted a room over the stables. The ceiling is at least 20ft high – it is as cold as the North Pole and just as draughty.

25 DECEMBER 1916

As on last Christmas Day both sides gave as little annoyance and provocation as is possible between two parties who are at war with one another. Even the divisional staff reduced their paper 'bombardment' to a minimum and graciously sent out their orders for the brigade 2 hours early so the DRs could get back to enjoy their Christmas dinner, at least that is how we looked at it, though in all probability the staff had their own dinner in mind.

I had an invitation from the sergeants' mess though I would much preferred to have been with the DRs. The company sergeants are all fine fellows but I missed the nimble wit and humour of the DRs' mess.

The sergeants' dinner was held in the Café de la Mairie. The head of the table was taken by the SM, a real old sweat who had seen service in India and China and fought in the South African war and also in several minor ones. I was the youngest sergeant. Madame and her niece superintended the cooking while the sergeants' cooks were relegated to serving and helping in the kitchen. Everything went off famously and as the liquor went around we heard some racy stories of soldiering in the old days. I wish I could remember some of them though the point of most was in the telling.

1 JANUARY 1917

New Year's Eve passed very quickly. We did not have a 'do' this year, everyone is spent up.

3 JANUARY 1917

This morning I was surprised to receive a letter and a telegram in quick succession from Frank [this is Frank Simpkin, Albert's brother] telling me he had arrived at Marseilles from Salonica and was on his way home on leave. Could I wangle a leave he asked, so we could be home together? I have not seen him since September 1914 when he left for Egypt.

My turn for leave is some months off on the present allotment, but I thought I would try my luck with the OC. I explained the circumstances, he was awfully decent over it, although he said he did not think there was much hope. At the same time he handed me several 'bouquets' over the work of the DRs in the last stunt on the Ancre which he said had been noticed by the staff. I was more than pleasantly surprised when he sent for me about 21:00 to tell me that he had got me a leave and I go tomorrow night. Wonders do happen, sometimes.

4 JANUARY 1917, LESTRUM – ENGLAND

I walked to La Gorgue station, which is 2 miles distant, to catch a train which was supposed to leave at 22:00. I arrived at about 21:30 and found quite a crowd on the platform. It was a beautiful clear moonlit night, quite mild for the time of year. The air was so still that the 'rat-a-tat-tat' of a 'humourous' German machine gunner could be heard as though only a field or two away. We whiled away the time singing songs, mostly of the type peculiar to the army. Every now and again some practical joker would call out 'Here she comes' and in a trice everyone was tumbling over each other in a mad scramble for packs and equipment only to find it was a false alarm. At any other time there would have been trouble for the joker but everyone was in the best of temper and spirits.

It was well past midnight when the train stole into the station as though ashamed of its late appearance. It brought a string of the most ramshackle coaches I have ever seen, the windows had hardly a pane of glass in them. We had a perishing cold journey, arriving in Calais at 05:00. We were marched across the town and packed into a cinema near the docks to await the sailing.

We disembarked at Folkestone and I travelled on via London to arrive at Sheffield at 21:30. I found my father waiting on the platform. He took me to the theatre where all the family was at the pantomime. My brother had arrived home a couple of days before. We did not go to bed until 02:30 that night, yarns unending.

14 JANUARY 1917, SHEFFIELD

Everyone has given me a splendid time and now my leave is over. I would not let anyone come to the station to see me off. Everybody is as cheerful as possible though the gaiety was a little forced. If anything should happen, far better that the parting should be remembered as a cheerful one.

I reached London and by the time I had crossed the city it was near midnight. I was undecided whether to spend the night in the station to make sure I did not miss the train or go to a hotel and get some sleep. The station waiting room was crowded with sleeping men so I went to a small hotel where I found half a dozen leave men having supper. Although it was well past midnight an old waiter was bustling around bringing pots of tea and plates of cold meat for those who wanted it. We were up again at 05:00 to find the old man getting breakfast, he must have been up all night. We felt quite touched by his kindness. Most of us handed over all the English money we had left, some with the remark: 'Here you are, Dad, I may not want it again,' which made the old man's eyes fill with tears.

The platform was packed with relatives and friends. An extraordinary scene: women weeping, others dancing and singing to concertinas, bugles blaring, drunks staggering around bawling, 'Are we down-hearted?' making it all in all a rather repulsive sight.

At 06:15 the train drew out and then we did get a wholesome cheer which made up for the tawdry scene we had been watching. The station out of sight, we sat back in glum silence, too depressed for words, but when the train reached the open country we were soon joking and exchanging experiences of our leave, sharing sandwiches and cakes pressed on us by friends on the platform.

We reached Calais at midday and marched to the rest camp. Why these camps are called 'rest camps' is a mystery – the frontline could be no more uncomfortable. The camp was flooded, rows and rows of tents were marooned in 'lakes' of water while the others rested on a quagmire of mud. A biting wind swept across the field like a scythe. I pity the poor devils who had to stay the night in this hell hole. We were lined up and sorted out for our various destinations. I was lucky enough to get away with the first batch. The train left at 18:00 and although we had less than 60 miles to go we did not reach La Gorgue until midnight. While on the train, I heard of an extraordinary accident which occurred on a leave train two or three weeks ago. Some fellows, seeing a coke fire in a brazier used to keep the water pipes which supply the locomotives with water from freezing, purloined it and took it into their compartment. When the train reached Dieppe they were all dead, poisoned by the fumes.

26 JANUARY 1917, LESTRUM

We have had ten days of continuous frost and there is no sign of a break. If anything the weather is getting colder. Yesterday at midday we had 12° of frost and at night the glass fell to 25° below. Fortunately it is a dry cold with practically no wind. The sun shines all day but it has no power and appears as a blood red ball which does not dispel the ground mist. This arctic cold is a new experience for me. One does not realise how cold it is until one rides a motorcycle. At 20mph the wind cuts through the clothing and takes one's breath away. The eyelashes become locked together with beads of ice and the tears which run down the cheeks and meet under the chin form a solid cake of ice like a bridle. Our 'Charlie Chaplins' [moustaches] become solid with ice.

27 JANUARY 1917

Yesterday we had a big bombardment on our front which lasted until nightfall. This morning we heard the reason for the disturbance. Our infantry made a raid on a German strongpoint, capturing an officer and eight men. The strongpoint lies in the ruins of a farmhouse which the tide of war has left stranded in no-man's land. Deep dugouts have been built under the ruins with shell-proof walls of reinforced concrete, with loop-holes for machine guns. A deep moat surrounds the house which makes it almost impregnable to infantry attack.

Deep snow lay on the ground and to enable our men to get near without being observed they wore white overalls. Their only weapons were Mills bombs and 'knobkerries', the latter being a heavy shaft with a head about the size of a pineapple, studded with horseshoe nails, looking something like a mace as used by knights of old.

The surprise was so successful that our men crossed the moat by a portable bridge which the Germans use, but had not taken the precaution to remove. We were among them before they realised what had happened. Some terrific hand-to-hand struggles took place and one of our men and a German locked in each other's arms fell into the moat and were drowned. Our losses were two killed, two seriously hurt and two missing. The enemy must have lost at least fifty killed and wounded.

31 JANUARY 1917

The weather is still intensely cold today. Last night when I came off duty, I found a most novel and interesting game in progress in the form of a competition to prove which is the best lice killer. As Joe explained, it was being done in the interests of science. Some six kinds of powder and ointment were offered for trial. I added a special kind of ointment which was supposed to kill anything from lice to wild game. One of the boys engaged in his daily de-lousing operation had no difficulty in providing some lively specimens for the trial. Each kind of powder or ointment was tried in turn but, believe it or not, all those lice were alive and kicking after an hour's immersion. Even petrol, which is supposed to be a sure killer, was no more deadly.

My experience of these fancy powders is that they may be rough on the lice but the user's hide bears the brunt of the attack. An hour after application one feels flayed alive. We therefore gave our considered opinion and solemn declaration that all these lice powders and ointments are a snare and a delusion. The only sure method is 'You must catch 'em and you must crack 'em one by one.'

1 FEBRUARY 1917

There was a surprising sequel to the raid of the other night. This morning one of our men who was missing and believed killed came into our trenches. He was wounded and had been sheltering in shell holes between the lines for three nights and days without food. He had endured the terrible cold; it is a marvel he survived. Each night he had crawled about trying to find his way back to his own trenches. He had lain outside the wire of both ours and the German trenches, listening for scraps of conversation which would give him a clue as to whose trenches he was near, but without success. Our patrols had been out each night searching for the bodies of the missing. He had heard them moving about but as he could not tell whether it was friend or foe he dared not attract their attention.

The day before he found his own trenches was fine and clear and there was a lot of aeroplane activity. He noticed that when our aeroplanes came from a certain direction they were not fired on until they were over the Lines and when they returned the firing ceased; this gave him the clue to which were the British trenches. It is a wonderful example of the moral of our men. He endured 3 days and nights of hell rather than take the risk of being taken prisoner.

8 FEBRUARY 1917

The cold weather continues and there is no sign of a break. There was a nasty smash at the railway crossing on the road to Merville. The Town Major of La Gorgue and a corps DR met head on. The Town Major was killed instantly and the DR died shortly afterwards. I will lay odds it was the Town Major's fault; I have had quite a few escapes from these officers riding motorcycles, very few have any experience. Only the other day, I avoided a head-on collision with an officer who met me at a corner, lost his nerve and took the wrong side of the road.

13 FEBRUARY 1917, NOEUX-LE-MINES

Moved to this large mining village, near Béthune, on high ground overlooking the surrounding country. It is shelled fairly often and many of the houses show signs of the shelling, especially around the colliery which is the main target. In spite of this and bombing from German aeroplanes a considerable part of the population still lives in the village.

20 FEBRUARY 1917

One of our Brigade HQs is in Vermelles, a modern mining village. People are still living in the village although it is little more than a mile behind the frontline. The Germans could raze it to the ground in a few hours if it suited them, but I suppose it is spared on the understanding that if you spare the village which shelters our Brigade HQ we will spare yours. A very convenient arrangement.

The signal office is in the offices of the colliery, quite palatial. The building has received a few direct hits but for the most part it is undamaged. 63 Brigade is in a large château at Mazingarb. The policy of forbearance does not extend to their part of the Line. The Germans make a point of shelling the château and the grounds at irregular intervals.

27 FEBRUARY 1917

From early this morning processions of French youths have been parading the streets decked in long red, white and blue streamers, carrying flags, singing and blowing bugles. One of the classes has been called up and they were celebrating the occasion. Free drinks have been the order of the day and by evening they were all pretty 'tight' and quite a few were taken home on wheelbarrows. To see the way French youths join up is in striking contrast to the whining tales many of our youths at home tell the tribunals and the 'artful dodges' they try to evade army service.

28 FEBRUARY 1917

A new sergeant major arrived today. Our old SM left us just before we pulled out of Lestrum. When the war broke out he had been retired on pension for several years but was called up to help in the training of the Kitchener's New Army. When we went to France he asked to go with the company although hc was well over the age limit for active service.

At first the DRs were a sore trial to him, they ran rough shod over all manner of rules and regulations which the old army hold as sacred. The 'Do-as-you-like Brigade', the 'Mad Mullahs' or the 'Third Lieutenants' he called us – 'Third Lieutenants' because we wore all manner of un-regimental clothes, coloured scarves, airmen's helmets, etc. 'They carry enough kit around for the whole company and damn me if some of them don't even sleep in pie-jammers.'

The DRs, when coming back from leave, made it a rule to bring him a bottle of whisky which would last him for a couple of days. He could carry his liquor like a gentleman. He would get a bit red around the gills and his voice would become a bit husky, but I never saw liquor get the better of him. We used to invite him to our dinners and he always said 'Those mad young devils make me laugh so much it takes me a week to get over it, it beats Pompey.' What 'Pompey' was I never found out.

News has come through that the Germans are retiring on the Somme and Ancre fronts. This seems extraordinary after the tremendous resistance they made in November last to hold their position astride the Ancre. According to the latest reports they have evacuated Grandcourt and Serre. These were the villages we tried to take and include in the ground won when we took Beaumont Hamel.

3 MARCH 1917

I have been off colour for several days. This morning I felt very cheap, headache, toothache, and a bit feverish so I paraded sick. The doctor prescribed that universal remedy, a No.9, which I promptly handed to some fowls outside his office. There was keen competition among them who should have it. I will bet they will not be egg-bound for a day or two.

4 MARCH 1917, MOVED TO NORREN FONTES

Weather intensely cold with occasional snow showers. The division is scattered over a wide area and our runs are very long. The only place we could find as a billet was a small stable. The floor was deep in dirty wet straw which we raked out into the yard in spite of the protests of the landlord, and demanded new straw. After a lot of grumbling and argument we got it. We know a thing or two about billeting from the French interpreters.

9 MARCH 1917, MOVED TO ROLLECOURT

This is a small village on the main St Pol – Arras road. Some 2in of snow fell during the night and this morning we woke to find our blankets covered where it had drifted under the tiles of our stable roof. A strong wind is sweeping the snow into drifts.

15 MARCH 1917

We changed our billet today, finding a reasonably dry barn in a farmyard and thought ourselves very smart, but now we find the place is out of bounds as there were several deaths from 'spotted fever' (a tick-borne disease) among some infantry in a barn over the yard. It was only by luck we did not take over the infected barn.

A batch of labour men arrived in the village a few days ago. They had come direct from England to work on the roads. Some of them have not been in the army more than a few weeks and they are all G3 class. I saw several cripples among them and some with club feet. Another man I noticed was so deformed in both legs that he walked with the greatest difficulty. One of the sergeants had only one eye. Today over 200 of them went sick and yesterday over 100 were sent away, the majority in ambulances. Of the 1,000 which arrived less than 2 weeks ago, half of them have left. It is a foolish waste of money to send a bunch of cripples to endure the terrible weather we have been having during the past 2 months. As everyone knows there are thousands of able-bodied men doing jobs at home, in and out of the army, which most of these people could replace.

17 MARCH 1917

Rumour has it that we are booked for a stunt on the Arras front. It is easy to see from the concentration of troops in this area that something is brewing. The OC gave me instructions that the DRs must know every inch of Arras, 'so they can find their way about the town blindfolded'. Every man has to spend at least 2 days there learning the run of the streets and the location of the dugouts. This confirms that we are going in the Line at Arras.

Picking out two 'volunteers', I set off for Arras. It was a bright sunny day and to me the journey was a pleasant break in the monotony of the past few weeks. We entered Arras by the Baudimont Gate, one of the town gates of ancient times which is still standing though badly shattered. Leaving our machines in a safe place we explored the streets on foot, searching for a number of dugouts and cellars which are going to be brigade and battalion headquarters. Most of the side streets are blocked with fallen masonry, only the main thoroughfares have been kept clear of debris which simplified our task of memorising 'all' the streets of the town.

Arras is a city of the dead, not a civilian is to be seen. I believe there are a few still in the town living in cellars but not more than a score out of a population of 20,000. The Grand Place is more ruinous than it was 12 months ago. The Hotel de Ville is all but razed to the ground. The surface of the Grand Place has several huge holes where the roofs of the cellars below have been broken in by shells. As the roof is 10ft thick, no ordinary shell could do this.

A network of tunnels and cellars run under the town in all directions, cut from the solid chalk. Dating from olden times they were made to protect the people from the cannon of the invader. History repeats itself. Few towns have a history as exciting as that of Arras. From the time of the Romans hardly a generation has passed without the town being besieged. The Spanish at one time held the town, long enough to leave their influence on the style of the buildings.

Some of the places we had to find were in the tunnels, the entrance to which was through the ruins of a butcher's shop. Sliding down a slope of wet clay we found ourselves in a tunnel with a wooden latticed floor which was supported on beams let into the chalk walls. Underneath the floor ran a swift stream. After walking some distance along this passage which was lit with electric lights, we came to other passages branching off right and left marked with signs such as 'The Bank', 'Liverpool Street', 'Piccadilly', etc. This explained the directions given in our list which had puzzled us greatly. At one place we found a series of small rooms cut out of the chalk with neatly boarded walls and floors fitted with forms and tables which is to be the divisional HQ. The tunnels continue right up to the trenches and it is possible to enter the tunnels in the centre of the town and emerge in the trenches without coming to the surface. Walking around in leather jerkin, gas helmet, tin hat and full equipment made us sweat. We left the tunnels by an outlet which comes out in Ritz Place which is used as a dump. We stopped for a smoke and a breather in the shelter of a wall enjoying the warm sunshine. Overhead there was a continuous screaming and roaring of shells but nothing seemed to be falling near enough to cause any hurry.

Suddenly there was the shriek of a shell and by a coincidence I had my eye fixed on the exact spot where it struck. I saw the wall crumble with the impact, and after what seemed to be an appreciable time the shell exploded and the next instant the view was shut out with smoke and dust, but remarkable to say I could see pieces of brick flying towards me. Instinctively I ducked and I heard the 'fizz' and 'crack' of the pieces of shell hitting the walls around us. It was lucky none of us was hit. When we had collected our senses we bolted down the street. Our way into the town lay through the station and across the station square. As we crossed the railway I could see a German balloon so close that the heads of the observers were visible above the top of the basket. They would be able to see every movement around the station.

In the station we overtook a stretcher party and a bunch of men going towards the town. Thinking to myself, we shall be lucky if we get across the square without an iron ration from 'Jerry', and sure enough we had just reached the middle when there was a tearing scream and a crash. As one man we threw ourselves flat, the poor devils in the stretchers meeting the ground with a bump. We were peppered with stones and dust, but no-one was hurt. It was a brace of 5.9s, one hit the pavé less than 30ft away and the other a low wall on the opposite side of the square. Jumping up we raced for the shelter of the houses but had to flop again as another shell hit almost the same spot. There is no doubt they were targetted shots directed by the balloon, and damned good shooting too. The square is a perfect hell hole at night and the transport gets cut up badly.

23 MARCH 1917

We went to Arras today to continue our lesson in local topography. This time we explored the northern part of the town, called St Catherine, which is built on sloping ground facing away from the line. It makes an ideal position for our batteries and I think that more artillery is concentrated in that area than in any other part of Arras. Some of the guns were concealed in the front rooms of private homes and were firing across the roads. I had the fear that at any moment we might walk in front of a gun and get blown to bits.

This 'hunting the slipper' game sometimes lands us into awkward situations. It is surprising what suspicions are aroused by the simple question, 'Whose dugout is this?' We usually address this question to the nearest NCO but before he can answer out bounces an officer, 'Who are you and why do you want to know?' I then explain, 'I want to know so that I can find it again when I have to do so.' It is amusing to watch the officer's face, first he thinks we must be spies, but as spies do not go about in threes he decides that the divisional 'Brass Hats' have designs on his dugout and fierce resentment takes the place of suspicion. He retires into his dugout grumbling and growling, leaving the NCO to answer my questions. A fool on a fool's errand never looked more foolish, but ours is not to reason why.

28 MARCH 1917

The weather has been very bad this past week, rain and sleet every day. The DRs have been taking a refresher course in the care and management of the horse. The horse lines are in an open field with the mud over the shoe tops and most of the time it rained and sleeted; in army language we have had a bellyful. The army horse must be the most helpless of all God's creatures. From dawn to dusk he must be watered and fed, exercised, groomed and have his nose and tail wiped. Even his sleeping hours must be watched over by a male 'nurse' to see he does not strangle himself, or kick his neighbour to death. Each time the animals go out they come back plastered with mud which means an hour of hard work cleaning them, not to mention the cleaning of their harness. I pity the men whose job it is to look after them. We have over fifty horses and mules in the company and not a quarter of them earn their keep. In my opinion, we could replace two-thirds by a couple of light lorries and a 3 tonner, in fact, half the horses in the army could be replaced by motor transport with a great saving of manpower.

30 MARCH 1917

This morning there was a collision on the railway which runs through the village. Two trains met head on, several waggons and vans were telescoped into one another and blown off the rails. This is the second collision within the last 12 hours, the other occurred last night a mile away which made it necessary to run the up and down traffic on one line, hence the second collision. Everyone ran to see what had happened just in time to see a crowd of drivers, firemen and brakemen walking up the track towards the signal cabin. This is run by a woman who was already outside with arms akimbo waiting for the deputation. Then commenced a furious argument, the lady against six train men but she was more than a match for them, she never stopped talking for an instant for a full 10 minutes. The men could not get a word in edgeways and finally gave up the struggle and retired from the field of battle. She was a wonder, I could not make out what she said but by the way she said it she must have flayed the very hide off those men. Even when they were 50yd away she still lashed them with her tongue. Nor was the lesson lost on the troops who had gathered expecting a little light entertainment, they were spellbound and slunk off feeling might sorry for their sex and so did I.

1 APRIL 1917

Heavy fall of snow and freezing cold. This is 'All Fools' Day', but no more foolish than any other day in these times.

5 APRIL 1917, AGNEZ DUISANS

Today we moved to Agnez Duisans, a small village which lies some 3 miles behind Arras. We are camped in a collection of Nissen huts outside the village. The terrible weather we have been having is showing its effect on the horses and mules, they are dying like flies from exposure and exhaustion. The sides of the roads are littered with their carcases. I counted almost a hundred between here and Arras.

7 APRIL 1917

Our camp was shelled in the early hours of the morning. The shelling started around 02:00, one shell every 5 minutes, with occasional intervals of 15 minutes. Each time there was one of these longer intervals we thought he had finished, but just as we were on the point of dropping off to sleep there would be another fiendish shriek as the shell flew over almost grazing the tops of the huts. The shelling lasted 3 hours, a refined kind of torture. The only thing we could do was to flatten ourselves on the ground and pray he would not shorten the range, which was 100yd too long.

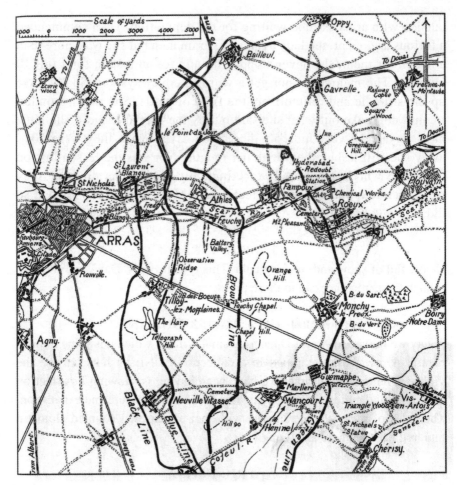

The Arras Sector, April 1917.

NARRATIVE THREE:

The Battle of Arras and the taking of Monchy le Preux

In April 1917, the Third Army, of which the 37th Division was a part, opened the spring offensive at Arras, taking the Vimy Ridge. The 37th Division's main objective was Monchy le Preux, a village some 3 miles southeast of Arras.

Our attack comes off tomorrow (9 April). The OC gave me an outline of what is going to happen. Our division will not be in the Line for the first attack but will jump the attacking division after the first and second lines have been taken. Our infantry will remain in Arras in the meantime. Each brigade and battalion will have a report centre and these centres are the various dugouts which the DRs have been so industriously finding and memorising in their visits to Arras. Zero hour will be 05:30 tomorrow morning. At 05:00 I have to report with three DRs to Wagonlieu where our general will make his temporary HQ until news is received that the objectives of the first attack have been taken, when he will give orders for our infantry to go forward and take up their position for the second attack. We have to take those orders to the various report centres in Arras.

When our troops are in the Line the Division HQ will be in the tunnels below the Ritz Place, which means that we shall have to cross the station square each time we go out. Yesterday the square was littered with wrecked waggons and dead animals which had been caught by the shelling.

We managed to get a few hours of sleep but it seemed as though I had only just lain down when I was awakened by an orderly shaking me, 'Ten to four, sergeant.' As we had slept 'all standing' it did not take long to put on our boots and collect our kit.

It was biting cold with a strong wind blowing. After 1 mile of byroads we reached the main road which was crowded with troops and transport on the march towards Arras, whilst an equally dense stream of ammunition lorries and waggons was passing in the opposite direction. It was a slow job weaving through the traffic and it was not made any easier by the treacherous grease on the pavé. I was on tenterhooks that one of us should have a skid and fail to reach Wagonlieu in time. As we neared Arras we could see that the fields on either side of the road were filled with resting troops.

We arrived a few minutes after 05:00. Telling the others to keep a lookout for the general I crossed a field to where the ground sloped away and I could look down on the valley in which Arras lies. The dawn was just showing but the light had not penetrated the valley below. Overhead the sky was a steely grey with banks of black cloud over the German position. A strong wind was blowing towards the trenches.

There was an uncanny silence, only an occasional gun fired, a stab of light in the darkness, the sound echoing around the valley. After weeks of continuous shelling the silence must have been noticeable to the Germans. Did they know what was coming? In a short time hell would break loose. At that moment thousands of guns were trained on their targets with the gunners standing by waiting for the order to fire, the greatest bombardment the world had ever seen. Tens of thousands of infantry in the trenches were counting the minutes waiting for the barrage to commence which would give the signal for them to go over the top. The dressing stations were working feverishly, getting ready for the deluge of shattered humanity which would shortly descend on them. Many then alive and well would, in a few minutes, be gasping their last breath. A greater number would be wounded, some to die, others to be patched up to feed the war machine again. Those whom the 'Fates' allow to come through unscathed will be put through the fire again and again until they are finally expended. War has no mercy. These were my thoughts as I sat waiting for Zero.

But for a freak of chance I might have been one of those waiting in the trenches, if I had dodged death so long. It was only a fierce hatred of walking which prevented me joining the infantry in 1914. At that time the despatch riders were very much in the limelight for their work in the retreat from Mons and it was supposed to be a highly exciting if not dangerous job. Times have changed.

Nowadays the DR's job is one of muddied ease and his chief preoccupation is keeping from falling under the wheels of the lorries and waggons, rather than running the gauntlet of 'shot and shell'. Perhaps when we get Jerry on the run in open country the DRs might qualify for a hero's halo.

Exactly at 05:30 the guns opened fire, a bit ragged at first but they soon got into their stride and settled down to a continuous roar. The darkness in the valley became a carpet of dancing flashes. Less than 10 minutes after the bombardment had started showers of red and green rockets and fountains of golden rain were soaring into the air. This firework display was the German SOS signal for artillery support but nothing could withstand that rain of shells.

It was now getting light and a short distance away a group of officers were watching the scene. It was General Allenby of the Third Army and General Snow of the corps with their staffs. I felt sure our general would be there so I returned to the other riders to warn them to get ready. A little later the officers left the field and as they passed I called my little group to attention and saluted. General Allenby, clad in a big cavalry coat with the collar turned up, a muffler around his neck and hands deep in his pockets, gave us a nod and a smile by way of a salute. I was surprised that our general was not among them.

Everybody seemed to be in a good temper and an ADC came across. 'Are you boys from the 37th Division?' 'Yes Sir.' 'Has General Bruce-Williams* arrived?' 'No Sir.' [*Major General Gleichen had been replaced in October 1916 before the Battle of the Ancre, firstly by Major General Scrase-Dickens and then by Major General Bruce-Williams.]

He then told us that our infantry had taken the first line and the Germans were evacuating their second line. We heard their cars move off and we were left alone. It was now 06:30 and the burning question was, 'Where was our general?'

It was biting cold and we stamped around to keep up the circulation. When 07:00 came with no signs of the general, I began to get a bit anxious. Had I come to the wrong place? We searched the map to see if there was another village with a similar name, but Wagonlieu is distinctive and quite uncommon for this part of the country. Besides, the ADC had enquired if the general had arrived, although he might have noticed our divisional signs and jumped to the conclusion that the general was expected.

As 07:10 came, then 07:20, the minutes passed like hours. I sent one of the fellows to try and telephone the old HQ at Agnes Duisans but there was no reply, everybody had left. He also tried to telephone the HQ in the tunnels in Arras but no reply.

It was now 07:30. I was getting desperate, I would send a man to Arras to find out what was happening. At that moment, the whine of a motor car could be heard climbing the hill and in a few moments the general's car came into view. The general got out followed by his staff officer. He looked around as though surprised to find the place deserted but catching sight of us he came forward and I went to meet him, army fashion.

'Sergeant, has the Army General gone?' 'Yes sir, he left half-an-hour ago.' I let him down lightly as in fact the Army General had been gone over an hour. He seemed to be taken aback by this information but after pondering a moment he turned to his officer, 'Look here, So-and-So, we must have breakfast earlier.'

These words cheered me immensely when I thought of the blue funk I had been in for the past hour, imagining everything from court martial to 'shot at dawn'. I was dismissed with 'Keep your men handy, I may want them at any moment.'

The general spent his time walking backward and forward between the signal office and his car, whilst we took shelter behind a low wall from the chilling wind.

At 11:00 the signal for our advance was received. The general came hurrying back from the signal office and his staff officer handed me the despatches, one for each brigade: 'You know what to do. Report as each man gets back'.

I handed each rider his despatch with a word of warning to take it easy. It was raining hard and the roads were deep in mud. A skid, and the message might not reach its destination in time and the result would be chaos. This was the climax of our month of wandering around Arras. I calculated that the first man should be back in 40 minutes and the others within the hour. I felt as worried as an old hen, but my anxiety was relieved when the first man got back several minutes before time and the others quickly followed: good going for 10 or 12 miles through traffic packed like sardines.

Apparently the attack had been held up and the advance was behind schedule, because each rider was greeted with 'Hello, where have you been? We expected you here before 08:00.'

Our division's objective is Monchy-le-Preux, a small village on the crest of the rising ground 3 miles behind Arras. Just in front of Monchy is the German fourth line, which overlooks a shallow valley over which our troops must pass to attack. We waited at Wagonlieu until 16:00, taking occasional messages to neighbouring divisions, when we were told to report to the Advanced Centre in the Ritz Place behind the station.

In Arras we found the streets blocked with all kinds of transport, most of it at a complete standstill because of a jam near the station. We made a detour by the back streets and reached the Ritz Place. The road on both sides was a solid mass of transport waggons, ammunition limbers and artillery unable to move in either direction. These traffic jams are extraordinary affairs, sometimes taking hours to disentangle. We wormed our way as near as we could get to the dugout entrance and left our machines in the safest position we could find. We were leisurely picking our way, clambering over fallen trees and piles of RE stores, when a shell hit a tree on the opposite side of Ritz Place. We dived for the stairway, just as another hit the sandbags protecting the dugout entrance.

I reported to the officer in charge of the signal station but as our brigades had not reached their positions there was very little to do. I decided to explore the various tunnels to get my bearings. A few moments after I had got back there was a tremendous roar overhead and the whole place shook like an earthquake. After waiting a little while I ventured out to see what had happened. The roadway was piled with wreckage of waggons, limbers, bodies of horses and mules lying in ghastly heaps, blood all over the place, like a slaughter house. The bodies of a dozen men were laid by the roadside.

An ammunition limber had been hit by a stray shell, exploding the ammunition which blew up other limbers in the column, killing or wounding every man and animal within a 50yd radius. From early this morning every part of the town had been searched with shellfire. The station square has been a death trap and the transport has suffered very heavily. This afternoon the bridge which carries the Cambrai road over the railway was blown sky high. Ammunition was stored under the bridge: a stray shell hit it and the bridge went up in a column of smoke 300ft high. It is said that a number of men were on the bridge and several others were killed by falling debris.

Towards evening the shelling slackened; the Germans, no doubt, were pulling out their artillery and taking it further back but they still kept up a desultory fire on the station square with their long range guns.

At 22:00, the OC told me to send a rider to search for our ration and store waggons which had not arrived. All the DRs were out so I went myself. It was a black night and it seemed almost impossible to find three or four waggons in the miles of traffic which filled all the main streets of the town. I wandered up and down the town for the best part of an hour when I found myself in the Grand Place where the traffic was inextricably mixed, officers and NCOs shouting orders to all and sundry but without producing the slightest movement. I had almost given up hope when by an extraordinary piece of luck I found our waggons with the SM standing alongside reduced to a profane silence. They had taken 4 hours to reach this spot from the entrance of the town and they had been stationary for the best part of an hour.

My knowledge of the side streets now came in useful. I found one which led to the outskirts of the town and when the traffic moved again we turned the waggons down this street and reached our store dump by a circuitous route. We had not noticed, however, that a string of waggons belonging to another unit had tailed on behind us. The officer in charge had not the slightest idea where he was; he wanted the Cambrai road. As I was returning that way I guided him to the station and there I left him.

I reported my success to the OC which so pleased him that he said I had better go back to the dump and see the waggons across the town in case they got lost again. I was just thinking about getting 'forty winks' which I shall certainly need before this show is over: I wished all transport in hell.

There is quite a lot of cavalry in the traffic, making for the front area which brings to mind a conversation I overheard between our general and the cavalry brigadier. The signal office and the staff office are only separated by a thin wooden partition and we can hear every word. The generals were arranging for a cavalry attack after our infantry have taken Monchy. The country beyond Monchy is clear of trenches and shell holes unless the Germans have dug another line of defence during this past few days.

Another interesting conversation I overheard was between our general and the brigadier of 111 Brigade who are going over the top in the morning to take Monchy. It was a conversation by telephone. As far as I could gather the brigadier was protesting that the wire was not cut and the attack would most likely fail. There was a heated argument ending with the general saying, 'They must go over whether the wire is cut or not'. There was some further conversation which ended with the general saying, 'My orders.'

111 Brigade attacked on the morning of 10 April at daylight and took Monchy in brilliant style. The Germans were taken by surprise. A good number of prisoners were taken – some were still coming down after dark without escort, wandering about not having any idea where to go. Some were impressed to carry stretchers. It was pitiful to see their servility, the slightest order from the scruffy 'Tommies' and they fell over each other in their eagerness to carry it out.

I am just beginning to know my way about the tunnels. There is a maze of passages running in all directions. The main passages are named for identification, such as 'King Street', 'George Street', 'Cannon Street', 'Glasgow', 'Edinburgh', etc. All the passages are lit by electricity and drinking water is delivered to all points. Tramway lines are laid along the principle passages for conveying stores and ammunition. There are several huge chambers, cut out of the solid chalk, lined with tiers of wire beds with tables down the centre. This is where the reserve troops spend time when not in the trenches. At each end of the chambers are flights of steps with notices, 'To the Front Line'.

The idea of living underground sounds like 'armchair warfare' but there is a fly in the ointment. There is a constant drip from the roof and unless one is entitled by rank to a cubby with a corrugated roof, one lives in a damned moist condition. The chalk floors are covered with white mud which makes walking a series of slips and slides, painfully tiring to the legs and trying to the temper.

In the afternoon, I went to find 112 Brigade whose HQ is in Tilloy, which was in the hands of the Germans yesterday morning. I had some difficulty in finding the dugout which was simply a trap door level with the ground. A flight of steps led to a small underground chamber which smelled strongly of the 'Hun'. The Labour Corps were busy filling in the shell holes and trenches getting ready for the heavy transport.

It was now snowing hard with a gale of wind, it had been snowing off and on all day. We never seem to have any luck with the weather for our attacks. The Ancre was just the same.

It was dark when I got back to the tunnels to find a state of panic: 'specials' to all brigades and neighbouring divisions. A big counter-attack is expected tomorrow. Our infantry who are holding Monchy are badly thinned out and the Germans are bringing up new battalions. All the DRs were out and they fastened on me to find the Reserve Brigade who seem to be lost. They are supposed to be in the town but no word has been received from them all day. The only direction I could get was 'try Rue de Fours. If they are not there we don't know where they are, you must find them.'

I found Rue de Fours, a street leading off the fish market, lined with large houses which must have belonged to the prosperous tradesmen. Most of them were badly damaged, some mere shells of walls filled with rubbish. I walked up and down the street several times and then searched the side streets. Every brigade headquarters should hang out a flag, but there was not a sign of a flag or other mark. The place was deserted, not a soul about to make enquiries.

Shells were shrieking over, directed on the roads entering the town, while our big howitzer batteries in the 'Citadel Gardens' were making hell's delight, the noise was deafening. I was up against a blank wall and I began to feel alarmed as no doubt the message was for reinforcements to be in the Line at daylight. What should I do? I remembered I had seen the sign of the Town Major in the fish market, I would ask him. I found him in bed but interested in my trouble. He said that any unit billeting in the town was supposed to report to him and he records their location but no brigade unit in Rue de Fours had reported to him.

He sent his orderly for the nearest traffic man who said that he had seen a waggon with our divisional sign loading stores in the Rue de Fours that afternoon. Back I went. I searched several houses and came to one which seemed to have been used recently. The floors were swept and one room at the back was cleared of rubbish. I shouted several times but got no response. I was about to leave when I noticed some signal stores in one of the corners. In a side passage, I found a stairway leading to a cellar and there I found the telegraphers asleep and also beautifully drunk. I wakened them and gave them a good cussing which brought down a 'hornet's nest' on my head. I handed in my message and left them to it. It was 04:00 when I got back to the tunnels. I lay down under the signal office table to get a nap but the procession of orderlies tramping in and out made sleep impossible.

Shortly after 06:00, the OC told me to take two DRs and report to a pillbox in the old German trenches behind Monchy. Yesterday these trenches were in the hands of the Germans. The general was going there; something was wrong, it was easy to see. We had already heard that the cavalry attack had failed and the brigadier had been killed. Using the main Cambrai road we managed to ride our machines to a point within 800yd of the pillbox. Beyond that it was impassable – a burnt-out tank lay across the road and the old trenches had not been filled in. Several batteries were in action on either side of the road without any attempt to conceal them. As the Germans are just over the ridge less than 1 mile away they are in for a rough time when the Germans have recovered their surprise.

Four aeroplanes suddenly came into view right ahead; flying at less than 300ft, they were following the road firing their machine guns continuously. As they got nearer we saw that the leader was going through some extraordinary antics, diving and twisting, as though trying to throw off a pursuer. We now saw that the first machine was one of our observation aeroplanes being chased by three Germans. Just before they passed overhead one of the enemy aeroplanes dived and we realised he was firing on the road by the puffs of dust as the bullets hit the road. It was all over in a few seconds, there was not time to take cover. The aeroplanes were so low we could see the pilots looking over the side and the flame from the muzzle of the machine guns.

I particularly noticed that the black crosses on the wings and tail were very small and inconspicuous. Our aeroplane, though of a much smaller type, put up a game fight for his life. As he topped the rise and disappeared from our view he was not much more than 100yd ahead and not more than 20ft high. It looked as though he was trying to land, but to land anywhere around Tilloy would mean a crash as there is not a dozen square yards of ground without a shell hole.

We now left the road to cut across the fields on foot. The ground was ploughed up with shell holes. Each one had some article of equipment showing our troops had used these holes as cover while advancing to attack. It was marvellous the attack had succeeded as the infantry would have had to advance up hill in full view of the enemy without any cover except these shell holes.

We found the pillbox already occupied by the general and some of his staff who were intently watching Monchy village, about 250yd away, which was hidden in a cloud of smoke from the tremendous bombardment. After reporting for duty, there was nothing for us to do for the moment so we took refuge in a nearby trench to shelter from the freezing wind and frequent snow showers.

A little later we were joined by Jock Cameron, one of our linesmen, who had just come over from Monchy. He gave us some details of the disaster to the cavalry that morning. From his description, they were manoeuvring to enter the village when the Germans saw them and sent over a barrage of shrapnel and high explosive which almost wiped them out. Their brigadier was killed. The survivors entered the village and joined the infantry in the trenches. Jock said the streets were choked with dead and dying horses.

News came through that the Germans were massing for a counter-attack. Our infantry had been badly thinned out and were hard pressed. An SOS had been sent for reinforcements, but unless they came quickly our infantry would be overwhelmed. Whilst we were intently watching the bombardment, a line of cavalry came into view, moving parallel to the line behind the village. It seemed madness to try and enter the village just then. As we expected, immediately they reached a point where they were in view of the Germans, a barrage hit them with deadly accuracy. Men and horses fell like 'ninepins'. In a few moments riderless horses were leaping over our trenches, many badly wounded, to stagger and fall. This second lot of cavalry shared the fate of the first.

The next scene in the drama was the welcome sight of several battalions of infantry advancing towards us in open formation. These were the reinforcements: Monchy was held. When the infantry reached us they got down into the trenches, evidently awaiting further orders. The Germans must have seen them because they sent over several salvoes of field-gun shells which dropped all around us for about 15 minutes, resulting in a few casualties.

When the shelling stopped I walked over to one of our abandoned tanks. A shell had pierced its plating and set fire to the petrol. Fortunately only one man was killed, the others escaped by taking shelter under the tank. It was called 'Lusitania', a name which seems to be unlucky.

Next we had a heavy snow storm which covered the ground like a mid-winter scene. The Germans gave us another taste of their artillery and this time it seemed to be more concentrated, showering the stones and dirt all over us, but with no casualties. Then the staff woke up and we were kept busy for the next hour carrying messages to various units and batteries in the area. The German attack had failed.

Occasionally there was a thundering roar overhead like an express train in a tunnel, from the passing of a shell from a big naval gun the Germans were using to shell Arras. We could see the column of smoke rise above the town after each burst.

A little later the general shut up shop and we were told to return to Arras. Arriving back at the tunnels we found all the DRs out. We had to go out right away, mostly to units inside the town, who have secreted themselves in all manner of queer places and the DRs seem to be the only people who can find them. When I protested to the Signal Master that these short distance messages could be carried by runners he said the staff say the operation orders must be carried by DRs.

Around 21:00, there was a 'special' for a battery whose map location showed it to be a short distance to the right of the pillbox where we had been that morning. Having had no sleep for two nights running, and no food but 'bully', biscuits and tea, I felt dead tired. I did not relish the job either as it was reported that the area behind Monchy was being shelled very heavily, no doubt trying to catch the reinforcements and ration parties for the trenches.

I found the Cambrai road crowded with pack animals taking up rations and ammunition. Horses and mules have a violent dislike of motorcycles, especially in the dark and I had to ride the gauntlet of hundreds of animals. Some lashed out with their hoofs while others adopted an attitude of passive resistance by turning broadside in my path. Several times I found myself in a mix-up which looked as though I was going to be knocked down, but when I buzzed the engine they gave me wide berth. The drivers' language was wonderful.

As far as Tilloy it was pitch dark but beyond there the ground falls away in a gentle slope and I had no difficulty in picking my way by the light of the flares from the trenches. The batteries alongside the road were belching dazzling white flame which lit the place like day. I hurried along to get away from their hellish noise so I could hear if the crossroads was being shelled.

Leaving my machine behind a bank of earth I waited and listened. If the crossroads was being shelled I would go across country as I did this morning, but if it was quiet I would keep to the road rather than cross the fields with the hundreds of shell holes and old trenches. All seemed to be quiet so I turned left down the track which leads to Rouex. The map location for the battery showed it to lie about 200yd to the right and the same distance behind Monchy. I expected to find the battery in action but there was neither sight nor sound of them and I began to think I was in for a long search.

I left the track and struck across the fields in the direction where I thought the battery should be. Walking warily, I was on the point of turning back when I almost bumped into a silent gun with no sign of the gunners. I shouted and someone in the distance answered. Making towards the voice I found a number of men digging a trench in the shelter of a low bank. A young officer clambered out and I gave him the message. He told me that they had been shelled several times that evening and they were digging a shelter. I was lucky to come across them at the first attempt.

These solitary wanderings behind the trenches in the darkness are the nearest approach to a nightmare I can imagine: the stabbing flashes of the guns, the soaring flares from the trenches lighting up the horizon, the stammering racket of the machine guns and the ear-splitting crashes on all sides, while overhead there is a constant roaring, screeching, swishing and moaning of shells passing over, each one adding its particular note to the hellfire chorus; Dante himself could not imagine a better setting for his Inferno.

Chapter Six

April – July 1917

12 April 1917, Arras

Our division is being relieved this evening and tomorrow we go back to rest and refit. Many of our battalions are badly smashed and the survivors are about 'all in' with this terrible weather. We shall not be sorry to get out of this hell-hole. At 20:00, the OC told me to take two DRs and wait at the Doullens entrance to the town. We were to act as guides to a fleet of motor lorries which were coming to carry our troops to their rest camp. The troops were to entrain in the Grand Place. The lorries were almost 2 hours late. I took the first lot sitting by the driver. We started off at the head of a procession of twenty lorries. It was a tortuous route, a wrong turn and there would have been chaos. In the narrow streets overhung with houses it was almost impossible to see one's hand before one's face but by good luck we reached the Grand Place without incident.

13 April 1917

We handed over to the incoming division at 07:00. We have returned to the Agnez Duisans camp but we are moving to Lignereuil tomorrow. Although we left this camp only 4 days ago it seems like 4 weeks. I have not had more than 6 hours sleep in the past five nights and I have not taken off my clothes. I do not feel particularly sleepy. When I ride my machine I feel quite normal but when I walk I am light-headed and dizzy.

We have had nothing to eat for over a week but 'bully', biscuits, bacon and tea. The cook house has been closed. Two days after we started this period of iron rations one of the staff asked me to arrange for one of our DRs when visiting the corps HQ to bring some soft bread for the general as the old man's teeth could not manage biscuits. He must be nearer 60 than 50-years-old. It was, of course, to be kept a secret.

14 APRIL 1917, LIGNEREUIL

Today we moved to Lignereuil, a small village near Avesnes le Compte. The village consists of a single street lined with cottages and farms with a château in the background. We are to rest in this place for a week after which we are to return to Arras for another stunt.

20 APRIL 1917

The OC unbent today to hand me a 'bouquet'. He told me the staff were pleased with the work of the DRs in the last stunt.

21 APRIL 1917, ARRAS

We moved back to Arras today. The signal station is in the railway cutting in front of Blangy. There is a deep dugout for the general and his staff. The signal station is simply a splinter-proof shelter. The Germans know every inch of this area as they held it previous to the attack; they lob their shells into the cutting like throwing potatoes into a bucket. The bridge can be seen from the German lines and receives the constant attention of their artillery, and from the amount of wrecked waggons and dead animals they have been pretty successful. The OC's car was left standing near to the bridge when a shell dropped under the front, blowing off the wheels and most of the engine. The car was a Sunbeam, the apple of the chauffeur's eye.

Two DRs have to be on duty at the cutting; as there is no shelter for them we have dug a deep narrow trench at the top of the slope opposite the signal office. From our cubbyhole we can look over the embankment. Authie is 450 yd in front. To the right we can see the chemical works at Rouex, about a mile away, while further to the right is Monchy, hidden in a cloud of smoke, bursting shells and shrapnel. The Germans hold Rouex and we still hold Monchy, but the Germans are making desperate attacks to push us out.

22 APRIL 1917, BLANGY

A fine bright morning. We could see Monchy and the woods beyond clearer than we have ever seen them before. The artillery fire has been heavy all day. The Germans put up a tremendous bombardment on Monchy from 14:00 till 18:00. Case was killed and Hall injured this afternoon. They were laying lines in front of the railway cutting: two of our best linesmen gone.

Things are not going too well but it seems fairly certain that our division troops have gained their objectives, also the left-hand division, but the right-hand division, which holds Monchy, has not taken their objectives, consequently the advance is held up. A fair number of prisoners have been taken.

23 APRIL 1917

Our main attack was made this morning. The barrage started at 04:30. It sounded truly hellish. Even when it was fully daylight the air was so full of smoke from the bursting shells drifting back from the Line that the flash of the guns showed bright red against the blackness. The staff are of the opinion that the Germans have brought up a lot more artillery as their retaliation was the heaviest since we started attacking Arras. One of our brigades took Gavrelle at the first attempt. Another reached the Rouex crossroads and entered the chemical factory. Later the Germans re-took the factory but we held all the other ground gained.

Last night, the German artillery was very active: the cutting and the bridge were shelled all night. The transport caught it badly, dead animals and smashed waggons are lying everywhere. I hear we had many casualties among the drivers. During the afternoon, the German naval gun starting shelling Arras and kept it up for 2 hours. The 51st Division HQ was hit causing several casualties. I was in the signal office in the cutting this morning when a priority message was received from a battalion in Monchy calling for immediate help and reinforcements. The German place great value on the strategic position of Monchy, which stands on high ground overlooking our side of the Line.

24 APRIL 1917

A beautiful day, not a cloud in the sky, but a very cold wind is blowing. Some distance behind the candle factory two of our observation balloons are at work. When they are up, the German long-range guns fire at them, around once every 5 minutes. The shells usually burst directly over our heads, the pieces come shrieking down, sometimes striking the ground like a gigantic hailstorm. I went up to the cutting this afternoon. A few minutes before I arrived, a transport waggon with two mules had been hit while crossing the bridge and had fallen into the cutting. They were shooting the mules, one had a broken back, the other also appeared to be badly wounded. As there is no wall and part of the roadway had been blown away, it is only wide enough for one-way traffic. If a team is hit or gets restive one wheel is sure to go over the edge and the whole lot has to go, a 20ft drop.

The Germans are counter-attacking continuously. The chemical works has changed hands several times today and who holds it at the moment is not known. They are also making desperate efforts to retake Monchy.

25 APRIL 1917

This morning we saw a fight between seven of our slow spotting aeroplanes and three fast German machines. They wheeled around manoeuvring for position but it was obvious the Germans were much faster than ours. Suddenly one of our aeroplanes burst into flames. The pilot made a great fight for life, diving almost vertically, the flames streaming behind for a distance of 30 or 40yd. His dive lasted for 30 seconds and then flattened out; by that time he would be about 400ft high but at that moment his tail fell off and he crashed to the ground. A trail of jet black smoke was all that was left to show the path of his dive to death.

A long-range 6-inch gun has taken up quarters alongside our dugout. About every sixth shell it fires is a 'premature' which, instead of exploding in German territory, explodes just as it leaves the muzzle of the gun, making an appalling crash which is the combined noise of the exploding shell and that of the gun. This morning I had a narrow escape of being a victim. A large piece of shrapnel from one of these 'prematures' flew past my head with a noise like a circular saw and buried itself in the ground a few yards away.

Late this afternoon the cutting was shelled very heavily. Corporal Cotton was badly hit and two of 63 Brigade signallers were killed. The sergeant of the Military Police and the Traffic Officer were killed this morning when directing traffic at the cross-roads near to the bridge.

26 APRIL 1917

The shelling of the cutting yesterday afternoon also caused another casualty. Corporal Grimshaw, the CRE's clerk, was killed. He had just returned from leave after getting married. Both his legs were blown off. He was quite cool, after making his will he remarked quite casually, 'Well, I'm no further use in this world so I had better be going.' He died a few minutes later. Another casualty: the ADMS's orderly was also killed this morning.

This signal office had a direct hit on the roof. Fortunately, it did not penetrate but all the lines were broken and some of the instruments were damaged from concussion. The Germans are making very accurate shooting, dropping their shells into the cutting sometimes in salvoes. It seems foolish to pick such a spot with practically no shelter except, of course, for the general and his staff. We have had more casualties in the last few days in the HQ than we have had during all the time we have been out here. We have to keep two DRs on duty at the cutting. I feel sure they have escaped due to my instructions to dig a deep narrow trench at the top of the bank.

27 APRIL 1917

The most spectacular part of the war is the air fighting. There is always a host of aeroplanes weaving backward and forward overhead. The slow observation aeroplanes occupy the lower strata of the air, spotting for the artillery or watching the movements of the enemy, their path strewn with puffs of shrapnel smoke from the enemy's anti-aircraft guns. Above them fly the two-seater fighters, whose duty is to guard the observation aeroplanes from enemy attacks. Higher still, with the heavens as their ceiling, the single-seater scouts range the blue skies like 'wolves' seeking their prey. Occasionally the 'wolves' elude the vigilance of the two-seaters on police duty and snatch a lone observation aeroplane or, if the odds are favourable they may attack the 'policemen'. Other times they can be seen engaged in a battle royal with their own kind.

An aeroplane falling in flames is an ugly sight. Even in the brightest daylight the glare of the flames streaming behind show blood red as the machine dives, leaving a trail of black smoke to mark the path of its fall. The pilot's death does not bear thinking about; it is neither swift nor merciful.

30 APRIL 1917

We are being relieved tomorrow and are going back to Lignereuil again for rest.

12 MAY 1917, LIGNEREUIL

We have now been at Lignereuil since the first of May. Spring has arrived. The weather is bright and warm. What a wonderful change the past few days of sunshine and warm winds have made to the countryside. A week ago hardly a leaf was showing but now the trees are green all over with their new foliage and the new corn has sprung up to 6in.

Four of us have fixed our 'bivvies' in the middle of the copse of noble beech trees which is part of the château grounds. Overhead the young leaves make a complete canopy which sheds a green light on everything below. The ground is a springy carpet of beech mast. At night time we hang a lamp in the branches and the effect is like a theatre setting for fairyland.

One night we were having a hand of bridge by the light of the lamp, when up walked the general and one of his staff officers. We all jumped to attention, but after pausing a moment he passed on without comment. As it was past 22:00 we fully expected to hear more about it, but the beauty of the scene and the novelty of the situation probably stayed his hand as we heard nothing further.

13 MAY 1917

I heard a story of a pathetic little incident which happened at the artillery HQ a few days ago. An old man and woman arrived accompanied by two French gendarmes. These old people were the owners of the farm whose cellars were being used as dugouts. The farmhouse had disappeared, all that was left of it was a mound of rubble which served to protect the roof of the cellars. They had come to recover some treasure they had buried before the German advance in 1914. They spent 2 or 3 days digging in various spots but they had no luck; either they could not locate the position due to the great change in the appearance of the site or, more likely, the Germans forestalled them. They departed looking very crestfallen.

17 MAY 1917

About 14:00 today, I was lying in my 'bivvy' taking 'forty winks' after dinner when I felt the ground give a tremendous thud, and after a couple of seconds came a rumbling roar which ended with a loud thunder clap. I jumped up and ran to the edge of the wood and could see a huge mushroom of black smoke in the sky in the direction of Arras. A few minutes later we had word on the telephone that the big ammunition dump as Wanquetin had gone up. This dump covers about 4 acres of closely-packed ammunition boxes.

18 MAY 1917

We hear we are going back to Arras again, this time to the right of the Arras – Cambrai road. I went up to Arras today to make arrangements for the DRs' work when we take over from the 56th Division. The Division HQ will be in Arras itself, near the Doullens gate, but there is a DRs' post on the Wancourt Road about 1 mile in front of Tilloy. I found the post, a filthy hole in a clay bank alongside a battery of 12-inch howitzers. All around was deep in clay mud and everywhere in a filthy condition. I passed a few raw remarks to the DRs in charge of the post; if they could not find a cleaner and better place, why had they not tried to improve it? There was plenty of material lying around. Our fellows would have got busy in their spare moments and made a shelter as clean and comfortable as possible under the circumstances, leaving it in better condition than when they found it for those who came after them. That is the army way.

19 MAY 1917

I went to Arras again today to make a further exploration of our new front. Coming back, I made a detour to pass through Wanquetin where the ammunition dump exploded 2 days ago. Half a mile before I entered the village the fields were littered with shells and empty cartridge cases. The village had the appearance of being heavily shelled. There is hardly a pane of glass left whole and not a roof with a full covering of tiles. Some roofs have been completely stripped, leaving the rafters as naked as when the house was first built. The streets are deep in tiles and debris.

The ground where the dump had stood is ploughed with large craters and hardly a shell to be seen; last time I passed the dump it covered 3 or 4 acres of closely-stacked boxes and neatly piled shells.

It is said the value was over £20,000,000, all expended in one big bang. One rumour has it that the dump was fired by a stray shell, another by an aeroplane bomb, whilst another rumour has it that it was caused by an officer examining a fancy fuse of a new German shell, but how do they know? There were several men in the dump at the time of the explosion but not a trace of them was found.

23 MAY 1917, ARRAS

Although the town is out of range of ordinary artillery fire it is shelled every night by a big long-range naval gun which is said to be mounted on a railway carriage and brought forward each night to fire on the town and taken back before daylight. It is said to be a 9.3-inch gun firing from a range of at least 10 miles.

Last night the shelling was directed at our end of the town. One hit the stable in the rear of our billet and another hit a house two or three doors higher up the street. Our billet is directly behind the Schramm Barracks which, although partly in ruins, are still used to shelter troops; probably the

Germans are aiming at the barracks and we are getting the overthrows. So far the shelling has caused more annoyance than actual damage; it keeps the troops awake and disturbs their rest.

26 May 1917

Today has been hot with brilliant sunshine. Sleeping on the floor of a three-storey building with 9-inch shells screaming past the windows all night long is too great a strain on the nervous system. We have moved our quarters and we are now sleeping under a large chestnut tree in the yard of a school near to St Nicolas Church. One end of the school is in ruins but there are two or three rooms on the lower floor which we can use as a workshop.

31 May 1917

After heavy artillery preparation the infantry of our division made a minor attack which we hear was only partially successful. The war seems to be settling down again to the usual trench warfare: our big attacks have come to a standstill.

1 June 1917

The hot weather still continues and the narrow streets of the town are unbearably hot and stuffy. These hot days we go swimming in a pool on the other side of the town. There are two pools side by side, one as clear as crystal with a weedy bottom but the other muddy. The clear pool according to a notice is reserved for men of the 29th Division, the muddy one, presumably for the outsiders.'Some 'opes,' I heard one lad say. A corporal runs around trying to separate the 'sheep' from the 'goats' but those not of the chosen simply undress alongside the muddy pool and jump into the clear one the moment the corporal's back is turned, and who carries divisional marks on their birthday suits?

An inter-division sports meeting was recently held on the cycle track on the outskirts of the town. There was some good running and jumping. The fellow who won the high jump was said to be a professional. After he had won he had the bar set still higher and gave a few exhibition jumps. Another very interesting competition was pole climbing by linesmen. Using their climbing irons they simply ran up the poles as though they were running up stairs. Unless I had seen it I would not have thought it possible.

6 JUNE 1917, LIGNEREUIL

Andy, one of our DRs who is attached to the artillery HQ which is still in Arras, called in today to find us living in peace and luxury. He says that nights in Arras are hell 'and then some'. The town is shelled and bombed all night long and everyone has taken to the cellars. There have been heavy casualties. We move again tomorrow farther north where we are to receive reinforcements to make up for the losses during the last few weeks. There we are to reorganise and go into training.

13 JUNE 1917, BOMY

It has been fearfully hot these past few days, the greatest heat I can remember. At midday it is unbearable, and the only thing we can do is to lie in the shade and sweat. Every day we go bathing in the mill pool although strange to say the water is too cold for comfort. The stream which feeds it comes from a spring nearby, which I suppose accounts for its ice-like coldness.

One day we had a bit of excitement at the pool which might have been a tragedy. Hobson, one of our DRs, was almost drowned in front of our eyes. He jumped in and started dog swimming with much vigour, shouting and bawling as is his wont. 'Hob' delights in noise, but this time it almost proved his undoing. After a few moments his head went under and he made gurgling noises. Still we thought he was joking, in fact, everyone thought he could swim. Suddenly, it dawned upon us that he was really drowning and there was a dash to his help, pushing him to the bank where he managed to clutch some overhanging bushes.

21 JUNE 1917

Today I went to Fruges, a small market town some 8 miles away from here to attend a medal presentation parade. The parade took place in the town square. Three sides were lined with troops and the fourth was occupied with 'medallists'. General Horne [Commander of the First Army] made the presentation and afterwards the troops marched past the heroes at the salute. In the evening, we 'wet' the medal in a small *estaminet*; I forget how many bottles of champagne we drank, but it cost me over 60 Francs. [The official diary of 31st Signal Company records that Simpkin and four other men were awarded the Military Medal 'for gallantry in the Battle of Arras'. *The Supplement to the London Gazette* of 18 July 1917, records the award with the standard generic citation 'for bravery in the field'.]

23 JUNE 1917

Moved to Steenbecque, a small village on the Hazebrouck Road. This village only differs from many others in so much that the local *estaminet* sells English draught beer which is served by two remarkably pretty girls with golden hair. The *estaminet* does a roaring trade, but it would be difficult to say which is the greater attraction, the beer or the girls. For myself, the beer tastes good and is no worse for being served by a pretty wench.

24 JUNE 1917

Moved to Locre, a village just over the Belgian border on the Ypres-Bailleul road. By a coincidence, we return to Locre after 2 years' absence, almost to the day. This is the front where our infantry went into the trenches to get experience when we arrived in France in June 1915.

I hear our division is taking part of the Line on the Messines Ridge which was captured on the seventh of this month after we had exploded several big mines. It was a fine bit of work and the Germans were taken by surprise or crushed by the weight of our attack as we had comparatively light casualties. Our line was pushed over the top of the ridge and now we are looking down on the Germans whereas previously they overlooked all our trench system and the country beyond. The gain was one of great strategic importance and this is shown by the efforts the Germans have made to recapture the positions. It was in these counter-attacks that most of our casualties were caused. They achieved very little and left a good number of prisoners in our hands. The German counter-attacks have now come to a standstill and all is quiet at the present moment, but rumour has it that our division is to make another attack very shortly to improve our position still further.

One of the sergeants of the signal company we were relieving told me how he had seen a German trick two of our aeroplanes a few days ago. He came down head over heels with our machines in close attendance, to within 500ft of the ground and then righted himself and made off to his own lines. Our aeroplanes dived and he had to come still lower to escape them and eventually landed in a field. Our aeroplanes flew off thinking they had finished him off. As our troops came running up to capture him he started off again, skimming along the ground jumping hedges like a partridge and got clean away.

25 JUNE 1917, LOCRE

Cloudy and heavy rain all night. Our signal office is in a barn. I have noticed that the barn wall facing away from the Line is heavily pitted as though from shrapnel or a bomb. I thought it rather peculiar but gave the matter no further thought. But today, I heard the reason for these marks.

Nearby is a cottage where lives a woman and her daughter who eke out a living selling coffee and washing shirts for the troops. The daughter speaks English quite fluently. Flemish people pick up English very quickly, there is some resemblance between the two languages. A few of us were in the cottage drinking coffee today when the girl said she had seen a German spy who is to be shot tomorrow, being escorted through the village. The girl then related how she had seen three of our men shot for desertion a short time ago. One day an officer came to their cottage and said that no-one was to leave the house for half an hour and a guard was posted at the door.

The girl was curious to know what was going on and went upstairs to look out of the bedroom window. She saw three men sitting on chairs, their legs bound to the chair legs, their hands tied behind them and their eyes blindfolded by a handkerchief. Before she could realise what was happening shots rang out and the men's heads fell on their chests. She had watched an execution of deserters. The chairs were placed along the barn wall where I had noticed the 'shrapnel' marks.

26 JUNE 1917

Better weather today. The troops have always given the people in these parts a bad name. My experience so far has been quite happy. True, one old farmer has locked up his pump, which has caused some hard swearing but it is easy to see that if all the troops used it the pump would soon run dry, and I do not suppose the army would come to his aid if his animals had no water.

27 JUNE 1917

Dull and close all day. A thunderstorm has been brewing all afternoon, the sky getting darker and darker until it was as dark as night at 19:00.

When the storm broke the thunder drowned the noise of the artillery. Man has a long way to go before he can produce a sound to equal the grandeur of a thunder clap. Just as the storm broke, it was my luck to have to take messages to all brigades. I was wet through before I had gone 100yd and at times I could hardly see where I was going, the rain came down like a solid wall of water.

28 June 1917

The weather is cooler. My birthday, the third out here. How time flies, yet when I look back to the day I joined it seems like 10 years ago. Every day brings a new sight and a new sensation. When will it end and where?

29 June 1917, Moved to Dranoutre

Raining in torrents all day, everyone drenched to the skin. Went up the Line to find the position of the brigades and batteries. Most of them are in dugouts in the old trenches just behind the big mine craters, which by the way are much smaller than the newspapers' descriptions would have us imagine. Everywhere the ground is water-logged and each shell hole is filled to the brim with water. I can see someone getting a ducking these dark nights.

The Division HQ consists of a collection of Nissen huts hidden in a small copse, and a large open field. The ranks have 'chosen' the field. The site was heavily shelled 2 weeks ago, causing a number of casualties when the last division was in occupation. The WCRE was killed. We expect the same attention at any moment.

4 July 1917

Early this morning five bombs were dropped on our supply column which is stationed outside Locre. A nasty affair – eleven killed and twenty injured, out of about fifty men. Emms and Oliver, their motorcyclists, were both killed. I had been trying to get Emms transferred to our section. I believe he comes from Norwich. I would not be surprised if it was not the same aeroplane which came over yesterday morning. It is said the bombs were not large but by a piece of bad luck, three fell in the space between two huts which were filled with men sleeping on the floor.

5 July 1917

Last night relays of German aeroplanes came over at 30 minute intervals bombing the towns and villages behind the Line. Almost 100 bombs fell in Bailleul and some on the hospital. It is said there were casualties among the hospital nurses. The artillery has also been very busy on both sides today, it looks as though a big attack is in preparation.

6 JULY 1917

Weather dull with misty rain. The artillery has been so quiet that there was a foolish rumour going around that an armistice had been declared. The correct explanation, no doubt, is the bad visibility.

8 JULY 1917

This afternoon I found one of our section dead drunk. I have noticed several times lately he has been pretty 'tight' and I wondered where he was getting it from. I have discovered that he and another of the same leaning, a corporal in the RAMC, have been concocting a drink composed of neat alcohol from the medical stores and other ingredients. I have threatened the RAMC fellow what I will do if it happens again and for our fellow I am nursing my wrath until he is sober again.

10 JULY 1917

Between here and Ypres there are five balloons floating at 880yd intervals. This afternoon we had a fine exhibition of balloon 'bursting' on a wholesale scale, by a German airman who fired three in as many minutes. Diving from a low cloud he took the first balloon in his stride which promptly burst into flames. Sweeping on to the next he fired that also before the AA guns had fired a shot. He then made towards the third balloon, but by this time the AA had put up a barrage around it and he headed for home. We were treated to the spectacle of two balloons burning at the same time. For a time we thought the third balloon had escaped, but it went the same way as the others, bursting into flames some 3 minutes after the German had gone. We also saw the unusual sight of six or more parachutes floating in the air together.

20 JULY 1917

A beautiful bright day with hardly a cloud in the sky. Our aeroplanes were up in swarms, the German AA plastering the sky with their efforts to hinder our spotting aeroplanes in their work directing the artillery fire. It is easy to tell whose AA is firing – our shells give white smoke, the German's black.

There was very heavy artillery fire all last night from both sides. The Germans were searching all crossroads and villages near the Line. They were using a lot of gas shells. Big shells were shrieking overhead, which we could hear bursting in Bailleul. It looks as though all civilians will have to leave the town very shortly.

22 July 1917

The Germans are using a new form of gas in their gas shells which is causing some excitement among the staff. It is said to blind almost immediately and to blister whenever it touched the body. The smell is like garlic; mustard oil is supposed to be one of the ingredients. When the shell bursts the gas, which is in liquid form, is sprayed into the air. This liquid evaporates giving off a most corrosive gas.

23 July 1917

Hot and sultry. The bombardment which has been intense for the past day or two still goes on, slackening in the daytime but breaking out at night again with renewed fury until the noise becomes one thunderous roar. The day of the attack must be getting near. Several times during the night, we could hear the German gas horns blowing so it looks as though we are getting a bit of our own back.

30 July 1917

The attack is timed to commence about 04:00 tomorrow.

NARRATIVE FOUR:

The Third Battle of Ypres

**Sergeant Simpkin's Division, now part of the Second Army
under General Sir Herbert Plumer, saw action in the area to the
south of Ypres, around Wytschaete and the Messines Ridge.
The battle took place in atrocious weather conditions which were
partly to blame for the tremendous loss of life in the campaign,
especially at Passchendaele, to the northeast of Ypres.**

I have been too busy to write up my diary these past few days.
The attack commenced at 03:30 on the morning of 31 July. I turned
in a little after midnight to get a bit of rest before we started what I
knew would be two or three days' hard going. It seemed as though I
had only been asleep a couple of minutes when I was awakened by an
orderly. 'All DRs to stand by immediately.' It was hardly light and there
was a low mist with a slight drizzle in the air. There was an intense
bombardment for 20 minutes before the infantry went over. At 04:30
a few of our aeroplanes came over and were quickly lost to view in
the low misty clouds. At 08:00 it was confirmed that our infantry had
gained all their objectives.

Shortly after 08:00 I had to take a 'special' for the Advanced Brigade
Post which is also to be used as a test point for the telephone lines. The
post was said to be on the highest point of the Messines Ridge in front
of Wycheart. No-one knew its exact location but it was 'somewhere
near Guy's Farm in an old German machine-gun emplacement'.

I rode as far as the craters and then started on foot up the track towards
the top of the hill. The mist, though low, was not actually touching the
ground. I had not been farther than the village of Wytschaete before.
The village is still recognisable by a few remains of walls and piles of

rubble. The most conspicuous object is an old iron lamp post which is still standing, badly pitted and chipped, leaning at a drunken angle but unconquered, which is remarkable after 2 years of constant shelling. It gives the name to the corner: 'Lamp Post Corner'.

To the right was a new track which ran along the top of the hill. I followed it, guessing it would bring me near Guy's Farm. The track, however, did not go very far but ended in a jungle of old trenches. Clambering across several of them I found myself on the top of the hill overlooking a great stretch of flat country. At the foot of the hill I could see the Comines Canal which is still in the hands of the Germans. The area near the canal was being shelled heavily and tiny figures could be seen scurrying here and there, but whether they were our men or Germans I could not tell.

I could find no trace of Guy's Farm but some distance away were two concrete machine-gun posts on the skyline. Crossing a stretch of ground broken by shell holes I reached the first box to find it occupied by two officers observing for the artillery. They remonstrated very strongly against my walking on the skyline. I apologised and explained the object of my visit. They advised me to search on the other side of the ridge as there was nothing in front of them. I scrambled back to the track. The mist had lifted a little and I could see a battery of field guns in action a short distance away. I went across to the nearest gun and enquired from one of the gunners who was in the act of pouring water down the gun muzzle to cool the barrel. He referred me to his officer who was sheltering with a telegrapher under corrugated-iron sheets. The telegrapher told me there was a test point about 100yd away in a small concrete emplacement. I made towards the spot he indicated and found it at the first attempt. It was flush with the ground.

I found two linesmen in possession but no signs of the brigade staff. The linesmen told me their shelter was in the midst of the shelling last night. They had two direct hits on the roof which stunned and deafened them for some time. They never expected to see daylight again. The shelling had not stopped, I saw quite a few shell bursts throw mud and stones into the air but our artillery was making so much noise that unless you actually saw the burst it was impossible to distinguish friend from foe. Having delivered my message, I returned to the main track down the hill where I found several motor ambulances being loaded with wounded. I noticed Captain Treherne of the Division HQ RAMC superintending the loading and bandaging. As I passed him I asked if he had any message for HQ. He said we are getting along very nicely. A lot of shrapnel was bursting overhead with a vicious crack but it could not be seen for the mist which was almost touching the top of the hill.

The devil himself seems to be in league with the Germans. I cannot remember a worse day since last winter. Rain commenced at midnight and has continued in torrents without ceasing. Everywhere is flooded which has brought our advance to a stop.

Captain Treherne was badly wounded through the spine this morning (4 August), when superintending the loading of ambulances near 'Lamp Post Corner'. He was conscious when they picked him up, but paralysed. He said, 'I am done for' and died shortly afterwards. He was very popular with all ranks. A little story I heard about him shows he was a gentleman and a good sport. Last week two deserters under sentence of death were brought to him for examination: all prisoners under sentence of death are medically examined before execution in case they are not mentally sound. While the prisoners were waiting for the doctor, his orderly who is a medical student from Dublin, feeling sorry for them tried to give them some tips on the art of acting insane, to give them a chance, though thin, of being declared unfit.

During the examination the first man forgot his lesson until the examination was almost over when he suddenly started to roll his eyes and twitch his face in a very amateurish fashion. The doctor could see he was shamming and asked him who told him to act like that. The man was so taken aback that he blurted out, 'The orderly, sir.' The doctor said nothing but passed him fit for the firing squad. It seems the man had deserted several times and had previously been acquitted. The other man was certified as being of weak intellect which would get him off. When the prisoners had left the doctor turned to his orderly and said, 'I do not blame you, I would have done the same, I do not agree with capital punishment.' This story was told me by the orderly himself.

CHAPTER SEVEN

August 1917 – April 1918

8 AUGUST 1917, MOVED TO SCHERPENBERG TODAY

Scherpenberg is a small hill which rises like a pimple from the Flanders plain. On the top is perched a windmill which is still working; I think it must be the nearest windmill to the trenches of any in France. It forms a landmark which can be seen from miles behind the German trenches and it is said that they take their bearings from it and this is the reason it has been spared – it is within easy reach of their long-range guns.

There are several similar hills on the plain, which no doubt was once a vast swamp, or perhaps it formed part of the seabed and these small hills would have stood out of the water as rocky islands. The sea coast would have been formed by the Messines Ridge and the low hills which form a semi-circle around Ypres.

We have pitched our 'bivvies' in a small field on the side of a hill next to the Line: we are hidden from view by a hedge and some tall poplar trees. On the other side of the hedge we get a fine view of Ypres and the trench system. To our right we overlook a small fertile valley and the wooded slopes of Kemmel Hill. To our left we look over the plain as far as the sea.

At the end of the field is a small farm which is occupied by an old farmer, his wife and two daughters. They are still carrying on the work of the farm, working in full view of the Line.

There was a big thunderstorm last night and today the air is exceptionally clear. I borrowed a powerful telescope from our signalling stores to have a look at the country behind the German trenches. I spent a most interesting time watching the roads and villages. The fields are cultivated right up to the trenches as they are on this side. I could see small villages, apparently untouched by shellfire and factory chimneys, some of which were smoking showing they were being used.

I could also see the outskirts of a fair-sized town, which I think is Wervec. The German transport was passing along the roads and the life of the town seemed to be very much the same as it is on this side. Whilst I was watching I saw a woman come to her front door and gossip with her neighbour, I am sure she did not know there was an interested spectator on this side. Behind their trenches the Germans have a complete network of light railways for transporting ammunition, stores, etc., but they seem to use horses instead of light locomotives to draw the waggons.

On our side, I picked out a dainty little château with an ornamental lake in front. Behind the château was a dark wood which made the house stand out like a wedding cake. It looked deserted and I wondered how so calm and peaceful a spot could exist within 1 mile of the trenches. I watched and wondered when suddenly a huge flame shot into the air which seemed to lick the walls of the house. The illusion was completely shattered, a heavy howitzer was hidden in the wood alongside the château. No, I am sure it would be impossible to find a calm and peaceful spot within 20 miles of this front.

11 AUGUST 1917

The shelling of back areas continued last night, causing many casualties among the civilian population. As our HQ camp is so conspicuous we have spent the day with our 'weather eye' open, expecting our turn at any moment. We have dug ourselves some 'funk' holes in a sandy bank. Everyone is wondering what is behind all this sudden activity of shelling back areas. Are the Germans thinking of making a big attack?

The division RE sergeant major was badly wounded last night. He has been living in a shack at the RE dump near to the Viastraat crossroad, to save himself the long journey up the line each day. Brigadier General McLaclan of 112 Brigade was shot by a sniper whilst making a round of the trenches this morning. His body has not been recovered.

12 AUGUST 1917

The RE sergeant major has died. It has been impossible as yet to recover General McLaclan's body which is lying in a very exposed position. When he was shot he was making a tour of the trenches which are very disconnected and in places it is necessary to walk over the top.

One of the farmer's daughters, who was ploughing a field at the foot of the hill, came running home in a state of great excitement. Her plough had turned up an aeroplane bomb, which she said looked quite new. She simply dropped the reins and fled.

14 AUGUST 1917

General McLaclan's body was recovered last night and was buried in the hospice cemetery at Locre where 'Willie' Redmond is buried. [Major William Redmond, who before the war was a barrister and Irish nationalist politician, was killed when leading his men in the attack on the Messines Ridge on 7 June.]

15 AUGUST 1917

I did a bit of detective work this evening. The DR attached to 111 Brigade reported his motorcycle was missing. He usually leaves his machine just below Wytschaete, which is the nearest point a motorcycle can be taken to the brigade dugout which is in the cellars of Onraet Farm. During the afternoon he had to take a message to Division HQ. As he came back down the duckboard track he could see his machine in the middle of a cloud of smoke and spouting earth. The Germans were trying to find one of our batteries which is concealed nearby. He sat down in a convenient shell hole and waited, but as the shelling showed no signs of stopping he left the machine to its fate and cut across country to the Viastraat road and got a lift on a lorry. When he got back a few hours later the machine had disappeared. To lose a motorcycle in these economical days means a Court of Enquiry and this we wished to avoid, as it is a nuisance to everybody.

I went up post haste to search for the missing machine. I walked over to a battery which is concealed in the wood nearby. Of course, no-one had seen the machine, but they confirmed that the ammunition lorries had been up that evening. This was quite obvious as there was a large pile of new shells by the track. They could not or would not give me the number of the column. There was nothing further to be done there, but I felt sure the ammunition lorries had taken the machine. I went to the Viastraat crossroads and enquired from the traffic men who were running up to the batteries around Wytschaete and by a piece of good luck he remembered the number.

I returned to HQ and looked up all the ammunition columns in our area and traced the column I wanted to a spot near Dickebusch, a few miles down the Ypres road. As I ran down the road I worked out my plan. I knew that if I asked if they had picked up a machine they would deny it, so I put on a bold front and said that I had come for the motorcycle they had picked up near the battery behind Onraet Farm. It worked. These ammunition column people are expert scroungers.

17 AUGUST 1917

A bright day. Shortly after 12:00, six German aeroplanes came over, flying very low. Our AA guns gave them a hot reception which broke up their formation. Whilst we were watching we saw several pigeons released from the aeroplanes, something I have not seen before. The probability is the aeroplanes were photographing the area behind our trenches to locate our batteries.

21 AUGUST 1917

It is reported that Abeel Station was bombed last night, causing many casualties among the men waiting for the leave train.

22 AUGUST 1917

The German bombing aeroplanes were over as usual last night. They arrived as punctually as a train. Immediately the last trace of twilight has disappeared, the drone of their engines can be heard in the distance, which is a signal for a great blowing of whistles for 'lights out' from the infantry rest camps, which are all around us. Last night Locre received their attention. One bomb fell through the roof of an infantry hut but failed to explode.

One's feelings about bombing are entirely different from those about shelling. A single sheet of corrugated iron over one's head seems to give a feeling of security against shelling, but not against bombing. Why this is I cannot explain, but everyone knows it is so. It is a peculiarity of the human imagination. We laugh at the ostrich who buries his head in the sand.

25 AUGUST 1917

The weather has been very wet with high winds for the past 3 days. Last night rain fell in torrents without ceasing. I was out on the early duty this morning, still pouring, everywhere flooded. All around Onraet Farm was like a pond. The ground around the Brigade HQ is honeycombed with shell holes, all of which were filled to the brim. The condition of the trenches must be terrible. Not a soul about and most of the batteries were silent, flooded out I have no doubt.

On the road back I met three prisoners, at the fork road leading to Wytschaete, being escorted down the Line. It is quite common to see prisoners early in the morning, the result of a night raid, or deserters who have come over in the night, but I never set my eyes on such miserable specimens as those I saw this morning. They were not more than 18 or 19 years-old, weedy and undeveloped as it is possible to imagine. Two of them wore glasses, great 'barnacle' affairs which made them look weedier still. We have some pretty poor specimens in our Labour Corps but nothing like these in our fighting units. If the Germans have to fill their ranks with these poor devils the end cannot be far off. What chance will they have when the Americans put their 2,000,000 picked men in the field?

The civilians in these parts are Flemish. They are mostly fair-complexioned and heavily built like the Dutch. They keep their houses spotlessly clean, which is a great contrast to the houses we used to see in the Somme district, though they have the same love of fierce and unholy stinks as their compatriots in the south. Every house has its midden (domestic waste heap) almost on the doorstep, the more prosperous the farmer the larger the midden, as [the author] Mark Twain noticed. The drainage system is an open sewer or swamp within a few yards of the house. The usual French peasant seems to live for nothing but work, and their life is little better than their own cattle. The people in these parts are bright and cheery in comparison.

1 SEPTEMBER 1917

The weather has been windy, wet and cold for over a week but today it showed signs of improvement. One consolation is, we have had peaceful nights during this bad weather.

2 SEPTEMBER 1917

A beautiful moonlit night, the moon almost at full. The air is as clear as crystal with little or no wind. An ideal night for bombing and both sides took full advantage of it. From 21:00 until early morning relays of aeroplanes were dropping bombs and firing on the camps and roads with their machine guns without cessation, which kept us in a state of blue 'funk' all night.

When I got back to Division HQ shortly after 11:00, I found they had had an exciting time while I had been away. Big bombs had fallen all around them and the camps and dumps around Reningeist had been bombed continuously for almost 3 hours and it was still going on. Several dumps could be seen on fire. Reningeist is like a thickly-populated town with rest camps, lorry parks, dumps of ammunition and RE material. It would be difficult to drop a bomb without hitting something. While we stood watching I suddenly heard a swishing sound overhead and, looking up, I saw the black shadow of an aeroplane swooping over the hill top and before we realised what was happening a string of bombs dropped right across the camp. We just had time to throw ourselves flat when one burst in the next field, the pieces whistling through the hedge like a charge of buckshot. The only casualty was a tent belonging to the Officer of the Guard, which was blown to ribbons; fortunately the officer was absent.

Living on top of this hill gives one that 'goldfish' feeling. After midnight the bombing seemed to go farther inland. The towns and villages received their turn. News has come in that over 100 bombs have fallen on Bailleul; many houses have been destroyed and the civilian population have had heavy losses.

4 SEPTEMBER 1917

I passed through Bailleul today and saw some of the damage caused by the bombing. Rows of houses on either side of the road leading to Merville have been razed to the ground, the debris falling across the roadway 10ft high. The Labour Corps were clearing the rubbish away in lorries. Over thirty civilians were killed and wounded. What earthly use is this bombing of women, old men and children? It neither helps nor hinders the war.

This morning I met Madelaine from the farm, leading a cow by a rope tied around its horns. She looked tired and dusty and by the way of a greeting I hailed her, 'Hello Madelaine, been taking the old cow for a walk?' She hesitated a second, then said 'No sergeant, I have been taking the cow to be married.' Not a shadow of a smile on her face. The girl is an absolute heroine. She is not more than 18-years-old yet she does all the outside work of the farm, even the ploughing. She is built in the true Flemish style, fair, with very homely features but her face radiates good nature. When she smiles it almost hides her face, displaying a strong set of regular teeth. Her sister Laura is a great contrast in type and feature, being small and dark, typically French.

The old father takes no active part in the work of the farm but sits by the stove all day and smokes. His age must be nearer 80 than 70 years. The mother is a lively old dame, as brown as a nut, eyes like black beads, quite a wit in her own way. Then there is an old aunt who seems to be an invalid who spends most of her time scolding; her tongue sounds sharp. This lady has a very poor opinion of soldiers.

One morning last week, we were surprised to see a little procession enter the field and march towards the farmhouse. In front were two boys in surplices, one carrying an incense burner and the other carrying a candle. Behind them came an old priest in most elaborate vestments. After the priest came a lesser priest also in robes of some sort. The procession disappeared into the farmhouse and we wondered what it was all about.

A few minutes later, Madelaine came running up the field asking for the doctor: the priest had fainted. We afterwards heard that the old aunt, thinking that she was on the point of death, sent for the priest to administer the last sacrament. Madelaine now says, in awe-stricken tones, that her aunt is getting better again. By all rights she ought to be dead and as far as the church is concerned she is in the burial register.

Yesterday morning there was a great hullabaloo at the Division HQ. The general's 'charger' had disappeared during the night, right from under the nose of the stable guard. To get the animal away, it had been taken down an almost perpendicular bank not less than 8ft high within 20yd of the sentry. It was an old hunter, a showy animal but long past its best. Today it was found standing in the vacated lines of the Australians who left yesterday. They had left it tied up with several worthless mules which is adding insult to injury.

5 SEPTEMBER 1917

Last night a colonel of the 140th Rifles was killed by a bomb in the rest camp behind the brasserie on the Vermorzeel road. I was in the signal office when the message came through.

12 SEPTEMBER 1917, ST JANS CAPPEL

Moved to St Jans Cappel, a small village behind Bailleul – the Division has gone back for rest and training. The village is in the centre of a large hop-growing area, and the harvest is now in full swing. Everywhere can be seen old men, women and children sitting in circles picking hops from the long vines. There is little to do and to while away the time we amuse ourselves helping the women pick hops.

20 SEPTEMBER 1917

We were called out at 04:30 to take 'specials' to all brigades. The 'push' has commenced. When we heard the news yesterday we thought it was at least a week away. After several days of fine weather it rained heavily all night, and this morning we had misty rain. We always choose wet weather for our attacks. It is extraordinary that the staff cannot get a reliable weather forecast. Fine weather is absolutely essential for an attack to succeed in the Salient. Later in the morning, we heard that the 19th Division went over at 05:45 and they were still going strong at 09:30.

29 SEPTEMBER 1917

We move tomorrow. We are taking a sector north of that when we were in the Line last time. I made a tour of our new area today, to find the position of our brigades and various units. I took Hill with me. We rode our machines as far as the Spoil Bank and then commenced walking as we were not sure of the road beyond this point. We followed a new plank road which runs parallel with the banks of the canal which in these parts stand above the surface of the land. The track is already much damaged by shellfire. Around 800yd along this track we came to a crossroad called 'Jackson's Dump'. At this point the track crosses the Verbrandenmolen Road.

The Brigade HQ is in a dugout under Hill 60, the entrance to which is in a railway cutting. We could see the approximate position of the HQ on the crest of the hill, so we made towards it, following the road up the hill until we reached a dressing station where we left the track and struck across country towards the railway cutting. We were picking our way over some rough ground, full of shell holes and disused trenches when we were surprised by some heavy shells bursting fairly close to us. We made for a shallow trench behind a battery of field guns and continued on our way up the trench, the end of which led out into the railway cutting. When we reached the end and looked around the corner towards the entrance of the dugout the cutting was full of black smoke and at that moment sheets of corrugated iron and pieces of duckboard were flying in the air.

When a lull came we made a dash for the dugout. All around the ground was broken with new shell holes still smoking hot. Reaching the entrance, we descended a flight of steps which ended in a low passage not more than 5ft 6in high. One useful purpose of the tin helmet is to protect one's head in these low passages. Every few moments one's head meets a beam with a crash which would fracture any ordinary skull. The stench was horrible, a combination of damaged graveyards, candle smoke, sweat, sewerage and stale cooking, with a temperature like an oven. The roof constantly drips water and the floor is deep in liquid mud. This is where the infantry spend their time in reserve. How they live without getting the plague is a mystery. We wandered around several passages, 'Bond Street', 'Piccadilly', etc., and eventually found ourselves at the place we started from. Making further enquiries, we descended to a lower set of passages by another staircase and found the brigade signal office. After passing the time of day with the telegraphers we borrowed a runner to show us the way to the adjacent brigade, which lives in another area called the 'Canada Tunnels'. Returning to the surface, the guide pointed out a low hummock around 400yd away, under which he said we should find the 'Canada Tunnels'. We could see a roughly-defined path leading across a flat land which was honeycombed with shell holes rim to rim. Not a blade of grass nor any sign of life, simply a waste of light-coloured clay, which becomes like glue in wet weather. A few shells were falling around the battery position so we lost no time hurrying along, 20yd apart as instructed by the notice board outside the tunnel.

The ground between Hill 60 and the 'Canada Tunnels' is under observation from the German side. In the distance we could see black smoke from bursting shells which seemed to be rising from behind the hill. As we got nearer we could see the mouth of the tunnel was being shelled, so we took refuge in a trench where we found a number of infantry also waiting to enter the tunnel. We spent an uncomfortable 20 minutes lying in the trench, listening to the bursting shells, never more than 100yd away. After several had exploded we decided it would be safer to risk a dash; we jumped out and covered the distance to the tunnel in record time.

These tunnels were even worse than those at Hill 60. The passages were mostly less than 5ft high, and in some places as low as 4ft. The place was crowded with infantry but nobody could give us any idea where we should find the signal office. Wandering aimlessly on, we found ourselves in another divisional area. We turned back, our backs and necks by this time feeling as though they had a bad attack of rheumatism. Even these low passages were lined with sleeping men. The air was even fouler and hotter than Hill 60.

The Germans were trying to burst in the tunnels by heavy, delayed-fuse shells which do not burst until they have pierced the ground for 20ft or more. Once we happened to be right under the spot where one of these shells burst which made the ground rock, the timbers of the roof and walls creaking like a ship in a storm. The tunnel has been breached in several places. I met an officer and he was able to direct us to the Brigade HQ where we found the signal office, which fortunately had a roof where we could unbend. After a few minutes' rest we set out for the entrance where we found the shelling was still going on. We waited a few minutes to get its measure and then dashed out, timing the shells so well that we were 50yd down the duckboard track before the next one arrived.

Our next search was for a signal post under Mont Sorrel, around 200yd away, but noted as one of the hottest spots around here. On the way we passed the body of a man who had been killed only a short time before. Scattered around him were some broken and squashed tomatoes which are not rations issued to the troops. Probably, he was an officer's servant who had been bringing up 'extras' to tickle his master's palate. Poor devil, lost his life so that some officer might have tomatoes with his bacon. We got back to St Jan after 16:00, not having eaten since early morning.

30 SEPTEMBER 1917, ZIDCOTE

We moved to Zidcote today, which is near Reningeist. It is a poor place for accommodation but we were lucky to find a shack which had been overlooked. This area is littered with camps and dumps and therefore attracts the German aeroplanes. The moon was almost at full and big bombs were dropping all around us which kept us in a state of blue 'funk' all night.

1 OCTOBER 1917

Fine and warm with clear skies. At 19:00 the moon was high in the sky, almost as light as day, so light we could see the German aeroplanes passing over, a thing which I have never seen before in night-time. I could read a newspaper with the greatest ease. The move seems to have upset the staff, as the brigade orders were over an hour late this evening. At 21:00 we were still hanging about the signal office grousing at the delay. Our grousing, however, was cut short by a deafening roar from a bomb which dropped in the adjoining camp and the next second we could hear the scream of another bomb dropping from immediately overhead. We threw ourselves flat on the ground as it burst. There was a sheet of red flame, a clap like thunder and the earth shook like a jelly. Walker, one of our DRs called out he was hit. We picked him up and carried him to the ambulance. He had a piece right through the calf of his leg – a beautiful 'blighty' made to order. The strange thing was, he was lying down in the centre of a group of fellows, none of whom was touched.

3 OCTOBER 1917

Our brigades are now in the Line, one at 'Canada Tunnels' and the other at Mont Sorrel. Considering the position of our frontline in the Salient, the Division HQ is in an extraordinary place, quite 6 miles away.

I went to 'Canada Tunnels' this afternoon. Instead of going by the 'Spoil Bank' track I followed the Ypres road as far as Café Belge and then to 'Shrapnel Corner', continuing along the Verbrandenmolen road until I reached 'Jackson's Dump'. 'Shrapnel Corner' justifies its name no longer; it is a health resort compared with 'Jackson's Dump', some 400yd further up the road, where very seldom 30 minutes passes without the Germans sending two or three reminders aimed at the crossroads. On the left of the road before reaching the crossroads is a high bank which provides emplacements for a number of heavy howitzers which also attract a lot of retaliation. Tall poplar trees once lined the road from 'Shrapnel Corner'; a few still stand, badly torn and shattered, stripped of all but their largest branches. Lodged in the topmost branches can be seen a man's arm and part of the shoulder blade.

Forward of 'Jackson's Dump' is the shallow valley encircled on three sides by low hills known as the Salient, which has been an arena for the fiercest fighting of the war. Miles and miles of trenches have been dug, only to be obliterated by the millions of shells which have been poured into this patch of ground until there is not 10sq yd of ground or trench which has not been torn open by shellfire. All the natural water courses have been choked and the land has become a morass over which a safe crossing can be obtained only by a system of duckboards and plank tracks. To leave the track means a mud bath and perhaps a miserable death if help is not at hand; many poor devils have lost their lives drowned in liquid mud.

As a rule we leave our motorcycles at 'Jackson's Dump' and walk, but today being dry I thought I would try and ride as far as Mont Sorrel to see if it were practicable. I was bumping along the plank track, picking my way around shell holes and displaced planks when I was startled by a 'whizz bang' shrieking past my head, burying itself in the ground 20yd ahead. If this shell was not one of our own it had come from across the Salient. A little farther on I passed some charge boxes blazing furiously and debris scattered over the track.

Where the track meets the 'Valley Cottages' to 'Tower Hamlets' road, the carcase of a grey horse makes a good landmark for the wanderer. Turning right the track runs towards 'Tower Hamlets' until it meets 'Moreland Avenue'. By the side of this short stretch lies a mass of twisted ironwork, which is the remains of three or four motor lorries which have literally been blown to pieces; probably carrying ammunition when they were hit by a chance shell which exploded their load. A short distance down 'Moreland Avenue' I was brought to a halt by a series of big shell holes, some still smoking, showing they were of recent making. Some 50yd of the track had disappeared, so I had to plough my way across by the aid of footslogging.

The next thing of interest I saw was a big Holt tractor hopelessly bogged in a shell hole and slowly sinking in the mud, apparently abandoned. Reaching Mont Sorrel I found Fonnereau, one of the DRs attached to the brigade, mending a puncture in the back wheel of his machine. He held up a tube of solution for my inspection which he declared had been cut in half by a piece of shell whilst he held it in his fingers a few moments before I arrived. It was certainly a most unhealthy spot for puncture mending, surrounded on all sides by 6-inch howitzers in full blast and the Germans retaliating every few minutes; no-one but Fonnereau would pick a spot like this to have a puncture.

Mont Sorrel: what a name to give to so foul a spot. Many times I have passed through Mount Sorrel, a pretty little village on the Leicester to Loughborough road. I can picture it at the moment, the yellow stone houses basking in the autumn sun. 'Mount Desolation' would be a more fitting name for this abortion.

4 OCTOBER 1917

There are rumours that a big battle in the Salient is pending. This must be the one which has been on everyone's lips for the past month. I have not noticed any particular preparation but it is difficult to judge because so many divisions are bunched together and the narrowness of the Front brings the artillery on top of one another, even in normal times. One thing however is certain – that the Germans have some of their best troops opposite us because the prisoners we have taken just lately are big hefty fellows.

5 OCTOBER 1917

The morning broke dull with low clouds and heavy rain, which continued all day. There was very heavy artillery fire all night. We hear that four divisions attacked at daylight on the left of the Menin Road and according to the latest reports they are going well. If this rain continues, the attack must come to a standstill and the tanks will be useless. Why do we always choose bad weather for our attacks?

7 OCTOBER 1917

Fairer today with rain at intervals. Last night, I had the fright of my life, probably more fright than danger. I lost my way and got stuck in a shell hole. At 22:00, a special message had to be taken to one of the brigades in the 'Canada Tunnels'. It was blowing a gale with fine misty rain, black as pitch. As there was no fear of aircraft I lit my lamp and got as far as 'Swan Edgar' where the traffic police got excited and made me put it out. The next 2 miles I rode in inky darkness, threading my way through a stream of transport, mostly ammunition limbers and pack animals, which took up the full width of the road. Being approached from behind, the animals were restive and swayed about a good deal. At 'Shrapnel Corner' there was a traffic block, officers and men in a raging temper. I fought my way through, every voice and hand against me. By the time I reached 'Jackson's Dump', I was sweating like a bull with the exertion of keeping the machine upright.

Two runners were supposed to have met me at the dump to convoy me up to the tunnels. They usually wait in the traffic men's dugout at the crossroad, but nothing had been seen of them so I set off expecting to meet them coming down the track. I had not gone far when I saw the red rockets of our 'SOS' go up from the trenches and almost instantly every gun within a mile radius, and there must be hundreds, started rapid fire. By the light of the flashes, I could see that every shell hole was filled to the brim and most of the track was under water, the planks floating, which sank as I stepped on them. To the right was the misty outline of Hill 60 thrown into relief by the Very flares from the trenches, but all around was a carpet of blackness, broken only by the stabbing flashes of the artillery. The noise and concussion bewildered me and my only thought was to get away from the hellish din.

I started to run, but I had not gone far when a shell screamed overhead, bursting somewhere behind, the mud thrown up fell around me. I then could see that others were falling quite close, sending a shower of sparks with a fountain of mud and smoke which showed for an instant against the flickering light, the sound of the burst being lost in the general uproar. Not taking much notice where I was going, I ran until I could run no longer. I took shelter behind a low bank to regain my breath, and while I was resting I took stock of my surroundings which I began to realise were not familiar. I was lost.

A short distance away a battery was in action, and by good luck I had stopped opposite a duckboard track leading to their position. I enquired from the men working the nearest gun for the way to the 'Canada Tunnels' but they had no idea and referred me to their officers who were in a dugout nearby. I found the dugout which was a short tunnel in a high bank of ground, the entrance covered by a blanket. Pulling the blanket aside, I found two officers pouring over a map on a table, the only light was a candle stuck in a bottle, the flame jumping and flickering with each bang of the guns outside. Explaining my trouble I asked to see their map. I found that I was at 'Valley Cottages', almost in Zillebec, a long way out of my area. I had taken the wrong turning at the 'White Horse Corner'.

Returning to the track, I turned back in the direction I had come. The noise was even greater than before, the air pulsated with concussions, which beat me with unseen hands. I set off at a trot, trying to watch the track and at the same time keep a look out for landmarks by the roadside. After 15 minutes of hard going, fighting against wind and rain, I began to think that I had missed the turning again, when I caught sight of a white patch in the ditch which I immediately recognised as my 'old friend' the grey horse carcase. I knew I was now on the right road. Even a dead horse has its uses.

My next shock was the black form of a man suddenly appearing in front of me. He was wounded and was trying to find a dressing station. I directed him to 'Jackson's Dump'. He said his chum had just been killed.

Shells were falling all around me, I could see the sparks as they exploded. I ran until my head began to swim and had to lie down to give my heart a rest. Getting up, I found I had almost reached 'Moreland Avenue': 200yd to go. The trenches behind 'Mont Sorrel' were a blaze of light from the soaring flares and the machine guns were firing continuously. There seemed to be a raid going on.

The ground behind the mound is a jumble of shell holes, broken planks and RE stores scattered by shellfire. I was carefully picking my way when a big shell dropped some 50yd away. I instinctively turned my head and the next moment I was up to the waist in mud and water. I tried to climb out but I could get no foothold in the mud and I sank deeper still. I dug my fingers into the clay and held on like grim death and shouted for help but it was useless thinking that anyone could hear me in the awful din which was going on. With the strength of despair, using my fingers, toes and knees I hauled myself out, the exertion and fright leaving me weak and trembling. The steep clay bank to the tunnel entrance I climbed mostly on hands and knees.

When I reached the signal office I was just about all in, a mass of clay from head to foot. I scrounged a tot of rum and in a few minutes I felt better. I was advised to start back right away as there was to be a bombardment by our artillery very shortly and it would be sure to draw a lot of retaliation on the back areas and our battery positions; that little effort I had experienced was simply an unrehearsed affair. Coming to the surface things had quietened down a lot. I hurried along, listening to the wail and plop of gas shells falling to the left of the track but the wind and rain was too strong for the gas to cause trouble.

I did not meet or see a soul all the way back to 'Jackson's Dump'. The traffic man asked me what it was like up the track; I replied suitably. The crossroads at 'Jackson's Dump' is one of the hottest spots around this district, they have had six traffic men killed or wounded within the last 2 weeks. Being away so long I half expected to find my machine missing, but honesty was abroad this night. Wiping the plug the 'old bus' started first kick.

9 OCTOBER 1917

I went to the tunnels early this morning. I saw the bodies of several men lying on the track who had been killed going up last night. A lot of infantry equipment also was lying about showing they had had many casualties. Hill 60 was being pounded as usual. Heavy shells which burst with a horrid metallic clang were spouting earth and smoke high into the air. The more I see of this spot the less I like it. An enormous amount of ammunition and stores of all kinds are lying in the mud and slowly disappearing. Someone will have to pay for it someday, I suppose.

10 OCTOBER 1917

A most miserable day, raining continuously with a biting cold wind. It was my turn for the night run to the 'tunnels'. The arrangement of the runners meeting us at 'Jackson's Dump' has fallen through; in any case they were seldom there when we wanted them. The OC has given orders that we have to work in pairs. I took Joe Torrey my side kicker along with me, He grumbled like hell, I did not blame him, he was out all last night.

It was raining hard when we set out, black as pitch, 'a night which almost makes one homesick,' as Joe said. We crawled along for 3 or 4 miles, overtaking a continuous line of motor lorries and transport, when just past 'Swan Edgar' Joe's handlebars broke in half so I had to go on alone. The traffic was an absolute nightmare, I could see only black shadows and at times I was jostling mules and horses, handing myself off motor lorries and saving my own life every few yards. At 'Shrapnel Corner' the traffic was jammed as usual. I pushed my way through, revving the engine to make the animals move to one side, officers shouting, 'Stop that bloody motorcyclist.' I shouted back, 'DR with special message,' which sounded awfully important and eventually I found myself at 'Jackson's Dump'. There were a couple of waggons smashed and several mules lying in the road, which explained the stoppage.

I threw my machine against the bank by the traffic man's dugout and made for the track. It was extraordinarily quiet, only an occasional gun firing just to let the 'Boche' know we were not asleep. I was grateful for this but I missed the flashes which light the track. Everywhere was under water and my experience of a few nights ago was still in my thoughts. Fortunately, I had a pocket flashlight with me, which though almost spent gave a glimmer. With eardrums at full tension to catch the sound of approaching shells I hurried along. The silence was uncanny. The flashlight came in useful when I came to the group of shell holes half way down 'Moreland Avenue', which seemed to be larger than ever. Someday, I shall find an easy way to the entrance of the dugout in Mont Sorrel. Trying to scale the high clay bank I slithered back down full length face downwards.

After delivering my despatches, I started back immediately as I was anxious to get away while things were quiet but I had not gone far when shells started to fall higher up the track, somewhere around the grey horse carcase. I judged them to be howitzer shells as they took quite 20 seconds to arrive. I could hear the thud of the German gun. When I got near to the spot where they were dropping I lay down to watch what was happening; one each minute: all falling more or less in the same spot. After the next burst, I jumped up and ran for what I guessed was a minute and then lay down again to wait for the next. I had not long to wait. First a faint thud then a couple of seconds' silence, then a faint whispering which gradually became a tearing scream. I flattened myself in my shell hole, feeling sure it was going to drop right on top of me. 'Crump', the mud spattered down, I jumped up and ran to get as far away as possible before the next arrived. A most methodical fellow is the 'Boche', I could imagine the battery officer saying, 'Keep firing on that target until I come back from dinner.'

At 'Jackson's Dump', I found a DR from another division trying to start a machine with a water-logged magneto, a hopeless job to remedy in the pouring rain. I gave him a lift on the carrier of my machine; against regulations but excusable on a night like this.

11 OCTOBER 1917

Another wet day, pouring rain with high winds. Yesterday, our infantry made an attempt to raid a German machine gun post. Today, I heard the story from an RE sergeant who took part in the affair, the object of which was to blow up a concrete emplacement of a machine gun which had been causing us many casualties. This sergeant had charge of twelve sappers carrying explosives and the infantry sent thirty men as a covering party. The attempt was made in broad daylight but due to our artillery barrage falling short it was a complete failure; the Germans were standing on the fire step ready and waiting for them, rifle to shoulder. Only five REs and nine infantry got back.

12 OCTOBER 1917

Weather a little better today but colder. Last night, I was on the 'Mont Sorrel' run, with Torrey as my partner again. By a coincidence his machine failed at the same spot as last time, a broken frame, but we managed to fix it. Near 'Shrapnel Corner', we had a surprise packet, a 'Boche' aeroplane passed over dropping a string of bombs. After I had counted eight getting nearer and nearer, I was just on the point of diving for the ditch when the supply ran short, but a few moments later he came back to give us a taste of machine-gun fire. That pilot was a hero – the night was pitch black, he would have had nothing but the flash of the guns to guide him. 'Valley Cottages' were being shelled – big stuff too. The shells were passing over us and the thought that 'Moreland Avenue' might be next on the list made us step lively. An aeroplane was droning around in the blackness. We could recognise him as a 'Boche' by the sound of his engine; the Germans employ mostly six-cylinder engines of the slow speed type while we use fast running engines of eight or twelve cylinders. Now and again he would swoop down and use his machine gun on the batteries in action. From the path of his tracer bullets he did not seem to be more than 200ft high. An aeroplane machine gun always stutters and stammers from firing through the propeller. He must run a big risk of getting hit by the stream of shells passing over as our aeroplanes always fly either under or over the path of the shells in their flight.

16 OCTOBER 1917

Moved back to St Jans Cappel.

28 OCTOBER 1917

We are still in this wretched village, the most forsaken spot imaginable. For want of something to do I have spent a lot of time exploring the country as far back as the Mont de Cats. Sometimes, when we have money we go to Bailleul for a feed but all the best places are reserved for officers, which greatly annoyed us until we found a place of our own. Even the 'Pip Squeaks' [junior officers], who a year or two ago were wiping their 'snotty' little noses on their cuffs for want of a handkerchief, may enter, while the highest NCO may not. This childish snobbery of the old army sickens me.

10 NOVEMBER 1917, MOVED TO SCHERPENBERG

It looks as though we are going to spend the winter in the Salient, not a pleasant prospect. One Brigade HQ is at the château in Kemmel and the other at the lock on the Ypres-Comines canal.

16 NOVEMBER 1917

A tremendous bombardment has been going on these past few days, mostly on the Passchendaele front. A constant stream of lorries carrying troops in the direction of Ypres is passing along the roads, probably reinforcements for Passchendaele.

18 NOVEMBER 1917

Two days ago Fonnereau, one of our DRs attached to the brigades who are in the cellars of the château at Kemmel, was placed under arrest 'under suspicion of being drunk on duty'. When it became known everyone said, 'Fonny's number is up.' He has so often been within an ace of being caught for the same offence. Whenever he can get liquor, and that is nearly always, he spends most of his time in a befuddled state. He was sent down to Division HQ for trial by the CRE but to everybody's surprise he was acquitted.

The tale of his exploit is rather humorous. Fonnereau had collected his rum issue and several others besides, the total making a full-sized sergeant-major's ration. Under its mellowing influence, he felt at peace with the world and full of brotherly love for mankind. Wandering around the dark passages of the château he met someone who he thought was a crony of his. Taking him into his arms he saluted him in the French fashion, a kiss on each cheek. 'Fonny' had made a big mistake – it was the Brigade Major, and a VC too. Fonnereau was put under arrest there and then.

20 NOVEMBER 1917

It is reported that three Zeppelins were seen over our lines this afternoon flying at a great height. I did not see them myself. The Germans are attacking at Passchendaele. There has been a very heavy bombardment all day, and this evening we had a gas warning.

21 NOVEMBER 1917

Fine but cloudy. This morning an aeroplane was shot down in flames, falling from a great height. It appeared like a ball of fire, leaving a ribbon of oily-black smoke behind. A black speck, which we took to be the pilot, came out and fell with fearful speed. A hellish sight.

1 DECEMBER 1917

Last night was another clear moonlit night. As soon as darkness set in the bombing aeroplanes began to arrive, we recognised them as Gothas by the beat of their diesel engines. They came in relays, dropping their loads of bombs and then returning for more until the early hours of the morning. Bombs were exploding all around us like thunder claps, sometimes so near as to make the ground quiver. We felt sure our HQ would be picked out, a high hill with a windmill on the top and a cluster of huts at the base makes one of the most conspicuous landmarks for miles around. It was not our turn however; the camps and dumps at Reningeist received most of their attention as usual.

6 DECEMBER 1917

Coming from the 'Spoil Bank' to the Brigade HQ at the lock, I was ambling along picking my way around the shell holes, which are pretty thick in these parts, my thoughts no farther than a yard beyond my front wheel when with a zip and a crash, a real 'stocking footer' passed within a yard of my head. There was a sound like the tearing of a gigantic sheet of calico, followed by a splitting crash, a shower of stones and earth and a cloud of smoke. Startled is not the word, every hair stood on end and hot and cold surges chased one another up and down my spine. It was just as though someone had crept up behind me and let a gun off in my ear. A shock a day keeps monotony away.

10 December 1917

A fine day. Shortly after noon a flight of six Gothas, surrounded by a dozen or more protecting aeroplanes, came over our side of the Line. They sailed slowly along about a mile behind the trenches, flying fairly low which enabled us to judge their huge wing spread. The wings are 'V'-shaped more than usual which gives them an ungainly appearance. At first we thought they were on a daylight raid but if they dropped any bombs it was immediately behind the Line, they did not come farther inland. Our AA batteries got very busy but their shooting seemed to be hopelessly inaccurate.

According to reports which came in later, they were on a reconnaissance and photographic flight and at the same time they were dropping propaganda leaflets in French, English and Flemish, giving accounts of the German victories in Italy. [A daring attack led by a young company commander called Rommel sparked off a major German advance through the Julian Alps. The Italian Army retreated 60 miles in 2 weeks.]

15 December 1917

The Germans are using a great number of gas shells of late. All night long their peculiar whine can be heard ending in a sound something like the drawing of a cork. If one did not know they were gas shells they might be mistaken for duds. The gas is in liquid form, which has a very low evaporation temperature. It has a terrible burning effect on the flesh and especially on the lungs should it be breathed. When the shell burst the liquid is sprayed around and anyone who is near may get covered with the spray and will undoubtedly breathe it if not protected by a mask. When the night is cold the liquid remains on the ground until the heat of the day evaporates it. One of the chief sources of danger is treading in the liquid and taking the gas into a dugout, gassing the occupants.

The Passchendaele attack seems to have simmered down and the Salient is comparatively quiet these days.

20 DECEMBER 1917

Very cold with strong winds which cut like a knife. Perched as we are on the side of a hill we cannot get away from its clutches. Riding a motorcycle chills one to the marrow. It looks as though we shall remain in this spot over Christmas so have decided to make the best of it and have a real Christmas dinner. Joe Torrey has been detailed to find a goose or turkey. We are a bit late starting, the land has already been swept as clean as a 'wolf's tooth' but we have good friends in every village between here and Amiens and if there is such a bird we will find him. Another has been sent off to find the drinks: champagne to benedictine and not forgetting the lemons for rum punch.

24 DECEMBER 1917

Our chief topic of conversation is our Christmas dinner which is going to be complete even to the sausages for the turkey and liquor.

25 DECEMBER 1917

Typical Christmas weather. Bitterly cold with snow on the ground. We sat down to dinner at 18:00, everyone 'poshed up to the eyes'. We should have been twelve strong but two were missing; Hill and Hobson went out at 14:00 and had not returned. The room where we have our mess is in an old farmhouse on the slopes of the hill. It is a large room with a low ceiling heavily beamed with dark timber. Pictures of saints and family portraits line the walls, staring stolidly at the unusual scene. The floor is of red bricks, swilled and scrubbed spotlessly clean. On one side of the room is the stove, the furnace fashioned like a Grecian vase which supports a coffin-like affair which is a combined oven and pan heater. This stove, bristling with bright knobs and shining like a mirror, is the pride of the Flemish housewife.

Nothing had been forgotten, coloured paper festoons were strung across the room and each picture had a halo of holly. Two large oil lamps hung from the beams of the ceiling, shedding a warm glow on everything. By the side of the stove sat the old man smoking his eternal pipe of home grown tobacco, while the old dame and her two daughters bustled around preparing the dinner, their shadows throwing grotesque shapes on the walls.

Torrey had surpassed our greatest expectations. Talk about groaning tables, those old tables had never carried such a spread before. Starting with soup and fish, we were to have turkey, pudding, dessert, not to mention all manner of side trimmings such as roast beef and pork etc., for the real trenchermen. Some of the boys had been fasting all day to do full justice to the dinner.

The drinks department were not far behind, they had kept up their reputation as expert foragers: champagne, red and white wine, whiskey and liqueurs, and bottled beers for those of simple taste.

My plate of turkey had just been placed before me when an orderly came to say that the staff were asking for the brigade returns. Hill and Hobson ought to have been back hours ago but I guessed what had happened: a dozen places to call at and a drink at each. It was my job to go and find them.

'It's snowing hard, sergeant,' was the parting remark of the orderly. I cursed Hill and Hobson, the weather and the orderly to all eternity and the boys sang 'Amen' in chorus. Hell! What a night, black as pitch, a gale of wind and a blinding snowstorm. I piled on all the clothes I could lay hands on and set out. Hill was on the brigade run and Hobson on the unattached units. I decided to find Hill first. His last call would be at the dressing station in Voormazeel. It took me about 30 minutes to reach it and by that time it had stopped snowing. I went down into the dugout and asked if the division DR had called. 'Sure, you will find him in the old barn across the way.' 'Is he alright?' I asked. 'You bet he is', and everyone laughed.

I found Hill lying across his machine apparently trying to stand on his head to look into the magneto. I asked him what was the matter. 'It won't go, something wrong with the magneto.' He seemed to find it a huge joke. I didn't, I was thinking of my spoiled dinner. 'Give me the despatches, if you cannot get it to go, get a lift on a lorry.' With that I left him.

A couple of miles down the road near Kemmel, I saw a black form in front staggering along and as I got near I heard curious sounds, it was Hobson singing at the top of his voice. He explained that he had skidded into a ditch and the shock had upset him. Some can ride when they cannot walk while others can walk when they cannot ride; for myself I can always ride. I took him on the carrier of my machine and we made uproarious progress, Hobson bellowing a 'Merry Christmas' to everyone he saw and when he was not bellowing like a bull calf he was making weird noises which he said was 'Christians awake'. I forgave Hobson, he was so cheerful about it.

When I got back to HQ, I had to go out again and did not get back for my dinner until 22:30; by that time Hill had managed to find his way home after many tumbles and a generally adventurous time.

At midnight the 'Boche' aeroplanes were bombing the slopes of Kemmel Hill.

29 DECEMBER 1917

Very cold with frequent snow storms. During the past few days we have had many snow storms. Two nights ago, I was out in a storm which lasted over 3 hours – rain and sleet. When I got back I could not straighten myself, my legs and arms were quite numb and dead. They gave me some rum which set the circulation going but I endured agonies when the blood began to circulate.

Kemmel château was on fire last night. When I passed the flames were gushing out of the windows and it seemed to be doomed.

30 DECEMBER 1917

Kemmel château is totally destroyed, only a shell of walls left standing. It was occupied by the Australians at the time which no doubt accounts for the fire – and the festive season. For 2 years the village of Kemmel was less than a mile behind the frontline. The church and all the houses are in ruins. In the midst of this desolation the château stood practically untouched. It was one of the wonders of the war. Only 2 months ago, I saw a civilian looking over the château. I was informed that he was the owner and he was very much upset at the damage done by the troops. His doubts are now set at rest.

1 JANUARY 1918

New Year's Eve passed very pleasantly. We had a few 'extras' for dinner but not the elaborate affair we had at Christmas. After dinner we had a sing-song. Sitting around the table, everyone in turn had to give a song or a recitation, no refusals accepted, everyone joining in the chorus. We found quite a lot of latent talent and plenty of unconscious humour. 'Auntie' started the ball rolling with his usual songs, mostly about love. He ought to know something about the tender passion, he affects to be a great 'lady killer' and the sight of a skirt makes him sigh like a porpoise.

Hobson gave us his famous song about a certain monk of great renown who had a liaison with a lady of the town. He treated the damsel with great cruelty and she died, but the old rascal, to save his reputation, or what was left of it, brings her back to life again. The chorus describes the old reprobate character in very broad language.

Someone then gave us 'The Gay Caballero', whose Don Juan exploits were both pleasurable and adventurous but fast living and old age overtakes him, curtailing his pleasures.

Some of these old songs must have been sung by the soldiers of Henry V at the battle of Agincourt, or at least by Marlborough's troops. One of the funniest was from little Oddy, who started to sing a sentimental ditty about 'Home and Mother', then wandered into an entirely different song and finished in a third.

We were getting down to the tail end when it came to Hill's turn. 'I can't sing and I can't recite, hic'. He was pressed hard but stubbornly refused and was inclined to be cantankerous. At last someone suggested that he should 'belch' us 'I wouldn't leave my little wooden hut for youuuuuu.' That brought down the house – Hill has a gift for raising the wind in a musical manner.

Someone than suggested that 'Granddad' should be asked for a number. The old boy had been taking his rum punch with the best. He gave us a recitation in Flemish, waving his stick and arms with great vigour. We began to have fears for his blood pressure when the old lady made him sit down. We then tried out a non-descript uncle who had drifted in. Uncle had a huge bushy beard and, as he recited, the wind whistled through his whiskers with dramatic effect.

Finally, Garnier performed his bottle trick which he usually does to prove he is sober. The trick consists of lying full length on the floor with a bottle balanced on his forehead. He then proceeds to rise, balancing the bottle all the time until he stands upright. Someone said, 'Damned good, but you couldn't do it if you were sober!'

At midnight we broke up singing 'Auld Lang Syne' with much vigour, too much for 'Fonny' who lost two bottles of 'fizz' and quite a lot of rum and punch. 'Fonny' is always unlucky. Thus ended 1917, nobody very drunk and nobody very sober. Our artillery saluted the New Year with several rounds rapid fire to remind the Germans of what was to come.

4 JANUARY 1918

The German aeroplanes were very active last night, bombing the dumps and camps; those around Reningeist as usual came in for most of their attention. I have been warned for leave on 12 January.

12 JANUARY 1918, SCHERPENBERG – SHEFFIELD

I caught the bus for Poperinghe where the leave train started. Reaching Calais in the early hours of the morning we marched to the rest camp. I went to a big shed which serves as an NCOs' mess and got some watery stew, and sat there till daylight. At 07:00, we were marched to the quay and, after hanging around for the best part of an hour, we embarked. The first lot on board had to go down to the lowest deck, then the second deck was filled and finally the upper deck, until the ship was packed with troops like a well-filled barrel of herrings. If we had been torpedoed there would not have been the slightest chance for those below.

I caught the 20:45 train from St Pancras. At one station three women got into the carriage, two dressed in fur coats. From their conversation I soon knew them to be munition workers. They were all a bit tight and were recounting an amorous adventure they had been having, probably for my benefit. They had a bottle of whisky which they passed around and I was asked to have some. Nothing lost I took a pull; it was pretty weak stuff compared with army rum. As I joke, I reciprocated by handing them a flask of rum to taste. One took a good swig and collapsed with coughing. It took her some time to recover her breath but when she did her language would have made an old army sergeant sit up and take notice. By the time we had reached Derby they had become very friendly and invited me to go home with them for the night. I excused myself on the grounds that someone was waiting for me at the station. They did not think this sufficient reason: 'What's the odds, you ain't married.'

I reached Sheffield at 02:45 and found my father waiting on the platform. As there were no trams or taxis we walked the 4 miles home to Norton Woodseats. I thoroughly enjoyed the walk, listening to news of home.

I found a big fire and a hot bath waiting for me after which we had supper and then to bed. After sleeping hard in any old spot it takes some time to get used to a feather bed again. My usual bed for a long time past has been a wooden door which we carry around as part of our stores. When this door is not doing duty as a mechanic's bench or a mess table it serves as my bed, the main idea being to keep it from clutching hands, not from any sympathy for the sergeant. When we move the usual remark when it is being loaded on the waggon is,

'What the hell is this for?' 'Oh, that's the sergeant's bed,' never, 'the mess table' or 'the mechanic's bench'.

There is very little one can tell the folks at home about life at the Front without unduly alarming them; half an hour was sufficient to tell my story. I was more interested in their experiences with the food rationing and the Zeppelin raids.

I spent most of my time taking long walks around the countryside. When I think of the French people living within 20 miles of the Line, shelled by day and bombed by night, our people have much to be thankful for that the war has not reached here. To be safe is a wonderful feeling.

An everlasting topic of conversation at the Front is, what one would do if peace came tomorrow. One said he would go to the best restaurant and order a dinner of all the things he likes best, another would take a Turkish bath, a peculiar idea, another would spend a week with the ladies, while another would take the first steamer back to India where he would at least feel warm. The fellows from South America long for the hectic nights of Buenos Aires and the Canadian longs for the solitude of his farm on the prairie.

For myself, I wish for nothing better than to lie in the heather on the top of the Derbyshire hills, without a soul in sight, with no sound but the wind and the birds where I can rest and think it all over.

17 January 1918, Manchester

I travelled to Manchester to stay with 'Ma' Dawson, my old landlady. Poor old soul she takes the war very much to heart, she never sleeps until the hospital train has passed in the early hours of the morning. What good it can do her I do not know; I suppose it is the same instinct which attracts women to funerals.

Food is getting scarce, potatoes and butter are almost unobtainable. People stand in queues for hours waiting for the shops to open. The old lady told me she often has to go home foodless because she cannot stand long enough to wait her turn.

I spent a week in Manchester, went to one or two shows, visited my old place of business, but felt pretty lonely, all my friends away. Women conductors on the trams, women on the railways, women everywhere but plenty of men to be seen on the streets too. I believe it is fairly easy to get an exemption if one is prepared to pay for it. I know one fellow at least who has managed to wangle an exemption so far by paying.

23 JANUARY 1918

In the train, I listened to the conversation of some men, evidently of the farming class. They were boasting that they never went short of anything. By an arrangement with the shopkeepers they exchanged butter and eggs for sugar and other luxuries of which there is a scarcity. I had the greatest difficulty in keeping my mouth shut. Good God, what selfishness, worse than dogs, a dog will not rob a bitch, but these farmers are robbing women and children.

The time hung very heavily, everyone cheerful but a trifle forced. I was glad when it was time to go.

25 JANUARY 1918, RETURNED FROM LEAVE

I caught the 23:25 train which arrived in London shortly after 02:00. As usual there were several of the old volunteer guides on the platform; they had a charabanc to take leave men across to Victoria or to the rest house. These old boys do good work in a quiet unobtrusive manner.

I put up for a night, or what was left of it, at a small temperance hotel, a frowsty old place near Victoria. There was an old waiter on duty who got me a supper of sorts after which I went to bed for a couple of hours. I was up again shortly after 06:00, had some breakfast – the same old waiter was on duty but he seemed to be ready to drop. He was very anxious to know how things were going out there and when was it going to end. He had a son in France. I shook hands with the old man and thanked him: a real hero.

The train left at 08:20. We had the usual scenes. Why do people come to the station to prolong the agony, making an exhibition of themselves?

There was a thick fog in the channel; the crossing took 3 hours. We reached Calais shortly after 15:00 and were marched to the rest camp, everyone sullen and moody. Rest camp is another name for jail, for that's what it amounts to, being surrounded by barbed wire with armed guards at the gates. Once inside we know nothing, we are told nothing.

At midnight, I lay down in one of the tents to rest. I must have dozed off for I was awakened by a banging on the canvas, 'All men for the 37th Division to parade at once.' It was 01:30. We were marched a mile or more to a siding where we entrained, the usual trucks, so many *hommes* (men) and so many *chevaux* (horses). We reached Hazebrouck about daylight when we were surprised to hear them calling for men of the 37th to get down. The Division had come out of the Line for rest, the HQ being at Blaringhem. I found the DRs had fixed themselves very comfortably in a small *estaminet* kept by an old man, his young wife and his niece. I also found that we had a new OC, the late OC having gone to the corps.

1 February 1918, Blaringhem

The new OC seems to be a good sport. He is an RE which will make things easier. Blaringhem is a mean little village of no consequence or distinction. It has one long street which staggers around like a drunken man and a distillery which manufactures alcohol from parsnips and mangelwurzels [a type of beet]. This distillery, no doubt, accounts for the winding streets. Every kind of spirit from whisky to cognac can be bought in the village, varying only in colour and the label on the bottle, they all taste alike: damnable.

The old man at the *estaminet* where we are billeted welcomed us with a gracious little speech, placing himself and his house at our service, 'But Gentlemen I ask of you two things, do not touch my wife and do not touch the till,' then as an afterthought, 'on no account must you touch the till!'

10 February 1918

Our runs are very short and we have little to do except clean and overhaul our machines. At the moment we have a craze for bridge. We have tournaments almost every day, a Franc a point, the winning pair dividing the proceeds. Play starts soon after breakfast and continues all day, usually ending late in the evening; once the last hand was played after midnight. My luck with the cards is notorious. In pure gambling games, I have the luck of the 'devil' but at bridge I generally manage to pick up a hand of 'tripe'. I always feel sorry for my partner but not as sorry as he feels for himself.

17 February 1918, Moved to Westoutre

We are taking over a sector next to the Menin Road, north of our last sector.

18 February 1918

Weather bright and sunny but a cold wind. I went up the Line today to find our various points of call. One of the brigades will be in the 'Jackdaw Tunnels' in front of 'Sanctuary Wood', one in 'Tor Top' and the other in 'Stirling Castle'.

There will be a relay post manned by the two DRs in front of Zillebeke. The directions given to me by the DR sergeant of the outgoing division sound quite homelike:

'Turn left at 'Shrapnel Corner' and continue until you strike the Menin Road, then turn left and proceed past 'Hellfire Corner' as far as the dressing station. A short distance past the dressing station, just short of Hooge Crater, you will see a duckboard path on the right. Leave your machine there and proceed on foot, a couple of hundred yards down this path you will find a relay post. Another 100 yards further on is the duckboard track which leads to 'Sanctuary Wood'. On the farthest side of the wood the track comes out on a plank track almost opposite 'Jackdaw Tunnels', the entrance to which is a short distance up the bank. 'Top Tor' you will find some distance to the right,' etc., etc.

I had no difficulty in following the directions to the relay post. I stayed a few minutes to pass the time of day, and while there two German aeroplanes came over, flying very low following the Menin Road, firing on any odd bunches of men they could see. I noticed they were tri-planes, the first German machines of this type I have seen.

'Sanctuary Wood' must have been named by some grim humourist – a fouler spot could not be found. What was once a lovely wood is now a 'cemetery' of dead trees, some still standing bleached white like skeletons, stripped of their bark and branches, but the greater part have fallen to the ground criss-crossed at all angles. The ground below is churned up with shell holes filled with stinking water. I hurried along the duckboard track listening to the hissing and wheeling of spent bullets clipping the trees. The wrecks of two aeroplanes lie in the far end of the wood, both ours, one fairly new.

Forward, the ground rises steeply and the entrance to 'Jackdaw Tunnels' is a short distance up the bank. 'Tor Top' is some distance to the right and gives a good view of the Passchendaele Ridge which at the moment was almost hidden in smoke from shelling. 'Hooge Crater' was also being shelled with high explosive and occasional shrapnel, the smoke drifting over the wood.

Returning through the wood, I was surprised to meet our general with two of his staff, red tabs and all; they seemed to be in a hurry. One of the officers, recognising me, asked if it was quiet forward; they had probably seen the shelling going on around the crater and thought it was dropping in the wood. It is comforting to know that even red tabs are not 'wind' proof.

25 FEBRUARY 1918, MOVED TO CAFÉ BELGE (DICKEBUSCH)

This is a bleak spot, in full view of the German observation balloons which hang on the skyline. Nissen huts for the men and concrete shelters for the general and his staff.

4 MARCH 1918

A big German attack on this front is expected at any moment. The place is 'lousy' with guns and troops. Every night there is a tremendous bombardment which lasts until daylight. Prisoners have been captured who confirm that the Germans are preparing a big attack. The staff have the wind up to the top notch, 'specials' every hour to all brigades and neighbouring divisions which keeps us out of bed at night.We have fixed a 'wind' gauge outside our hut with a dial and pointer, 'No Wind', 'Wind Normal', 'Much Wind' and 'Wind Vertical'. I saw one of the staff officers examining it the other day but he could not make anything of it, a good job too.

6 MARCH 1918

Very cold with hard frosts at night. All night we have tremendous bombardments ending in a perfect frenzy just before daylight, which makes us think that the Germans are attacking.

7 MARCH 1918

Last night, a sergeant and a private of one of our battalions went out in front of the trenches and penetrated to a point 300yd behind the German frontline. Lying in wait they surprised a German sergeant major and his batman and brought them into our lines. The batman gave information that an attack is timed for tomorrow morning.

8 MARCH 1918

Bright and clear first thing. The promised attack for this morning did not happen, but after bombarding our sector all day, which was thought to be in retaliation for our usual nightly strafe, the Germans made a surprise attack in massed formation at around 18:00, and got as far as our support trenches. Before our infantry could make a counter-attack it was dark.

9 MARCH 1918

Last night the Germans were in our trenches and everyone expected them to make another attack at dawn. Our artillery went mad. If the Germans were concentrating behind their lines to follow up their attack they would have a bad time. Our infantry made an attack at daylight and recovered the lost trenches at one bound, killing the Germans almost to a man. From news received, the Germans also broke into the trenches of the division on our left and were ejected later in a furious counter-attack. It looks as though they are testing the strength of our troops holding the Line.

12 MARCH 1918

The Germans have made no further attacks but our artillery gives them no rest at night, always ending with a 30 minute hurricane bombardment of their front line and supports, just before dawn.

We have an unwelcome neighbour in the shape of one of our 12-inch railway guns which is brought up every day to a position behind 'Scottish Wood' and fires directly over our camp, once every 30 minutes. If the Germans can range its position we stand a good chance to catch anything which drops short. I went across to watch the process of loading and firing. At least five charges, each the size of a Cheshire cheese, follows the shell into the breech, which shows that one third of the gun's length must be taken up by the charge chamber. After the breech is closed, the locomotive with the van which carries the ammunition, moves a short distance down the line. The gun is then elevated and laid on the target and then fires, sitting down on the recoil chamber and returning in a slow and dignified manner, just like an 'old dame' making a curtsey. The noise and concussion heard from alongside the gun is not so much as one would imagine, in fact I think we feel far more concussion some 800yd in front. The first time it fired all the canvas windows in our hut were blown in.

The staff have a new craze, everyone is to put their spare time to gardening. We are to grow vegetables, but where the seed is coming from nobody seems to know. We are filling in shell holes and digging over the ground ready for sowing. An old plough has been found and put into service and we have all tried our hand. The result would not please a farmer, but I suppose that the cabbages will grow just as well in crooked rows as in straight. The burning question is, who will gather the fruits of our labours? We shall not be here long enough to reap the harvest. I have no doubt the main idea is to keep the troops from brooding over their troubles.

24 March 1918

Prisoners captured a few days ago gave information that there was going to be four days of bombardment of all areas and towns behind our lines. Little notice was taken of the information but sure enough the bombardment started. For four days, every village and town within 20 miles of the Front has been intensely shelled day and night. The clock tower of the Town Hall in Bailleul was smashed down in the first few hours and by the second day hundreds of shells had been poured into the town and hardly a house was whole. The civilians have fled, but not before there were many casualties.

26 March 1918

The morning was beautifully fine and bright, everyone hard at work packing stores and getting our machines ready for the move. We are going south to take over from the divisions which have been smashed by the German attack in the Somme. Their advance in the south is getting pretty serious, very shortly they will have reached the old line which they evacuated in 1916. It looks as though our Intelligence has been asleep to allow the Germans to concentrate four or five divisions for each of ours without our knowing it. Since the Russians went out of the picture the Germans have brought all their troops released from the Russian Front to France and it was known that they were preparing for a big attack. If the number of divisions we have concentrated around Ypres is any indication it looks as though the British Army staff expected the attack to take place here.

27 March 1918

We move tomorrow. We shall be glad to get away from this place, not because it is a little 'hot' but because there is no shelter of any kind, not even a trench, and the ground is waterlogged.

Dickebusch and the crossroads just below our camp have been shelled all morning, sometimes those hitting the pavé throwing up a cloud of white stone dust. In the middle of the afternoon, shells began to fall among our waggons which were ready for the move, riddling several including the one carrying our motorcycles, ruining a bunch of tyres. Two horses were killed, one the general's charger and another of lesser rank. One shell smashed a hut where a number of men had just left to attend a pay parade.

28 MARCH 1918

We moved off at 10:00 and were told to make for Frévent. The staff were to be there at 16:00. A gale of wind blew dead against us, blowing dust and grit in our faces which stung like shot. On the way down we stopped at several of our old haunts for drinks. Late in the afternoon, the wind died down and it poured with rain. When we reached Frévent, I heard that Munro, one of the brigade riders, had been taken to hospital with a broken wrist, from a skid.

As the infantry were going by train there was very little for us to do. We found a cellar and with some new straw made ourselves comfortable for the night, but around midnight two riders had to turn out to report to Doullens to be there when the infantry arrived in the early hours of the morning. A foul night, raining in torrents and pitch darkness, roads packed with transport.

29 MARCH 1918

Arrived at Doullens at 10:30 to find quite a pack of troubles awaiting me, one man had broken the back wheel of his machine, another was missing since the previous day, and we had to find someone to ride Munro's machine. These matters being straightened out I went on to Toutencourt, a small village which lies off the main Doullens to Amiens road.

Toutencourt was crowded with troops, many were stragglers who had lost their units in the retreat and in some cases they were the only survivors. We heard many accounts of the German attack from these men. It was made after a very short bombardment under the cover of a thick ground mist. It came as a complete surprise and in some cases the Germans had reached Division HQ before it was realised that the attack was more than a raid.

The Germans came over wave after wave, sometimes with linked arms. As fast as one wave was mown down another would take its place. They must have had terrible losses. Our infantry were swamped, many machine-gun posts held out but the German infantry simply passed between them and pressed forward like a football crowd. Our line was broken in several places and the Germans advanced unopposed, we having no reinforcements within a day's march. There is no doubt that we were completely surprised.

Our retreating troops are now falling back on the old trenches we held before the German retreat in 1916. In some parts of the Front, we do not know how far the Germans have advanced and it is said there are several gaps in our line.

Weighed myself today on the scales in a village shop. Just under 12 stone (168lb). Height 5ft 11in.

30 MARCH 1918, TOUTENCOURT

I turned in about midnight after a very strenuous day chasing units who had no map reference or if they had they could not find it. I was sleeping like 'a log' when an orderly wakened me at around 04:00. The OC wanted to see me. Wondering what it was all about I went to the office, which was all lit up. In a few minutes, the OC came out and said 'We want you to go to Pas and find out who occupies the château and deliver this message to the Town Major. Do not get there before daylight and do not go beyond the village.' He did not give the reason but a wink is as good as a nod. As the village lies in a hollow, I decided to enter from the Doullens end which gives one a 'bird's eye' view. Reaching the outskirts I stopped, looked and listened. The place seemed deserted. Last time I saw Pas it was crowded with troops. It was not quite light so I dropped down the hill without using the engine and pulled up in the square. Not a soul about. I waited a little while and then rode from one end of the village to the other but could find no Town Major.

Thinking he might be in the château, I went there and an old lady came out. 'Are there any British army people in the château?' I asked. 'No, they went away some days ago.' I then went down to the château farm where we used to be billeted in 1915. There was nobody about but I noticed the outbuildings were full of army stores, apparently unguarded. I knocked on the farm door and a woman's head appeared at an upstairs window. She recognised me. All she could tell me was that the British had left in a hurry some days ago because the Germans were coming. I looked sceptical but she was very emphatic that the Germans had been seen outside the village. She told me that the Town Major used to have his office in a house opposite the château gates but he had gone with the rest.

To make sure, I decided to call at the house. The front door was ajar. Stepping inside I found myself in a long passage with doors on either hand. Choosing a door at random, I walked in to find a big four-poster bed, from the depths of which two old ladies bobbed up, dressed in white night gowns with mob caps on their heads, alike as two peas. For a moment I was too surprised for words, but at last I managed to blurt out in my best French, 'Is this the office of the Town Major?' 'Yes sir, but he has gone.' With that I beat a hasty retreat. Reaching Division HQ, I gave the OC an account of what I had seen and done and he hurried off to tell the staff.

1 APRIL 1918, MOVED TO PAS EN ARTOIS

The Division HQ will be in the château, thus we return to where we started from in July 1915. It looks as though we are being rushed to fill a gap in the Line which is wide open without defence.

3 APRIL 1918

Our troops are talking up their positions, holding a line which runs along a ridge between Bucquoy and Puisieux, where we join the Australians. On our side of the ridge there is a shallow valley bounded by Gommecourt and 'Pigeon Wood' which is a cover for the batteries. The Germans overlook this valley. This morning, I went up the Line to find various points of call. At the Bucquoy end we have an advanced brigade post in the old German dugouts under Rettemoy Farm. As the Germans know its position to a yard it will be a pretty hot spot. A second brigade will be in the dugouts under Fonquevillers church, a forward post at Gommecourt and the reserve brigade at Souastre.

On the way back, I stopped to have a look at the Gommecourt Redoubt where the 46th Division was cut to pieces in July 1916. Standing on high ground it gives a good view of the ground our infantry would have had to cross in the attack. It was easy to see that most of our barrage had fallen short, the wire was still in good condition. A complete division was lost attacking Gommecourt and 'Pigeon Wood'. Out of 10,000 men less than 1,000 returned. I remember seeing the survivors, plastered with mud, their clothing in tatters. I happened to be in the signal office, looking over the shoulder of the telegraphist as he took down the messages reporting the progress of the attack. 'Our troops are entering Pigeon Wood.' That was the last progress report received. Our infantry entered the wood but never came out again. They were mown down by concealed machine guns.

6 APRIL 1918

We found the Germans alright. Their artillery has wakened up and no mistake. Fonquevillers is being shelled very heavily, big stuff too. The crossroads near the church is a spot to avoid, we have had one casualty already: 'Fonny' was hit in the arms and legs. How he picked it up is rather humorous. 'If you are going past the church I should wait a bit, they are giving Blighties away.'

'Giving Blighties away are they?' said 'Fonny', 'That's just what I am looking for,' and off he went. A little later someone saw him being carried away on a stretcher. Recognising a pal, 'Happiest man in France' he shouted.

They say it is not very serious, for which I am glad, but not sorry to lose him. He has been my bête noire ever since he joined the section. Slovenly and inefficient, he was continually in one scrape or another which caused me endless trouble. After one affair, I told the OC 'Either he goes or I do.' There is no doubt he had a friend among the staff. He got away with 'murder'.

A short time after the 'kissing the major' incident I gave him a little fatherly advice. He was very apologetic and told me a bit of his past. At one time he was destined for the RC Church, but his weakness for liquor thwarted this worthy ambition in his novitiate days at the college. During supper in the refectory the brothers took turns to read the lives of the saints. One night, when it was his turn, he was so fuddled that he got the saints and the sinners mixed. The next day he was posted, an ornament lost to the church. He was the son of indulgent parents who used to send him a bottle of whisky almost every week which meant a couple of days' fuddle. The parcel also contained tinned delicacies and cakes which he gave to anyone who would take them but the whisky he never shared with anyone.

Before he joined our section he had been in the infantry and the Military Police, speaking French and German fluently. I understand his mother was German and his father French ('Fonny' was a nickname, his full name being Fonnereau). In his sober moments, he had a pretty wit and a command of English which comes only from a classical education. Exit 'Fonny' aged about 24-years-old, twice wounded, the only man in the British Army who has kissed a VC major.

8 April 1918

I had a narrow escape and a severe fright today. Whilst overtaking a line of motor lorries in a narrow street, I skidded and fell right in the path of one of them. When the lorry stopped, the front wheel was resting on the back wheel of my machine and nipping my thigh. Fortunately the lorry had good brakes or I should now be a cold and sticky corpse. My own fault, I was in a hurry and took a chance. I gave top marks to that driver, he undoubtedly saved my life. He was too upset to give me a good cursing which I deserved.

NARRATIVE FIVE:

German Spring Offensive

**In the spring of 1918, the Germans launched two major
offensives on the Western Front. Sergeant Simpkin referred to
the first of these in his entries for March. Here he records his
view of the second offensive starting on 9 April, when his division
were in the line at Gommecourt, between Arras and Albert.**

This morning I took the early run to the brigades. I heard that we were making
a minor attack to straighten our line but expected nothing unusual. Instead the
Germans made a full-scale attack with the idea of continuing their advance.

Firstly, I called at Souastre and then intended to proceed to Fonquevillers
by the direct road. When I reached the outskirts of Souastre I could see the
road was blocked by a line of motor lorries, some of which were on fire, they
were being shelled with 5.9s. The road was under direct observation by the
Germans. I waited a while to see if the shelling would slacken when a line of
German prisoners, marching down the road, were shelled and several men fell.
I decided to take a round-about route through Bienvillers and enter from the
Hannescamps end.

Reaching Fonquevillers, I found a group of officers and men watching
the shelling; the village was almost hidden by a cloud of smoke and spouting
debris. It looked most uninviting, but I knew the longer I watched the more
'funked' I should be so I barged through the crowd and raced towards the
village. With head down and eyes glued on the road I steeplechased over shell
holes, bricks and rubbish, the machine bucking like a broncho. The noise was
deafening and the air was full of gas. Reaching the shelter of the dugout under
the church I felt I had a grievance, not having been warned about this uproar.

My first words were, 'Say, what the hell do you call this? What's happening?'
'The Germans are attacking', was their reply. Everyone seemed very tense.

'How do we stand?' was my next question. 'Nobody knows, all lines are down.' 'What about the runners?' 'We haven't seen any.' All this sounded ominous, if we are pushed back the Germans will be in Fonquevillers in 30 minutes.

My next call was Rettemoy Farm. Returning to the surface, I found the stairway and the entrance crowded with men taking shelter, some with gas masks on. I waited a bit to see if the shelling would ease but I could see it was getting worse. Taking myself by the scruff of the neck, as it were, I started off for the Gommecourt turning which was less than 100yd away. I had all but reached it when there was a crash and the wall of a house poured itself into the roadway. I made a wild swerve and was so scared that I missed the turning and went straight on. When I realised my mistake I turned around and dashed off like a scalded cat.

The next thing I remember was getting a shower bath of liquid mud: the road was flooded. The engine started to splutter and at the Gommecourt crossroads it gave up the ghost. Leaning the machine against a low bank I tried to find the cause of the trouble when there was a scream and a crash from a shell burst, not 20yd away, and in a few seconds another came, showering me with earth and stones. Looking up, I could see that shells were bursting all around me, no doubt a barrage on the crossroads. I jumped up and ran for 100yd down the road which leads to 'Pigeon Wood' and then lay down in a shell hole to get my wind. Shells were now bursting all around the machine. Having abandoned it, I must now walk a good mile to the farm. The usual way is by a track which skirts 'Pigeon Wood' but the wood was hidden in a cloud of black smoke from bursting shells from the German artillery trying to find our batteries which are hidden there. A few yards from where I had been lying there was the body of an infantry man with half his head missing. He had not been dead long, the blood was new. The track past 'Pigeon Wood' was impossible so I decided to make a 'beeline' across the valley to the farm, cutting diagonally across the old German trench system. Our frontline trenches lay over the crest of a high ridge on the right. A big attack was going on, clouds of smoke were rolling along the crest but above the thunder of the shelling, the machine-gun fire sounded like a gigantic hailstorm on a tin roof. I had covered about one third of the distance when a solitary shell burst fairly close. I hurried along thinking it might be a stray when I was bracketed by six, some of them gas shells. I panicked and ran for the nearest trench; the shelling followed me, mostly gas. Reaching the trench I took a flying leap and landed in a foot of mud and water. It was an old broken-down trench about 10ft wide and not more than 4ft deep. I lay full length behind the steepest bit of wall I could find and put on my gas mask.

Shells were now coming in salvos showering earth into the trench and the air was full of whizzing metal.

I thought it was time to find a deeper trench. Jumping up, I slogged through the mud, bent double, puffing and blowing through my mouth piece until I began to feel faint. The gas mask is not meant for violent exertion; I had to resist the greatest temptation to take it off. I lay down full length, expecting 'Kingdom come' at any moment. I never felt so lonely in my life.

As soon as I was able I set off again, forcing myself to keep a slow pace. Backward and forward around the traverses I toiled, feeling I was in a world of my own, when I was brought to earth by the sight of a well-developed backside of an infantry man digging a cubby hole in the side of the trench. I lay down beside him to get my wind. What a feeling of safety a companion gives one. I had been thinking, if I get hit nobody will find me.

Waiting a while for the gas to clear, we left the trench and walked on top. Reaching the dugout, I felt pretty limp, covered with mud and wet through with sweat. All lines were down and the linesmen could not keep pace with the breakages. They had had no communication with HQ for over 2 hours. I was told the Germans had made a big attack but had been beaten off, but more attacks were expected. I had to wait some 20 minutes for the returns.

Going on top, I could see Hobson in the distance, coming towards the dugout. He was badly shaken and spewing, the gas had got in his stomach. He had a 'special'. I waited while he delivered his despatch so we could return together. I decided to return the same way that I had come. The bombardment seemed fiercer than ever. Keeping close to the trenches in case we wanted shelter we hurried along, Hobson spewing every few yards. When we reached the lower part of the ridge where the Germans had a view of the valley the shelling commenced. It was evidently a sniping battery. We took refuge in odd bits of trench and shell holes, hopping in and out. Fortunately there was no gas. Once we nearly got it and Hobson got a crack on the knee with a piece of shell but was only bruised. He wanted to take refuge behind a burnt-out tank but I would not let him, a derelict tank is always a mark for artillery fire.

We got within 100yd of the Gommecourt crossroads and sheltered in a big shell hole to watch what was happening. Gommecourt seemed quiet and we could see my machine lying on its side, half covered with earth and stones and all around the ground was ploughed up with big shell holes.

The skyline on the ridge was a rolling cloud of black smoke. The Germans were attacking again. Could our troops hold them? We half expected to see them appear on the skyline. Hobson suggested that we should leave my motorcycle to its fate, but I have a great love for that machine, which I have fitted with all manner of gadgets, a polished copper exhaust pipe and a blue and white pennant on the front mudguard. Incidentally, this pennant was painted by a professional artist for the London theatres.

The sniping batteries had got tired of chasing us and the big 5.9s that had been shelling the cross roads were waiting for something worthwhile. I ran to the machine and picked it up. It looked alright, so I jumped on and started freewheeling down the hill towards Fonquevillers, with Hobson on the carrier. Letting in the clutch, to my surprise the engine fired spasmodically and we managed to reach the outskirts of the village where it gave up the ghost completely. Hobson now left me to retrieve his machine in Hannescamps. I found the exhaust valve needed more clearance. After adjusting this I had another call to make, the Australian Brigade at the opposite end of the village. Since morning, the village had received such a pasting that the main road through the village was blocked with bricks and debris and the infantry were clearing it away, so I left my machine at the church and walked to the Australian Brigade. Outside the entrance there were some new shell holes and a lot of blood. They had had several killed that morning.

I reached Division HQ around midday to meet the general face-to-face at the door of the signal office. The OC came running up. Had I seen Hobson? I told him I had and I knew he had delivered his 'special'. The general, overhearing this, seemed satisfied and the OC handed him the despatch I had brought. There had been no communication with the forward brigades since early morning and the 'old man' had been pacing up and down in front of the signal office for the last hour or so. Being on the wrong side of my breakfast, I went to the cookhouse to try to get a cup of tea but began to be sick so I went to the medics to get something for it. Hobson came in a few minutes later, like myself a picture in different colours of mud. He looked pretty seedy, I suppose I must have looked the same.

Yesterday's event was supposed to be a minor attack on our part to straighten our line, but unexpectedly it turned out to be one of the biggest and fiercest fights our infantry have had for a long time. By a coincidence, the Germans had staged a major attack a few minutes before ours was due to start. The German idea was to continue their advance, which if it had been successful might have meant that Arras would have had to be evacuated. They were beaten back with great losses and I am afraid our losses were fairly heavy too. It is quite evident that there was gap in our line and we arrived just in time to prevent the Germans pushing through without obstruction.

CHAPTER EIGHT

April – August 1918

13 APRIL 1918, COUIN

There is an epidemic of motorcycle stealing. No doubt it is our 'Botany Bay' friends next door. To baulk this we generally remove the high-tension cable to the sparking plug when we have to leave our machines unattended, and thereby hangs a tale.

Last night, I had a special for the brigade who live in the dugout under Fonquevillers church. Returning to the surface after delivering my despatch, I was walking to my machine when there was a shriek and a crash, fairly close too. I kick-started vigorously, anxious to get away before the next came, but the engine would not start. At that moment another came, somewhat closer, which spurred me to greater efforts, but nothing doing. Then came another which made the ground tremble and bricks came raining down. It was getting too hot so I dashed back to shelter, cursing the machine, then I remembered I had the cable in my pocket.

14 APRIL 1918

We are moving to Authie for rest and training. We are being relieved by the 24th Division: my brother was in the artillery with the division in Gallipoli. When in Couin we took possession of the village blacksmith's as a workshop. It was an absolute museum of ancient tools and the old 'smith who sports a long white beard is Exhibit No.1. The old man is always in a hurry. He comes into the smithy at a gallop, mumbling in his whiskers, and starts rooting among his bits and pieces for something he never finds and then dashes out again. Sometimes a villager comes in to ask him to do a job, but his stock reply is, '*Beaucoup travail, beaucoup travail*'. I have yet to see him do a job of work. He is a decent old chap though; he does not mind us using his tools.

The countryside is being laced with a network of trenches and barbed-wire entanglements, evidently we do not mean to be caught napping again. The news from the north is depressing: Locre, Kemmel, Dranoutre and Bailleul all lost. It seems incredible, only a few weeks ago we were running in and out of these places which, except for the long-range shelling and occasional bombing, seemed to be as far from the war as being at home. Lestrum and Merville are also gone. Lestrum we knew well, with happy memories. The villagers were kindness itself and we spent 6 weeks there, one of the happiest times I can remember out here.

16 APRIL 1918, AUTHIE

Authie is a small village lying in a shallow valley with wooded slopes which gives good cover for troops and transport. A stream meanders through the village, providing good watering for man and beast. The villagers have been warned to clear out as a big attack by the Germans is expected on this front. All the bridges and crossroads are mined. The *estaminets* are selling out their stock; we have been drinking all the best vintage wines at 6 Francs a bottle. The old man at our farm has been selling his stock of cider which he says is 20-years-old. There is a thick scum at the bottom of the bottle but the liquid is clear as crystal. It tastes like the finest dry champagne — I have never tasted cider like it.

18 APRIL 1918

It is confirmed that von Richthofen, the crack flier of the German Army, was brought down yesterday in our trenches whilst chasing one of our 'spotting' aeroplanes. He was killed.

24 APRIL 1918, HÉNU

Moved to Hénu today. The Division HQ is in the château. I made a trip to find our various points of call. Fonquevillers is still in our area, also Gommecourt. The right-hand brigade is in an area which was once in the German line.

It is very interesting to explore some of the places which used to be mentioned so often in operation orders: La Brayall Farm, 'Sniper's Square', the 'Z', the 'Sunken Road'. The wire in front of the old German line is a wonder even today, three belts each 30 to 50yd wide, still in good condition. No wonder our attacks failed in July 1916.

3 May 1918

This front is very quiet and beyond the routine runs to all units we have little to do. To kill time, I went exploring the country behind Fonquevillers. I came across a lot of farming machinery, ploughs, tractors, all practically new, sent by the American Society of Farmers. If I know anything about the French peasants they would have been far more pleased with an old-fashioned plough and a pair of horses.

4 May 1918

A beautiful warm day. For some days past, shells have been falling in the fields in front of the château where the transport men water their horses. I thought it was strange that 'Fritz' should waste ammunition on the off-chance of smashing a few horse troughs or killing a few horses when there was a divisional HQ in a château full of officers and lesser fry a short distance away.

Today, I had just laid down in my 'bivvy' for my usual forty winks after dinner, when I heard the 'ping' of a long-range gun firing directly towards us, and at the same instant there was a terrific screech like the tearing of a gigantic piece of calico with a thunderclap. I put my head out of the 'bivvy' to see a cloud of black smoke hanging over the château. In a few moments the staff and their servants came running out to see what had happened. Their curiosity was soon satisfied, there was another screech and one of the outbuildings used as a canteen went up in dust and before they had recovered their surprise another arrived, this time a 'dud' which buried itself in the paddock in front of the château.

This was too much and everyone took to their heels, senior officers and all and did not stop until they had put 100yd behind them. There we stood, expecting to see the château go up in smoke. After firing some twelve rounds he stopped and we filtered back to see the damage. One shell had hit the top branches of one of the large elm trees which line the drive leading to the château. This shell exploded in the air, killing a sergeant of the machine gunners, almost decapitating him. The sergeant of the APM's was wounded in the knee. The only material damage was to the shack which we use as a garage and workshop for our motorcycles. If it had been an hour earlier there would have been some DRs in the garage cleaning and adjusting their machines, also the mechanic who works there most of the day. The shelling was directed by an aeroplane which circled over the château at about 10,000ft. Undoubtedly, it was a big naval gun on a railway truck firing from 20 miles away. Pretty good shooting, only 50yd out for a direct hit.

5 MAY 1918

The machine-gun sergeant who was killed yesterday had only been on the Division HQ staff for 2 weeks after spending a year in the trenches without a scratch.

18 MAY 1918, AUTHIE

Moved to Authie today for rest and training. We have pitched our 'bivvies' in the old spot by the stream.

4 JUNE 1918

Our rest comes to an end tomorrow when we move south. While we have been here we have had a fairly easy time though it started badly with an inspection by the general which caused us days of spitting and polishing. After the inspection we had company sports; everyone was very keen. The DR section did well, taking second place in the mile, the event of the day, and second in the hundred yards. We also won the 'boat race' which consists of eight men standing astride and supporting a telegraph pole. On the word go the crew run backwards guided by their cox who is the only man who runs forward. The main idea is to keep in step.

5 JUNE 1918

The division moves tonight after dark. It is said that the Germans move their troops at night; apparently we are taking a leaf out of their book. It is the first night move we have made to my recollection. It is said that we are going to the Soissons – Reims front where things are not going too well. We are to travel light, nothing but regulation kit to be carried. The company had kit inspection today and loads of private kit had to be dumped which caused much heart burning.

6 JUNE 1918

We were out most of the night chasing units on the move. I hope the move went alright but it seemed an awful mix-up, as our troops met a French division also on the move. Soon after daylight we were told to report to Cavillion, a small village which lies a few miles behind Amiens. The staff have made their HQ in the château; the remainder of the village consists of some six wattle-and-daub farmhouses.

7 JUNE 1918, CAVILLION

Fine and hot. We have lost one of our riders, Musto, who collided with a French staff car last night. His leg is badly smashed and he has other injuries; not much chance of him being a DR again. Quite a good sort but not much of a rider.

8 JUNE 1918

This morning I was awakened by geese which were standing in the opening of the 'bivvy' honking defiance at me. I threw a boot at them and went to sleep again. The next time I woke, I was startled to find them squatted down inside the 'bivvy'. They appeared to be quite tame, evidently someone's pets. What a gift from the gods, if only we had the time and the facilities for cooking.

First thing this morning the OC told me to take two men and explore the roads behind the line from Montdidier to Villiers Bretonneux. It looks as though we are going to take over part of that sector.

10 JUNE 1918, AILLY

Weather fine and hot. We moved today to a small village about 12 miles south of Amiens and 2 miles north of Conty. We seem to be in reserve to the French, to be used in case of necessity. As far as we know there are no other British troops within 10 miles of here.

17 JULY 1918

We have been here over a month waiting for something to happen. The German advance on the Marne has come to a standstill and the Compiègne push has also failed. A big attack is now expected at Villiers Bretonneux towards Amiens.

We are still under orders to move at a few hours' notice. On 14 July, we spent a day exploring the roads immediately behind the line. Starting at La Faloise, we passed through some beautiful country, a great contrast to the flat country of the Somme. For miles, we ran along a deep valley with thickly-wooded slopes and in some places chalk cliffs. A clear stream wanders along the bottom of the valley in a wide marshy bed. We passed through several tiny villages, hardly touched by shellfire although not more than 2 miles behind the Line. Each village had its church and each church had a different shaped spire.

The French troops we saw were taking life very calmly and most of the batteries were silent. Defence not defiance was the order of the day and quite in keeping with the sylvan surroundings. As we got nearer to Amiens we found more violent signs of war, shell holes in the road, broken down trees and ruined houses, and the countryside was networked with the white chalk thrown from the trenches.

The next place, Longueau, is a big railway junction with locomotive sheds and sidings. The railway track was torn up by huge shell holes and several locomotives were stranded. Continuing through Longueau we came to the Amiens to Albert road. The crossroads looked decidedly unhealthy, all houses were badly damaged; we did not linger, especially as we could see shelling going on some distance up the road.

We decided to go into Amiens and find a restaurant as our souls longed for civilised fare. The station and all around is badly damaged and some of the houses nearby have been flattened out. Most of the civilians have left and the town is deserted except for a few military. No-one is allowed in the town without a pass except DRs and 'brass hats'. We searched the side streets for an eating place but everywhere was shuttered, so we gave it up and set off for Ailly by the main Boves road. A few miles down the road we found a wayside *estaminet* open where we managed to get some '*oeufs* and chips' which we washed down with *vin ordinaire*.

20 JULY 1918

We are moving tomorrow back to Pas, much to our disgust. Although we must not be ungrateful for the long holiday, we were hoping for a change, somewhere near Ailly for preference, which would have been cushy, until we had stirred up the old 'Boche' as we always do.

21 JULY 1918 , MOVED TO PAS

We are taking over from the 23rd Division.

23 JULY 1918, MOVED TO HÉNU

So, after two months wandering we come back to where we started from, without doing any actual duty in the Line. As the old soldiers say, they can do anything with you in the army except put you in the family way.

31 JULY 1918

Today, I was walking along a duckboard track behind the village of Bailleuval when I met face to face a man in officer's uniform but without rank distinction or cap badge and, what was more unusual, a bearded face. I hardly knew whether to salute or not. I put him down as a sort of padre until I was told it was John Sargent, the artist. He is a fine figure of a man and looks about 60 years-old.

On the way back I noticed twelve or more infantry sergeants lined up in front of one of the main dugouts. I enquired what it all meant. They had been picked out to take commissions. The 'wastage' of second lieutenants in these days is greater than the supply. Poor devils, almost a sentence of death.

We have now passed the third year out here and commenced the fourth and still no sign of the end.

9 AUGUST 1918

We have had an extraordinary epidemic of influenza which the doctors call the 'Spanish Flu'. Men went down in hundreds. The hospitals were filled to overflowing and men had to be treated where they lay. Fortunately it was all over in 3 or 4 days in the majority of cases. It started with a slight headache and a temperature, which quickly increased to fever heat and the next 12 hours was spent in torture from a head which wanted to burst but could not, and then it went away as quickly as it came but leaving the victim as weak as though he had been ill for weeks.

My side kicker, Joe Torrey, was one of the first victims. He was taken to hospital as it looked as though it would turn to pneumonia. When he could take notice of his surroundings, he wrote me a frantic letter asking me to get him away or he would be sent down to the base. I saw the OC who was a good sport and arranged for him to be brought back and he soon recovered. By that time most of our fellows had been down and recovered. There was only Hill and myself who had not had it, and I began to think that I should escape, but I was caught at last. One evening, I developed a headache and felt a bit feverish so I went along to the ambulance room for a pill. 'You have got it alright, go and get under some blankets and I will come along presently with a draught.'

That night I was extremely fevered and felt completely unwell, everything went round and round and every sound echoed tenfold. At noon next day, I felt better and the following morning I wanted to get up but I was told to stay where I was. Towards evening however, I got up for a short while but what a surprise I had, my legs would hardly carry me. It took me about a week to get back to normal. From information received by our Intelligence the Germans have had the epidemic worse than ourselves. In fact, it came from their side. There is no doubt that the extraordinary quietness of the Front for this past month is due to half their troops being down with the 'flu.

20 AUGUST 1918

Weather fine and hot. A week ago there was not a cloud on the sky of our blissful content. For 8 weeks we have been rusticating in a perfect Arcadia, watching the corn grow and ripen, wakened in the morning by the cooing of wood pigeons and lulled to sleep by the wind in the trees. Tomorrow all this comes to an end, the division is attacking at daylight. This morning the OC told me to go to Battalion HQ in the trenches behind Bucquoy and to find out how near we could get to it by motorcycle as it might be used by the GOC during the attack.

I collected one of the DRs to accompany me and set off. It was stinking hot and the roads were deep in chalk dust. Wherever we went we left a cloud of dust which must have been seen from miles away. Passing through places which are under observation from the German side, I felt sure we should have a 'ration' from 'Fritz' to help us on our way but we did not raise even a 'whizz bang'. Our artillery was giving the Germans hell, but there was very little retaliation. We had no difficulty in riding right up to where the communication trench starts, where we left our machines in the shelter of an old gun pit.

When we got back to HQ, the first thing we met was a runner waiting for the 'next DR'. All the DRs were out so we had to go out again. All for a good cause, but it is difficult to appreciate it on an empty stomach.

NARRATIVE SIX:

Final Allied Offensive

August 1918 marked a turning point of the war: the German successes of their Spring Offensive were reversed and the Allies made a decisive breakthrough. The 37th Division were once again in action north of Albert where they had been in the spring.

(21 August) The attack was made at 4:30 this morning. After a 20 minute bombardment our troops went over. There was a thick ground mist at zero hour and it is said our infantry were in the German trenches before the Germans realised that it was an attack. By 10:00, our right had taken Achiet-le-Petit but our left was held up in front of Logeast Wood which is full of machine guns. At present our artillery is raking it from end to end. From what we heard our infantry had a fairly easy time, taking Bucquoy with few casualties.

The transport has been moving forward all day and the dust on the roads is beyond description. We cannot see more than 10yd ahead. I have been riding with a handkerchief over my mouth and nose to keep out the dust which aggravates my hay fever. We can scrape the dust off our faces. This evening the Division HQ moved to Fonquevillers. The staff have taken cover in a deep dugout at the Hannescamps end of the village.

(24 August) I have not had time to write up my diary for the past few days, and so much has happened that my memory on dates is a bit hazy. After the infantry had gone forward, all the transport moved up to the valley which runs behind the old trenches; transport, batteries in action, infantry and store dumps all in glorious confusion. Trying to find anyone in this lot made one feel like a dog in a fair. I started out early one evening with several messages, some for units in our own division and others for strange units. By midnight, I had found two and it was getting daylight when I had found the last, and

by that time I began to feel like a gibbering idiot. I was not the only fool in the fair, there were officers who had lost their units, transport who could not find their way, and ammunition columns who could not find their batteries.

After the Germans had been cleared out of Logeast Wood, the village of Achiet-le-Grand was the next objective. The village proved a hard nut to crack. It was guarded by a line of trenches in front and a deep railway cutting on the south, the banks of which were tunnelled with dugouts which gave cover to a big number of German troops.

Our tanks made an attack during the afternoon but without success. I was in the signal office whilst the reports were coming in. One message read, 'Tank attack on Achiet-le-Grand failed, four tanks knocked out.' A little later a message was received by aeroplane that cavalry had been seen crossing the railway south of Achiet-le-Grand.

At 18:00 our infantry made a dash for Achiet-le-Grand and reached the outskirts of the village, but an hour later they were pushed back again by a heavy counter-attack. The Artists' Rifles on their left were also pushed back almost as far as Logeast Wood, which made the position of our men rather serious. The Germans next tried to rush the trenches held by our men but got a terrible cutting up, leaving a big number of dead and wounded in front of our position.

By this time, our artillery had got into position again and gave the Germans around Achiet such a hammering, which broke up any idea the Germans may have had of attacking in the morning. The troops of our division were then taken out for rest and reinforcement, and went back again about 4 days later. At the first attempt, 63 Brigade took Achiet-le-Grand, capturing over 1,000 prisoners. The Germans then fell back to a line through Bihucourt and Loup Wood. This position was on a slight eminence overlooking our line.

Our Division HQ is still in Fonquevillers which makes our runs very long. The hot weather continues and the roads are deep in chalk dust. We are smothered in it, we breathe it and we eat it.

One day the Army Commander General Haig called unexpectedly at Division HQ. If we had known he was coming we would have stopped the war and 'poshed up' a bit. It was most inconsiderate of him.

The DRs covered themselves with glory as usual. Just as the general was emerging from the dug out, one of our section arrived at the entrance and they met face to face. The general stopped and stared at the apparition before him, smothered in dust, looking like a miller's labourer.

Smiling a sickly smile the general passed on with the remark: 'You fellows are very busy these times.'

Hail the despatch riders, the sergeant major's pride and joy. Our work has been more laborious than exciting. We are now so far in arrears with sleep that whenever we have a spare moment we spend it sleeping. Immediately a fellow comes in and he has not to go out again right away, he dosses down. I saw Hobson fast asleep with a half-eaten hunk of bread and cheese in his hand.

We lost one of our number, a newcomer who had been with us only a few days, due to an accident. He struck a shell hole in the dark and crashed, some part of his machine pierced the lower part of his body, rather serious I believe. An officer said to me, 'When I see you fellows bumping about on those motorcycles I often wonder if you are fully sexed.' I assured him that at times we wished that we were not. The other day, I came across one of our fellows sitting by the roadside, his face as white as death. I thought he was badly hurt, but between his groans and curses I gathered that he had hit a bump and sat heavily on his sex.

After the Germans had been pushed out of Achiet-le-Grand they retired to a line running through Bihucourt and Loup Wood. The next day they were forced out of this position by a combined tank and infantry attack. A few hours before the attack, operation orders had to be delivered to the Tank HQ. There were two messages, one whose map reference showed it to be in front of Achiet-le-Grand and the other between the railway and Loup Wood, which I imagined would be our frontline.

Garnier and myself were next for duty. I gave him the choice which he would take. He chose the one in front of Achiet. We rode together as far as the corner of Logeast Wood where we parted, he to go straight ahead and I to the right by a track which I had noticed before, but not explored.

It was a dark night, but there were plenty of Very lights [flares] and gun flashes to light the way. Our artillery was in full blast, pounding the enemy's position and their back areas preparing for the morning attack. I soon found that the track was badly cut up with shell holes and half-filled trenches. All our artillery seemed to be on or around the track and I was scared stiff for fear I should get in front of a gun just as it was letting off. I had a struggle to get the machine across some half-filled trenches and at one place I came across a bunch of shell holes still smoking hot. In my anxiety to get away I narrowly escaped riding head first into a trench, so I decided to walk. There was a howitzer battery close by so I asked them to keep their eyes on my machine in case it 'strayed'. I had no difficulty in following the track, which was sunk 2 or 3ft below the surface of the ground, and eventually I struck a metalled road running at right angles which I guessed to be the main road between the two Achiet villages.

I had memorised the position before I started and if the track which I had been following had not been altered I ought to meet the railway right ahead. Then 200yd to the right and 200yd forward I ought to find the place I wanted – if the reference was correct. Small groups of men were scurrying past, so I shouted several times asking if they had seen any tanks about but they could give no proper answer – everyone was in a tearing hurry. 'Whizz bangs' were screeching overhead and gas shells were bursting with a splitting crash; I wondered how Garnier was getting on.

I went forward in what I thought was the direction of the railway, and in a few minutes I almost flattened my face against a tank lying behind a low bank which I found was the railway line. Following the railway for about 200yd as I had calculated, and then striking inland for the same distance, I found a concrete shelter which was the Tank HQ. For once the map reference was correct, but I take a little credit myself for making a 'bull's eye' first time. I smiled to myself, however, when I thought how I had placed the spot somewhere in the frontline. Loup Wood was some distance ahead, showing on the skyline as a black hump against the light from the Very lights which were falling well beyond the hill crest.

It was getting light when I got back to Fonquevillers. Garnier had raced me home by 30 minutes. The general and his staff have moved up to Achiet-le-Grand, installing themselves in an old German dugout just behind the village. Now that we have reached the area where every house and every tree was destroyed by the Germans in their retirement in 1916, accommodation for the 'Brass Hats' is getting very scarce.

CHAPTER NINE

September – November 1918

1 SEPTEMBER 1918, FONQUEVILLERS

Our infantry are out of the Line resting and the DRs have very little to do. Searching around the trenches we found a small concrete shelter which had been overlooked by everyone so we took possession. It was complete with door, a small window and four wire bunks. From a tablet on the door it had belonged to a Brigadier Beob of the German infantry: I wonder where the old boy is now? The Germans are past masters in the art of making themselves comfortable. The British Army's idea of comfort is polishing buttons.

The dead are still unburied; there must be at least twenty bodies lying within 100yd radius of our shelter, mostly Germans who were mowed down in their counter-attack on the 24 August. The stench is terrible. Around the station the slaughter was even worse: the dead are lying in heaps.

While in the signal office today, a message was received reporting a combined tank and aeroplane attack on a German position which threatened to hold up our advance. This is a new idea of warfare.

Near our shack there is one of our latest 'Whippet' tanks standing on its nose, a casualty of the last attack. It had tried to cross a deep trench at an angle and got stuck. From the thousands of pit marks on the armoured plates the Germans had played their machine guns on it, but without piercing it. Last night, we had a grand firework display in the southern sector. Rockets of all colours were soaring into the air and we wondered what it was all about. This morning we hear that it was the Australians celebrating. They had found a German rocket store or something similar and proceeded to let them off.

4 SEPTEMBER 1918

Fine and warm. We are moving into the Line again tomorrow. Early this morning the OC told me to go and explore our new sector, but before I had time to start, word came through that the 'Boche' had retired during the night and the infantry had advanced 2 miles to get in contact. I had to wait for our new position.

I took Joe with me. We passed through Sapignies and Beugnâtre where heavy fighting has taken place these last few days. We explored all the roads to make sure they were passable. Except for a few shell holes and an occasional trench across the road they were in surprisingly good condition, far better than those on our side. The Germans are now holding Beugny and Fremicourt on the Bapaume to Cambrai road. There is no trench system, the fighting is from village to village: when the 'Boche' are pushed out of one village they retire to the next.

Favreuil is to be our Division HQ. The Germans had a big field ambulance in this place. There were the remains of several marquees which have been used as operating and dressing stations. In a field at the back is a cemetery, a number of bodies on stretchers, some stark naked, were lying where they had been left unburied. Apparently the Germans strip their bodies before burial. All along the roads and in the villages bodies were lying where they had fallen. We seem to have been living for the past few days without being able to get away from the stench of rotting bodies.

Over 300 prisoners were taken in this village. The prisoners' cage was full: a mixed bag, many young boys and several officers among them. Some of our infantry noticed that one of the German officers was wearing a pair of British officer's field boots. A crowd gathered and a few hot heads threatened to shoot him. The situation began to look very nasty but fortunately the officer guessed that something was afoot and took refuge in the crowd. As a rule our 'Tommies' are over-sentimental with the prisoners, giving them cigarettes and food: 'Trying to make them feel at home' as a Jock put it.

5 SEPTEMBER 1918, FAVREUIL

Moved to Favreuil today. Most of our work at present is keeping in touch with neighbouring divisions. Positions are changing hourly, map references are of very little use these days, it is a case of 'last heard of at so-and-so.'

We found the wreck of one of our aeroplanes in the wood which adjoins one end of the village. A low mound nearby showed where the pilot had been buried. The body had only the thinnest layer of earth over it and the poor devil's hands were left uncovered.

6 SEPTEMBER 1918

The weather has turned wet with high winds. Last night, I was searching for some artillery who were supposed to be in our area. It was pitch dark and raining hard with a gale of wind. I came to a crossroads with several ruined houses. The place seemed deserted and I was on the point of riding away when I saw the shadow of two Nissen huts in the distance. When I got there, I could see they were badly knocked about. Shining my flash light in an open door I had the shock of my life, the hut was full of German dead lying in all manner of postures, their faces absolutely phosphorescent, their hands with fingers curved like claws as though trying to clutch hold of life itself. An ugly sight for the daytime but a real hair-raiser for a dark night.

7 SEPTEMBER 1918

Today at daybreak, our infantry reported that there was no reply from the German side. It was then found that the Germans had retreated during the night, but how far no-one knew. The country about here is slightly undulating with copses of trees scattered about, very like the English countryside. After a short time, our infantry could be seen advancing across the fields towards a wood in open formation. Heavy firing, both artillery and machine gun fire, then broke out in the sector on our left, which showed the next division had found the enemy.

10 SEPTEMBER 1918

After some stiff fighting the Germans have been pushed out of their positions in Havrincourt Wood and have fallen back to Trescault village and Gouzeaucourt Wood.

12 SEPTEMBER 1918, MOVED TO VÉLU

Today Division HQ was moved forward taking possession of a German Army HQ lately occupied by Prince Rupprecht of Bavaria. If the prince was responsible for the building of the HQ he had good taste and a keen eye for comfort, nothing rough and ready for him. It might have been the hunting lodge of a king. Electric light, duckboard paths, and a balcony where the weary 'Brass Hats' could rest after their labours and count their losses in 'cannon fodder', and all the comforts of a home. Some of the boys say there was a red lamp, but I do not believe that.

The prince's chalet has a dining room with a large fireplace with over-mantle, and the walls tastefully painted. The showplace, however, is the bedroom, with an extraordinary bed which has a wooden 'counterpane' made of massive timber which can be lowered over the bed to protect the occupant from bomb splinters. There must have been some good pickings in the way of souvenirs for the first arrivals. I saw one of the HQ grooms carrying a wooden plaque around. I recognised it as having hung over the fireplace of the prince's dining room. It had the Bavarian coat of arms painted in colour. I gave the groom a few Francs and he was pleased to part with it, so I have come into possession of one of the best souvenirs I have seen.

Another good souvenir I saw, but too big to 'lift', was a large chalk drawing of the Kaiser and the Crown Prince on a piece of black tarpaulin decorating the walls of what had been a German canteen. It was splendidly drawn, undoubtedly the work of a skilled artist. Nothing was left of the canteen stock, except a few broken packets of German war tobacco, which seems to be nothing more than shredded beech leaves.

13 SEPTEMBER 1918

We have been kept in a state of blue 'funk' all day by long-range shelling. The Germans must know the wood is occupied by a Brigade or Division HQ. Fortunately, most of the shells fell short of the Division HQ in the top end of the wood. We spent a lively night listening to the shriek and crash of shells and to fill up quiet moments we had aeroplanes over dropping bombs. I was on night duty and found it was quite a relief to get away up the Line where it was much quieter. It is said that over 300 shells have fallen in or around the wood during the last 24 hours. It is an old soldier's superstition that the first few days after returning from leave are unlucky. I do not suppose that one day is more unlucky than another, but last night some men returning from leave were killed which seems to prove the superstition. Unable to find their units in the darkness they turned in to sleep in an old German stable until daylight. In the early hours of the morning, a shell came through the roof killing three and injuring several. This has caused a lot of head-wagging among the old sweats.

15 SEPTEMBER 1918

Last night, as soon as the last traces of daylight had gone, the German bombing aeroplanes began to arrive, first the smaller types criss-crossing our back areas with strings of bombs which kept us on the jump. A little later we heard the drone of the double-engined Gothas in the distance and as soon as they had crossed the trenches they began dropping bombs aimed at our batteries, big fellows, which burst with a crash like thunder. The roaring of their engines filled the skies. Everyone held their breath, listening with all ears for the scream of falling bombs.

Our searchlights were waving their beams backward and forward searching for the raiders. Suddenly they caught one in the light and immediately several other searchlights fastened on to it, making the aeroplane stand out like a huge white moth. In a moment the machine guns were chattering madly, their flaming bullets rising like a bead curtain, and the AA joined in, bursting shells twinkling like stars.

The Gotha made a slow clumsy turn and made off towards the Line. In our excitement we forgot all about bombs, but we got a stunning reminder when he dropped six which exploded almost as one, shaking the ground like an earthquake. It was quite clear he had dropped his load and taken to his heels.

There was an uncanny silence, even the artillery in the Line ceased fire to watch the spectacle. Suddenly a stream of tracer bullets flew towards the Gotha, fired from a position high above his tail. It seemed to have no effect, he sailed on but still held in the remorseless light. Our aeroplane was still on his track, flashing through the searchlights as he manoeuvred for position. A moment later, another stream of fiery beads ripped across the blackness, a longer burst this time, the rattle of the machine gun faintly reaching our ears.

Missed again we thought, but a small flame began to show on one of the wings and in a few seconds the Gotha was a flaming torch lighting the sky a blood red. It seemed to stagger in its stride, and then began to dive, gently at first but getting steeper and steeper until it was falling vertically with a wake of flame like a meteor. We could hear the roaring of the flames. Up to that time, we had been watching the Gotha fight for life in breathless silence but now a tremendous roar of cheering broke out, rolling around the countryside like a gigantic arena. We heard afterwards that even the troops in the trenches stood up and cheered. The Gotha hit the ground with a tremendous thud, the fire flared up for a short time and then died down. It was all over, the most thrilling sight I have ever seen. It fell some 800yd away.

16 SEPTEMBER 1918

This morning I went over to look at the wreck of the Gotha. It had fallen in the triangle of the railway junction outside Beaumetz. Its size was amazing: it looked like the wreck of a Zeppelin, a mass of twisted tubes and wires. The tail, which was as large as an ordinary aeroplane, had fallen 200yd away. It was one of their latest super Gothas, having a wingspan of 124ft and four engines. It carried a crew of eight. Among the wreckage was a small engine and dynamo for supplying the electricity for the wireless. The engine was a copy of that used in the Douglas motorcycles. I also noticed some fire extinguishers in the debris, which had availed them nothing.

The bodies of the crew were scattered around where they fell, half buried in the ground by the force of their fall. Two were frightfully burnt, a crisp brown, while the others were either shapeless masses of flesh or flattened out as though a steam roller had passed over them, their heads as flat as pancakes. Only one of the crew escaped. He fell among some Nissen huts in Beaumetz and broke his leg, so it is said. The parachute was made of a mixture of silk and cotton. I cut sufficient to serve as a handkerchief.

17 SEPTEMBER 1918

During the afternoon, the Germans made a counter-attack which was the biggest attack they have made since the advance. It commenced with a terrific bombardment of our trenches and the area immediately behind our front line. Havrincourt Wood was lashed from end to end with gas and high explosive and all roads leading forward had a barrage fire put across them. After 30 minutes' bombardment the German infantry attacked in three waves. The first and second waves never reached our trenches, they were mown down with machine-gun fire. Most of the third wave took refuge in a sunken road which our machine guns could not reach. At one point, by sheer weight of numbers, they entered our trenches but were overpowered. We captured over forty, all youngsters, whose average age was not more than 19 years-old. Our infantry say the Germans were all young troops who seemed to have had very little training. They came over almost shoulder to shoulder and simply walked into the fire without any idea how to take cover. It is said the older German troops refuse to go over the top.

While the attack was on, the staff had the 'wind up' to the top notch. All lines forward were down and there was no communication except by DR for over 2 hours. Everybody thought the 'Boche' had broken through. Three of our DRs had not returned from the brigades. I wanted to go and find out what had happened but the OC told me to keep all DRs standing by.

About 17:00 the artillery fire began to slacken and news came through that the attack had been completely smashed. The missing DRs had been held up in Havrincourt Wood: they took refuge in a dugout until the storm passed over.

In the early evening, two of the prisoners were sent to HQ for inspection. They must have picked out two of the ugliest and weediest specimens. Neither was more than 17-years-old, their 'coal bucket' helmets resting on their shoulders. One had glasses, thick barnacle affairs, tied round his ears. They were the object of some curiosity but the general remark was, 'It is a bloody shame to put such kids in the trenches. If the Germans are reduced to using material of this kind the end cannot be far off.'

21 SEPTEMBER 1918

Today we were relieved by the 42nd Division and moved back to Achiet-le-Grand for rest. We looked forward to occupying the little dugout so kindly left us by Brigadier Beob, but found it had been smashed down by the Australians.

24 SEPTEMBER 1918, ACHIET-LE-GRAND

Achiet is now a big rail head. Alongside the station is a park of captured artillery and a pair of tanks painted in camouflage colours with the German cross on either side. I examined them closely. They are well-finished in detail. The armour plating is thicker than that used on our tanks. The 'caterpillar' arrangement however is very light and flimsy in construction, I am sure it could not cross a good-sized trench. They seem to be designed more as mobile machine-gun posts than armoured cavalry which is the object of the British tank.

It is very interesting to compare the German methods and ours in the treatment of ammunition. The German shells are all protected in some way or other. Some are packed in wicker baskets; others have tin covers over the nose cap, while all have the copper driving bands protected by a wrapping of webbing. Their charges are packed in well-made boxes with watertight lids and spring clasps. This method of packing is very costly no doubt but in the long run it must pay as the cost of a big shell far exceeds the cost of a wicker basket.

The British waste of ammunition is enormous. Our shells have little or no protective covering; they are simply dumped on the ground in the mud exposed to the weather. In the Ypres Salient, more ammunition was lost in the mud than used by the guns. From the number of unexploded shells one sees lying around the captured trenches we must have a large percentage of 'duds'. This is more than likely due to rough handling and lying out in the weather.

5 OCTOBER 1918

Today we moved up to a spot just behind Gouzeaucourt. The HQ staff have gone to earth in some old dugouts cut into the side of a low hill. We have left the flat plains of the Somme, the country is now undulating. Our part of the Line runs in front of Vauchelles and then down the side of a deep valley at the bottom of which runs a river or canal: we hold one side of the canal and the Germans the other.

Booby traps are the topic of the day, and orders have been issued that no troops are to enter dug outs until they have been examined and passed as safe by the engineers. The Germans are leaving all manner of mines and bombs behind which can be set off by the unwary handling some object or tripping over a wire which releases a firing device which fires the mine. Sometimes, the object to be handled is an attractive 'souvenir' such as a spiked helmet casually left on a table or shelf. They have also a very ingenious delayed-action arrangement for firing charges several days after the device is set. It consists of a copper wire passing through a bottle of acid. The acid slowly eats away the wire and releases a trigger which is held back by a powerful spring and so fires a detonator. By this arrangement, several days may elapse before the mine is sprung.

Shortly after midday we were startled by an aeroplane, one of ours, skimming over our heads not more than 20ft high. It just cleared some old trenches and landed in a belt of wire entanglements, practically undamaged. The wire acted as a brake and prevented it crashing into another maze of trenches. The pilot climbed out and asked where he was and where was the nearest telephone. He was directed to the signal office. While he waited for the RFC tender, Joe Torrey invited him to our shack for a spot of rum. He spoke with a strong 'Yankee' accent or perhaps it was Canadian, and I also noticed that he wore pale lemon-coloured civilian shoes, the effect of which was almost as startling as when he swooped over our heads. He said he was well over the German lines when his motor began to fail and finally stopped altogether. He then planed down, making the glide as long as possible, but until he saw the khaki uniforms he thought he was landing on the German side. He said it was very difficult nowadays to know where the frontline lies.

7 OCTOBER 1918, MOVED TO BOIS LATEAU

After several days fighting, the fiercest since the Hindenburg Line was taken, our infantry have crossed the canal. The 'canal' is in reality a river and a canal, running side by side. Fringed with trees it winds along the bottom of a deep valley, passing through two small villages, Banteux and Bantouzelle. The sides of the valley are thickly wooded which gave good cover for the enemy's machine guns. The crossing of this canal will be one of the epics of the war when it is told. Isolated patrols managed to swim across but in face of terrible machine-gun fire our infantry were unable to get across in numbers strong enough to make an attack. I saw telegrams reporting failure of our attacks again and again. The engineers also made several attempts to throw a pontoon bridge across the canal, but each time their work was destroyed by shellfire long before it was completed. From their positions the Germans could see our every movement.

The German position was then bombarded with an intense fire for 2 days when our infantry attacked again. Swimming and floating across, they managed to get a foothold on the opposite bank which diverted the enemy's attention whilst the engineers put three pontoon bridges at different points over which reinforcements crossed to attack. Next morning, it was found that the Germans had retired to the crest of the valley some 1,500yd back. The line they now occupy is the Hindenburg support line, sometimes called the Siegfried Line.

8 OCTOBER 1918

These HQ moves always mean plenty of hard work for the DRs. We have been on the go for the last 24 hours with hardly a moment's rest. Two of our brigades are on the other side of the river. The bridge at Vaucelles is well marked by the German artillery. I saw four or five drowned horses with an ammunition limber lying in the water below the bridge. The water seems to be about 8ft deep, clear as crystal.

9 OCTOBER 1918

I was awakened this morning by someone shaking me, 'Get up sergeant, it is seven o'clock. Come and see the tanks chasing Jerry out of it!' I went on top. It was a fine morning, the mist of last night had disappeared. From our position on the hilltop we could see the tanks advancing towards Crevecoeur with the infantry following behind. Large black crumps were bursting around them. The tanks and infantry disappeared over the brow of the hill into the valley which leads to the river and 30 minutes afterwards groups of prisoners were being hurried to the rear. Great columns of black smoke from burning dumps were rising high into the sky on the horizon and now and again the air was shaken by tremendous explosions which showed that the Germans were burning their stores and ammunition.

Last night, I almost walked into the German Line. It was all quite simple, nothing exciting. I was taking a message to the brigade who were in some old trenches, along with the infantry, well forward ready for the morning attack. I got my directions from one of our DRs who had been there earlier in the evening. 'Half a mile beyond Vaucelles you will come to a battery of field artillery in a sunken road. Leave your machine and climb the bank into the field and you will find a line of telegraph poles; follow the poles and you will come to a group of trenches near to a copse of trees where you will find the Brigade HQ.'

I found the battery alright and started across country following the poles which stretched right ahead. Here and there I passed groups of infantry squatted in trenches sometimes with a small fire reflecting on their faces. The nights are getting cold. I had walked the best part of 800yd when a sudden burst of machine-gun fire pulled me up with a jerk; quite close too. Could I be going wrong? The poles still showed ahead. I stared around trying to pierce the blackness for a sight of the 'copse of trees'. A lot of shells were passing over and bursting a mile away to the right but straight ahead all was quiet. Should I go forwards or backwards? Whilst I was debating the point with myself a Very light fell in the grass some distance ahead. I flopped. Two more came, the light reflecting on a cluster of houses about 200yd away. Where was I? Somewhere near the frontline if those Very lights were in their right place. I waited a little and then started back a good deal faster than I had come. I had almost reached the battery from where I started, when I saw another line of poles branching off to the right. It then dawned upon me – I had followed the wrong poles! If it had not been for those Very lights goodness knows where I should have got to.

10 OCTOBER 1918, MOVED TO HAUCOURT

Our artillery was very active all night but there was practically no reply from the Germans. This morning it was found that they had retired during the night and our infantry advanced without opposition. At 10:00, the whole division was on the move forward and that evening the divisional staff made their HQ in the village of Haucourt which is very little damaged. The houses are full of furniture, just as they had been left by the inhabitants, who appeared to have left at a moment's notice. After living for over 2 months in a belt of country where every village has been razed to the ground, desolation and destruction whichever way one looked, it was a welcome change to enter country with green fields hardly disfigured by shell holes, trees with foliage and villages with houses almost undamaged.

I passed a nasty sight in a sunken road beyond Lesdain. The bodies of at least twelve Germans lay in the mud – their transport had been running over them in the night. They must have been killed by shelling or bombing as our infantry advanced over this part without opposition. The DRs have been handed a bouquet for their good work during the past 2 weeks.

18 OCTOBER 1918

The division has come out of the Line for rest. The Germans are still retreating and our troops are now entering villages where the inhabitants have remained behind. They could get very little news from the Germans, except when the news was bad for the Allies, but the people had an 'underground' news service which was passed from mouth to mouth and generally they had a good idea of what was happening. During the past month, the Germans had relaxed their restrictions a good deal and yesterday they told the inhabitants that their friends the English would be with them in the morning. In spite of 4 years of occupation, tricolours and bottles of wine made their appearance when our troops marched through.

21 OCTOBER 1918

Tomorrow we move forward into the Line again. The Division HQ will be in Briastre in the cellars of the brewery. I went up this afternoon to have a look around. The village lies at the bottom of a deep valley astride a stream called the River Selle. Although the Line only rested on the village for a few days the place has been smashed to pieces, not a house is whole. The Germans made a big effort to hold us up at this point and the crossing of the river cost us many casualties. Many of our dead are still unburied; most of them are lying near to the road leading to the railway crossing.

The Germans now occupy the opposite ridge of the valley which gives them a good view of all the roads leading into the valley on our side. There was a good deal of shelling going on while I was there, most of it seemed to be falling around the brewery, a pleasant prospect for tomorrow.

22 OCTOBER 1918, CAUDRY

The Division HQ will be here until the 5th Division have attacked when we take over near Briastre. Caudry is a fair-sized town with several large factories for making lace. The Germans have smashed or dismantled most of the machinery.

About 11:00 this morning, the railway bridge at the lower end of the town blew up with a tremendous roar. At first we thought it was a bomb or a big long-range shell, but it turned out to be a delayed-action mine which the Germans had set under the bridge. The civilians had said that they had seen the Germans digging there. The engineers searched but could not find the mine. A team of horses was killed and six men injured.

23 OCTOBER 1918

The Germans are now in full retreat behind Beaurain. Last night and early this morning, the village was shelled very heavily, causing us some casualties in the brigade sections going up to take over from the brigades of the 5th Division.

30 OCTOBER 1918, BRIASTRE

The division is now out of the Line for rest. The first few days we were in the cellars of the brewery, but when the shelling had subsided we took over a house alongside which was more or less intact except the windows were all broken and the roof had disappeared. We boarded up the windows and for the roof we prayed for fine weather. We cleared out loads of rubbish and cleaned up the place. Joe mended the clock whose ticking made the place quite home-like, and everyone had a spring bed. Unfortunately after a few days, the weather broke and we were forced to take refuge in the cellars to escape the dripping water.

As they retreat the Germans are looting very thoroughly, taking everything of value. They even cut the red plush covers from a set of gilt chairs in the priest's house. What they cannot carry away they damage or destroy.

Our rations are a bit thin these days. The nearest railhead is a long way back and the transport is having great difficulty in keeping up supplies. The roads in these parts are very narrow, pavé, with a high camber and the lorries slide off the road in wet weather.

The engineers are working night and day repairing the big viaduct across the valley near Solesmes. The Germans blew up three arches. At night they work by flares, which are likely to attract all the enemy aeroplanes for miles around. The place is ringed by searchlights and AA guns for their protection; all the same it must be nervy work.

4 NOVEMBER 1918

We moved to Neuville today. The weather is bad, pouring rain with high winds. Our part of the Line lies in front of Ghissignies. The Germans are holding the railway cutting about 250yd in front of the village. As usual they have chosen a position which gives them a good view of our side of the Line. Nothing can enter Ghissignies without them seeing it.

We hear that the attack of the 17th and the 21st Divisions on the Mormal Forest failed with heavy losses. The New Zealanders however have pushed deep into the flank of Le Quesnoy but they cannot go any further until the line is straightened out in front of the forest.

5 NOVEMBER 1918, NEUVILLE

At 21:00 there was a 'special' for the brigade in Ghissignies. It was my turn out. After the reports of the afternoon I did not relish the job. I made myself unpopular with some infantry on the march towards Ghissignies who protested about the noise of my machine. I overtook the head of the column and slipped down the hill into the village. Here I left the machine. It was pitch dark and I could not see a soul about. Then I saw two dark figures run crouching across the road and disappear behind a wall which seemed to be the grounds of a château.

'Where is the Brigade HQ?' I shouted. 'Go back, it is not down here.' By the way they said it, I guessed I was going wrong. I cursed myself for not making proper enquiries before I left Division HQ, but I expected to find the usual group of runners hanging around the dugout. I went back to where I had started and searched in the opposite direction. At last I found two of our linesmen and they put me on the right track. The brigade was in the cellars of an old mill. When I told them where I had been they laughed. 'If you had walked much further up that road you would have walked into Jerry's line.'

I had to wait some time for the answer and by then the artillery had warmed up and it looked as though it was the beginning of a long bombardment of retaliation when neither side knows when to stop.

Returning to the church I collected my machine and opened out, guiding myself by the gun flashes and trusting to luck that nothing was in the way. I must have been doing 40mph when the machine hit a shell hole and over the bars I flew, landing like a shot rabbit, rolling over and over. I expected to find the machine completely smashed but, beyond a buckled wheel and bent bars it was none the worse. I was beginning to feel that this was my unlucky day, nothing had gone right. I was crawling along, the machine rolling all over the road when I became conscious that shells were bursting in the fields at both sides of the road. I wanted to hurry but if I did so the front wheel would probably collapse.

Suddenly there was a screech and a crash, one burst not 10yd away; unconsciously I opened the throttle and the machine shot forward and strangely it handled better at speed than it did when going slow. (This was the last time I had a close acquaintance with a shell. I could find the exact spot today – it was just at the entrance to the village of Salesches.)

6 November 1918

The brigade was supposed to have moved to a spot on the Le Quesnoy road, but the infantry were still held up just outside the village by concealed machine guns which the artillery had failed to silence. Later in the day, we heard this gun caused us many casualties before it was located in a Calvary (a wayside shrine) hidden by hedges lining the road. Fire was concentrated on the spot and a German came out with a machine gun on his shoulders and started to run but he was riddled before he had gone 20yd. He was found to be a youngster not more than 18-years-old.

Another story I heard from one of the infantry sergeants: about a German machine gunner who fired his gun to the last and when he was cornered, stood up and pointed to his chest where he wanted it; he got it, though there were some who would have let him off, but a machine gunner gives no mercy and receives none.

NARRATIVE SEVEN:

The Armistice

**In the days leading up to 11 November 1918, the 37th Division
were resting behind the rapidly advancing frontline. Rumours
of an end to the fighting abounded and the troops naturally
looked to the despatch riders for confirmation.**

(7 Nov) Le Quesnoy has surrendered. This small town has been besieged for the past 2 days, our troops simply went past leaving it to be captured or surrender at leisure. As it was full of French inhabitants it was not shelled. A complete German transport column was capture4d. I met them early this morning coming down the road towards Ghissignies: waggons, horses, officers and NCOs on horseback, all riding in correct military formation and being escorted by six grinning 'Tommies'.

There are persistent rumours that the German people are in revolution and that their navy has mutinied. One rumour has it that the German army have given their High Command 6 days in which to make peace or they will make terms themselves. We have heard so many of these tales before that we usually put them down to the latest latrine yarn, where most of them are born. Today however, I saw something which has set me thinking that there may be some truth in the latest rumours. I was chasing a unit but was finding it impossible to catch up with them, they were always 'just gone'. I came to a small deserted hamlet near to Mormal Forest. The Germans had been using the mairie as their HQ. One of the interior doors was chalked in very German writing: 'To TOMMY 6TH ---- 7TH ---- 8TH ---- 9TH ---- 10TH ---- LA GUERRE FINI. FRITZ.'

The Germans are now retreating so rapidly that it is becoming a rout. The roads are lined with abandoned guns and lorries. Practically the whole of Mormal Forest is in our hands. Prisoners are coming down the Line in thousands. Most of them are quite clean, showing they have seen little fighting. There must be far more prisoners than British troops behind the line in these parts.

The DRs have managed to find an old cottage in the outskirts of Neuville. Last night, thanks to Joe's ingenuity, we nearly set the whole place on fire. He had put a large bundle of cordite spills on the mantelpiece above the fire to be used as pipe lighters. A spark set the whole lot off, causing a big sheet of flame that licked the ceiling from end to end. Fortunately, no harm was done but we were pestered by swarms of crawling insects which we eventually identified as flies that had lost their wings in the 'Great Fire'. We were unanimously of the opinion that Joe's ingenuity ought to be curbed.

(9 Nov) This afternoon a message was issued by Army HQ to all divisions that read roughly as follows: 'If a German officer carrying a white flag should approach our lines he is to be allowed to cross and conducted to the nearest Division HQ who will advise the Army HQ of his arrival.' This has set everyone talking and guessing.

Almost every hour has brought some piece of news that will be history for future generations. The Kaiser has abdicated and fled to Holland. A delegate from the German army has passed through our lines and has been in conference with our army heads. Nothing is known definitely about the object of his visit but it is a foregone conclusion that it is to negotiate peace terms. The Germans have had enough, they are finished.

(10 Nov) This has been a day of days. The Germans have been given until 11:00 tomorrow to accept our terms for an armistice. 'Will they accept?' has been the burning question of the day which has been discussed from every angle. The general opinion is that they will accept.

The troops seem to think that a despatch rider knows the contents of every message he carries and everything that goes on, even the whispering of the 'Brass Hats'. Every time we stop we are mobbed by a crowd of 'Tommies'. 'What is the news, is it peace?' To give an answer one way or another is dangerous. 'Now boys, you know as much as I do,' is the answer I have given a dozen times today.

Shortly after midnight Garnier, the last man in from the brigades, brought the news by remarking quite casually as he entered: 'It's all over.' He had seen a message accepting our terms which had been intercepted a few minutes after midnight. The news caused no excitement and after a few commonplace remarks silence reigned again and in a short time the sleepers resumed their slumber songs.

I lay awake for some time thinking. I had often wondered how peace would come. I had always imagined it would be heralded by a fanfare of trumpets with great dramatic effect so beloved by the politicians. A week ago there was not a break in the war clouds and now peace has stolen in by the back door. Whilst the politicians have been watching the front door it has sneaked in by the back.

The artillery roared and rumbled in the distance making the place tremble. Around me lay my comrades rolled in their blankets, their boots as their pillow, their feet towards the fire, the embers still glowing. Now and again a rider on night duty would enter, bringing in an icy blast, to search for a pair of gloves or a coat, or an orderly would put his head in the door bawling, 'Next DR' and get heartily cursed for his pains. In a short time all this will be over. At 11:00 the guns will stop firing and all will be silent. Tomorrow we shall sleep relaxed without the fear of bombing aeroplanes or long-range shelling. It will seem an entirely different world.

(11 Nov) The day broke fine with a slight frost. The war was still going on. In fact the artillery fire seemed more than usual, and much of it seemed to be concentrated on the villages immediately behind the Line. The thought passed through my mind than some poor devils will get pipped on armistice morning. It was comforting to think that our division was out at rest and well behind the line.

It was my turn for early duty which usually starts at 06:00 but the post was an hour late. I had several points of call and I knew I was carrying the despatches confirming the armistice. As I entered the first village every barn spewed men when they heard me coming, half of them without trousers, shirt tails flapping in the breeze as they tried to keep pace with me, all shouting, 'Is it peace?' It was quite evident the news had spread by the grapevine. Reaching the signal office I found a crowd waiting, all bleating 'Is it peace?' 'What's the news?' I pushed my way through the crowd and found a group of officers waiting. I handed over my despatch. It was opened and read aloud. When I got outside there was a larger crowd than ever, half of them still without their trousers. 'What's the news?' As I had heard it confirmed I felt I was safe in saying: 'There will be an armistice from eleven o'clock this morning.'

There was no cheering but a murmur of satisfaction and smiles on all faces. Not the sardonic smile such as we are used to but the smile of pleasure one sees on the faces of children. I had no need to kick-start my engine, six men pushed me off. It was the nearest I have been to being a public hero.

I got back to HQ at around 09:30. Found the cook had some hot tea waiting while he fried me a special piece of bacon. Washed and shaved. By then it was 10:30. After setting my watch by the signal office clock, I walked down the road until I was well outside the village. I sat down to wait for 11:00.

Away to the right was the grey-green of Mormal Forest. Straight ahead, the ground rose in a gentle hill which shut off the view of the country towards the Line which was now a good 10 miles away. It was a beautiful bright morning with blue sky and banks of white fleecy clouds riding slowly across the sky.

The artillery was hammering away in a frenzy as though trying to use up as much ammunition as possible before 11:00. Swarms of aeroplanes were patrolling the Front and I could swear I saw an air fight with several aeroplanes engaged and at least one was brought down, but there was a very bright sun and it was a long way off. As the hour drew near the firing grew louder and louder as though the guns were disappointed at losing their prey. Eleven o'clock came and the noise died down, not suddenly, but gradually over a space of two or three minutes and even after this there were several isolated shots by some gunner trying to have the honour of firing the last shot of the war. Then the aeroplanes came droning home and finally silence.

It was an uncanny feeling; night and day over 3 years, with the exception of brief periods when we were on leave, we have never been without hearing the sound of guns. The sound had become part of our daily lives: our ears were so attuned to it, we could tell the type of gun firing and any strange sound put us immediately on our guard.

When the silence was complete, I went back to the HQ. Everybody was standing around as though waiting for something to happen. Nobody seems to have grasped that our job is finished and in a short time we shall be back in civilian life again.

Whenever my thoughts turned to my return to civilian life, assuming I was lucky enough to get back, I always thought of starting my life again where I left off, but now my ideas have changed: I am a different person. Before the war most of my leisure time was spent in search of mildly dangerous sports: motor cycling, speed trials, hill climbing. I lived on a motorcycle mostly for business. All that is over, I have had enough excitement for a lifetime, all I want is the peace of the English countryside and the solitude of the hills, lying in heather listening to the gentle hissing of the wind.

Chapter Ten

November 1918 – February 1919

14 November 1918, Caudry

There is a howling famine in liquor, not a spot of rum, whisky or even beer to be had. Things looked pretty glum and we wondered how we were going to celebrate the Armistice, when Joe found an old friend who was doing duty as a Town Major who gave him a chit for twelve bottles of whisky. Two riders went back to the nearest canteen, which was 50 miles away, to bring it home.

15 November 1918

Last night we had a party – it was a great night. We had invited several friends including some members of the division concert party. We had all the old numbers and several new ones besides but the 'Old Monk' as usual was a prime favourite. Although its morals may be bad, it lends itself to good harmony.

As the guests began to get a bit the worse for wear two men fell in, one for each arm, to see them safely to their billets. One fellow however insisted he would get home himself. He went outside, steadied himself to get his bearings and then set off at a run, but unfortunately his direction was bad and he ran full tilt into the back of a motor lorry. Nothing worse than a bloodied nose.

A dozen bottles among about twenty is going some but it is only once in a lifetime we shall have the opportunity to celebrate an Armistice. When all our guests were gone we called the roll and found Joe was missing. The search party found him sleeping peacefully in the garden with hoar frost on his clothes. There were some pretty thick heads this morning, few could face their breakfast and some tried the old dodge of taking 'a hair of the dog'. I went for a long walk over the fields to get it out of my system.

20 NOVEMBER 1918

For the past week there has been a constant procession of refugees through the town. They are mostly old folks, women and children, some pushing handcarts and wheelbarrows but the majority carrying bundles, large and small. It was a sad sight: some had come over 100miles. I have met them on the roads at 03:00 in the morning, anxious to get back to their homes but many, I am afraid, will find only ruins. The weather has been fine with moonlit nights, which is a blessing.

21 NOVEMBER 1918

Some of our men who have been prisoners working behind the Line have turned up, looking like scarecrows. Most of them have managed to keep some part of their original uniform although it might be buried under a crowd of patches, like Joseph's coat. Their physical condition was terrible, some of them like walking skeletons. They had been fed on food only fit for pigs: potato peelings boiled with scraps and the leavings of German troops. The German prisoners in England are better fed than our own people in many cases.

Already there are signs of unrest at the delay in issuing definite information as to what is going to happen and how and when we are going to be demobilised. Everyone wants to get home and naturally those who have had the longest time out here expect to go home first.

28 NOVEMBER 1918

We have had a lecture on the subject of demobilisation. The idea seems to be that a certain class of men called 'key' men will go home first without any regard to their length of service. These men are mainly butchers, bakers, plumbers and similar small fry. Now everyone knows these men were the last to join and the great majority are conscripts. The troops are up in arms against this idea, the whole army is buzzing like a beehive. Many say they will go home whether they are demobilised or not. Everyone blames Churchill.

1 DECEMBER 1918, GOMMEGNIES

We have moved from Caudry to a small village called Gommegnies which is about 6 miles north east of Le Quesnoy. We have very little to do and our chief occupation is killing time. I spend a good part of my time wandering over the fields around the village. It is very interesting to study the defences hastily prepared by the Germans to protect their retreat. They must have worked hard as the whole countryside is littered with short lengths of trenches used by their rearguard.

[From December 14 to 28, Albert was on leave, spending his time in Sheffield where his brother was also on leave, and in Manchester.]

It was good to see the English countryside after the monotony of the French plains. I visited my old place of business where I was employed before the war and was pleased to hear they had kept my place open for me. I hope everyone will be as fortunate, but I am afraid not. Already there seems to be a feeling of resentment against the returning army. The stay-at-homes are all nicely dug in and their nests well feathered. I have heard them say that they wouldn't have minded if the war had lasted another two years. They think the army should be demobilised very gradually so that the country shall not be upset in any way: the country, of course, being themselves. I told some of these gentry that if the army was not demobilised soon they would find them on their doorstep having demobilised themselves. They do not appear to have heard what has happened in Germany.

There is sure to be a boom in business very shortly which should find work for all, but in any case the men have a right to come home to the country they have fought for.

[After a rough Channel crossing, 3 days in a rest camp at Boulogne and 2½ days on the train, Albert re-joined his unit in Belgium.]

We found the Division HQ in the village of Gosselies. The first person we met was Joe Torrey who gaped with astonishment as though he had seen a ghost.'Well! We didn't expect to see you again, what have you come back for?''Why shouldn't we come back?' we replied.'Don't you know there is an order out that all men on leave need not return!' This was the last straw. After what we had endured in the rest camp and on the train, living on bully and biscuits, unwashed, unshaved, our great coats plastered with grease from lying on the filthy floors of the trucks, this was a knockdown blow. We found everyone living very comfortably in civilian billets, sleeping in beds. I was billeted on an old couple who seemed to be among the leading lights of the village. They made a great deal of their hardships during the war but I doubt if they suffered as much as the French people behind the German lines. One night I came back rather earlier than usual and found the kitchen table covered with stacks of paper money and the old couple busily counting.

They were rather taken aback but explained that it was German money which was going to be redeemed.

As time went on we realised that this part of Belgium had been very prosperous during the war, working for the Germans. The people here seem to be a very mixed lot: Belgian, French, Dutch and German, they call themselves Walloons. Their patriotism is a very flexible matter.

We have very little to do, our runs to the brigades have been cut down to twice per day. These runs take us through some very historic country. We practically encircle the battlefield of Waterloo. Napoleon is supposed to have slept in Gosselies the night before Waterloo. Early next morning he rode to his battle headquarters at Belle Alliance – now a short row of cottages on the main Brussels road. It does not seem to have altered much since the day when Napoleon saw the flower of the French Army wilt and break against the British squares. The march of industrialism does not seem to have reached this bit of country which will always be sacred to the British Army.

We cannot settle down to anything, not even bridge, which used to be eternal. Everyone is thirsting to get home, so fed up are we with army life. Letter writing is our main occupation: writing to anyone who we imagine can influence our discharge. It is very difficult to get one's discharge unless one has a definite job to go to. One loophole has been discovered: to declare oneself as a student desirous of continuing one's studies. One of the boys has got away on this pretext, which has riled quite a few who had not thought of this dodge.

JANUARY 1919, GOSSELIES

Having nothing better to do I went down to Charleroi to see the sights. 'Down to Charleroi' describes the journey graphically as the road runs downhill all the way. A narrow gauge tramway runs between the two places and as the troops travel free the trams are well patronised. During rush hours the carrying capacity of the trams is only limited by the number who can cling to it, inside or out. Half way down, the brakes refused to act. The driver got tremendously excited because he could not stop at the appointed places, but everyone took it as a huge joke. Fortunately nothing got in our way and the tram kept on the rails and finally expended its energy in the last mile which is flat.

4 FEBRUARY 1919

I am now at home finished with the army I hope, though I am still in the Reserve. The day after my discharge papers arrived I was on my way home.

My last impression of Belgium was the sight of an old man sitting on the bank of a canal, fishing. A thick mist lay over the land, not a breath of air to ripple the water: the old man might have been a statue.

There is no more peaceful sight than a man fishing.

Index

Note: towns and villages in France and Belgium are not indexed – see Itinerary

Aeroplanes,
   Albatross, 43
   flying levels of, 111
   Gotha, 144, 181–2
   night flying, 30, 134
   Taube, 15
   triplanes, 153
Airships, 40, 53–4, 61, 143, 150
Allenby, Gen. Sir Edmund, 38, 97
Ammunition, comparison of, 183–4
Anzacs, 49, 53
Artists' Rifles, 73, 174
Auto Cyclists' Union, xii, 3

Bainbridge, Brig. Gen. E.G.T., 19–20
Barnes, Maj. Gen. R., 23
Bate, Jim (blacksmith), 40
Bideford (Devon), 2, 20
Birthday celebrations, 43
Blakeway, Cpl J.B., 7–8, 21, 28–30, 32, 38–9, 48, 50
Booby traps, 184
Brigades,
   63rd, 47, 110, 174

100th, 19
110th, 47
111th, 40, 45, 100–110, 127
112th, 72, 101, 126
Bruce-Williams, Maj. Gen. Sir Hugh, 97
BSA motorcycle, 5
Buxton, xii, 5–8

Cameron, Pte Jock, 103–104
Case, Pte, 108
Cavalry, use of, 103–104
Chatham, xii, 4–5
Christmas meals, 21–2, 81–2, 145–6
Churchill, Lt Col W.S., 23
Cotton, Cpl, 110
Crossley Brothers, xi–xiii

Dawson, Mrs Emma, xi, 25, 150
Declaration of war, 1
Demobilisation, 196–8
Deserters, execution of, 58–9, 117, 123
Divisions
   5th, 188
   9th, 59–60, 62

17th, 189
19th, 132
21st, 47, 53, 189
23rd, 170
24th, 165
29th, 114
42nd, 183
46th, 45–7, 159
51st, 109
55th, 43, 45–6
56th, 112
63rd (Royal Naval), 73
Douglas motorcycle, xi, 3, 5,
    11, 182

Emms, Cpl, 118

Farming,
    Belgian, 125, 129–31
    French, 61, 71, 167
Fonnereau, Spr R., 136, 142–3,
    148, 160

Garnier, Cpl B.D., 81, 148,
    175–6, 192
Gas,
    effects of, 23, 43–4, 120,
    125, 144, 162–3
    precautions against, 23
George V, King, review by, 10
Gleichen, Maj. Gen. Lord
Edward, 10, 97
    German ancestry of, 52–3,
    59
Grimshaw, Cpl, 110

Haig, Gen. Sir Douglas, 23, 38,
    174

Hall, Pte, 105
Hill, Cpl C.W., 146, 148, 171
Hitchin, 8–9
Hobson, Cpl W.T., 115, 146–7,
    163–4, 175
Horne, Gen. Sir Henry, 115
Horses,
    care of, 34, 92
    stampeding, 37, 57

Kitchener, Field Marshal Earl,
    39–40

Labour Corps, 89, 101, 130
Larkin, Cpl, 78
Leave, 11, 20–1, 24–5, 82–4,
    149–51, 197
Lice, 58, 69, 85–6
Looting, 29–30, 32

Manchester, xi, 1–2, 25, 150
Map reading, 8, 53, 66–7
Marples, Pte, 78
Mascots, 36
McLaclan, Brig. Gen., 126–7
Messines Ridge, 116, 121, 125,
    127
Military Police, 20, 29, 58–9,
    110
Mills bombs, 48, 85
Minenwerfers, 21, 23
Monchy-le-Preux, 35, 95–106,
    108–10
Montagu-Stuart-Wortley, Maj.
    Gen. The Hon. Edward, 67
Morris, Cpl, 6
Motorcycles,
    accidents, 7–10, 15, 32, 86,

160, 169, 190
modification of, 22, 39–40,
    78, 164
problems with, 9, 26–7,
    127–8, 141, 147, 158, 162,
    165
    see also BSA, Douglas,
    Rudge, Triumph, Zenith
Mount, Cpl, 78
Mules, xix, 10, 93, 99, 105
Munro, Cpl, 78, 157
Musto, Cpl P.V., 169

Norman, Cpl, 6, 9, 13, 15, 29,
    32–3
Notts and Derbys (Sherwood
    Foresters) battalion, 46
Nunn, Cpl, 10–11

Observation balloons, 27, 91,
    109, 119, 154
Oddy, Cpl, 148
Officers, preferential treatment
    of, 26, 142
Oliver, Cpl, 118

Passchendaele, Battle of, 121,
    142–3
Pigeons, use of, 42, 61–2, 128
Prisoners,
    British, 60, 196
    German, 62–3, 65–6, 72,
    128–9, 136, 156, 178, 183

Railway gun, 155, 167–8
Rats, 14
Redmond, Maj. W., 127
Rest camps, 84, 151

Royal Army Medical Corps,
    119, 122–3
Royal Engineers, 153rd Field
    Company, 57
Royal Field Artillery, 2
Royal Flying Corps, xii, 28,
    38–9, 42
Rudge motorcycle, 5
Rupprecht, Crown Prince of
    Bavaria, 179–80

Saywell, Miss Lily (future
    wife), xiii
Scrase-Dickens, Maj. Gen. S.,
    97
Shaftoe, Cpl L., 8, 21, 65
Simpkin, Albert,
    birth, xi
    joining up, xii, 1–4
    training, 5–12
    promotion to sergeant, 7
    award of Military Medal,
    115
    demobilisation, 198
    marriage, xiii
    emigration to Argentina,
    xiii
    death, xiii
Simpkin, Lt Frank (brother), xi,
    1–2, 28, 82–3, 165
Spanish 'flu, 171–2
Spies, 38, 41–2, 54
Sports, 114, 168

Tanks,
    first sighting of, 69
    German, 183
    Whippet, 177

Tidworth, xii, 9–12
Torrey, Cpl J., 139–40, 145–6,
    173, 178, 184, 188, 192,
    195, 197
Treherne, Capt, 122–3
Triumph motorcycle, 11, 37

Vimy Ridge, 56, 58, 95

Walker, Cpl, 134–5
Wigg, Cpl C.B., 24, 39, 42

Ypres Salient, 15, 125, 132–45,
    184

Zenith motorcycle, 5
Zeppelins *see* Airships